Continuous-Time Self-Tuning Control

VOLUME II — IMPLEMENTATION

MECHANICAL ENGINEERING RESEARCH STUDIES

ENGINEERING CONTROL SERIES

Series Editor: **Professor C. R. Burrows,** *University of Bath, UK*

Continuous-Time Self-Tuning Control

VOLUME II — IMPLEMENTATION

P. J. Gawthrop
University of Glasgow, UK

RESEARCH STUDIES PRESS LTD.
Taunton, Somerset, England

JOHN WILEY & SONS INC.
New York · Chichester · Toronto · Brisbane · Singapore

RESEARCH STUDIES PRESS LTD.
24 Belvedere Road, Taunton, Somerset, England TA1 1HD

Marketing and Distribution:

Australia and New Zealand:
JACARANDA WILEY LTD.
GPO Box 859, Brisbane, Queensland 4001, Australia

Canada:
JOHN WILEY & SONS CANADA LIMITED
22 Worcester Road, Rexdale, Ontario, Canada

Europe, Africa, Middle East and Japan:
JOHN WILEY & SONS LIMITED
Baffins Lane, Chichester, West Sussex, England

North and South America:
JOHN WILEY & SONS INC.
605 Third Avenue, New York, NY 10158, USA

South East Asia:
JOHN WILEY & SONS (SEA) PTE LTD
37 Jalan Pemimpin #05-04
Block B Union Industrial Building, Singapore 2057

Library of Congress Cataloging in Publication Data
(Revised for volume 2)

Gawthrop, P. J, 1952–
   Continuous-time self-tuning control.

   (Mechanical engineering research studies. Engineering control series ; 1–2)
   Includes bibliographies and indexes.
   Contents: v. 1. Design — v. 2. Implementation.
   1. Self-tuning controllers.   2. Automatic control.
I. Title.   II. Series.   III. Series: Mechanical
engineering research studies. Engineering control
series ; 1, etc.
TJ213.G374   1987   629.8   86-29760
ISBN 0-471-91417-7 (Wiley : v. 1)
ISBN 0-86380-088-2 (v. 2)
ISBN 0-471-92429-6 (Wiley : v. 2)

British Library Cataloguing in Publication Data

Gawthrop, P. J.
   Continuous-time self-tuning control. — (Mechanical
   engineering research studies. Engineering Control Series)
   Vol. 2, Implementation
   1. Computer systems. Programs. Algorithms
   I. Title   II. Series
   005.1'2'028

   ISBN 0-86380-088-2

   ISBN 0 86380 088 2 (Research Studies Press Ltd.)
   ISBN 0 471 92429 6 (John Wiley & Sons Inc.)

Printed in Great Britain by SRP Ltd., Exeter

Continuous-Time Self-Tuning Control
Volume 2 — Implementation
(IBM PC Disk)
P. J. Gawthrop

PROGRAMME DISK AVAILABLE

The programme CSTC described in this book is available on disk for your IBM PC (and most compatibles) with a floating point coprocessor. The Pascal source is also provided and can be recompiled, using a suitable compiler, for use on other computers.

Order the programme disk, priced £25.00/$45.00 (including VAT), by cutting out and using the **original** form below. Send the completed form to:

John Wiley & Sons Ltd
Customer Service
Distribution Centre
Shripney Road
Bognor Regis
Sussex
UK PO22 9SA

(Site licences are available for this software. Further information can be obtained from the Publisher, Research Studies Press Ltd., 24 Belvedere Road, Taunton, Somerset, UK TA1 1HD.)

Please send me Gawthrop: Continuous-Time Self-Tuning Control, Volume II — Implementation (IBM PC Disk) at £25.00/$45.00 (including VAT). ISBN 0 86830 101 3.

Please add £1.50/$3.00 to cover postage.

Tick boxes as appropriate.

I require the disk in the following size:

☐ 3½"

☐ 5¼"

☐ Remittance enclosed: £/$ .... (payable to John Wiley & Sons Ltd.)

☐ Please send me an invoice for prepayment.

Series Editor's Preface

Professor Gawthrop's concern and motivation is to help engineers to apply self-tuning control to industrial problems.

In his first book he described the design of self-tuning control algorithms. The object of this second volume is to reinforce those ideas and to reduce the effort needed to apply these algorithms to industrial plant.

C.R. Burrows

Preface

Volume 1 of this monograph discussed and described the *design* of continuous-time self-tuning controllers; this volume focuses on *implementation* issues. This emphasis on implementation is particularly important in the context of the continuous-time approach: digital implementation of continuous-time algorithms is less obvious than that of discrete-time algorithms. Thus a purpose of this volume is to convince a reader of volume 1 that continuous-time algorithms can be implemented in a digital form.

This volume is designed to be read in conjunction with volume 1. Corresponding section numbers are indicated where appropriate; thus

    1.1.1. [1.2] Transfer Functions

implies that section 1.1.1 of this volume must be read in conjunction with section 1.2 of volume 1 with the same name. In addition, references to equations and sections in volume 1 are prefaced by 'I'.

On the suggestion of the Series Editor, Professor C.R. Burrows, a computer program **CSTC** has been developed to accompany this text. The text itself contains the full program together with numerous illustrative examples of its use. In addition, the software is available separately (for use only with this book) on an IBM type disc for use on and IBM PC or compatible. The Pascal source code is provided for those who would rather recompile and run the software on a different computer. The software is designed not only to simulate the illustrative examples that I have created but also to help readers create their own examples. It is my hope that this will help those starting to do research in this area to rapidly pass through the learning phase and on to new research ideas and results.

Access to a computer and the software is not essential; but interaction with the software will enrich the appreciation of the contents of the book.

Development of usable software is not an easy task. I must give special thanks to T.C. Tsang of Oxford University and A. Plummer of the University of Bath for evaluating the software and making numerous helpful suggestions for its improvement.

The ideas embodied in the software arise from those in Volume 1, and once again I would like to acknowledge the help given by those listed in the Preface to volume 1.

I hope that this experiment in enhancing the written word with computer software will prove to be a fruitful way of disseminating continuous-time self-tuning control.

University of Glasgow   P.J. Gawthrop
Gilmorehill
August 1989

Contents

CHAPTER 3. EMULATOR-BASED CONTROL

CHAPTER 6. SELF-TUNING CONTROL

CHAPTER 10. TWO-INPUT TWO-OUTPUT SYSTEMS

CHAPTER 11. CSTC: THE PROGRAMME

VARIABLE INDEX

PROCEDURE INDEX

CHAPTER 0

Introduction

0.1. INTRODUCTION

The traditional means of conveying the results of a research project to others (whether in academe or industry) is via the printed page; volume I of this work is an example of this process. However, this by no means conveys all of the efforts and achievements of the project. If the reader of a book wishes to implement the the algorithms described there, he has a long and daunting task ahead of him: he will repeat mistakes and resolve problems. Even worse, he has no way of knowing if he has provided a correct implementation of the author's ideas. Moreover, such a reader may be frustrated by the illustrative examples provided: he may ask "But what if the parameters of the simulation were changed?", but will have no direct means of finding an answer.

Many of us are now used to complementing our bookshelves of printed material with personal computers. This provides the opportunity of conveying the intellectual capital tied up in software to others, and so overcoming the problems inherent in the printed page. In the context of this volume, I perceive two advantages arising from the use of this new medium of communication: the book becomes a computer-illustrated text, and the algorithms implementing the ideas of volume I are precisely described in executable code.

As a computer-illustrated text, the reader can use the text examples as *starting points* for investigation of the properties of continuous-time self-tuning control; both advantages and disadvantages are there to be examined and discovered. A wide range of such starting points has been provided; at the risk of some repetition, the examples have been made largely independent of each other: they do not have to be examined serially.

0.1.1. ORGANISATION OF THE BOOK

The book is organised to reflect the chapter arrangement of volume I. Thus chapter 1 of this volume contains material corresponding to chapter 1 of volume 1 and has the same title. Starting at chapter 1, each chapter has two major sections: a section on *implementation* followed by a section containing *examples*.

Implementation

The implementation section provides a guide to the way in which the algorithms have been implemented in Pascal. It should be read in conjunction with the programme (listed at the end of the book) together with volume I. The connection to the programme listing can be made via the *cross-reference listing* following the programme. The connection to volume I is indicated by the section number in square parentheses after the appropriate section number. Thus section 1.1.1 [1.4] refers to section 1.4 of volume I. Alternatively, when scanning the programme listing itself, reference can be made to the textual descriptions of individual functions, procedures and variables by means of the *procedure and variable* index at the end of the book. These procedure and variable names are emphasised by the use of boldface in the text.

Examples

The examples section provides worked examples which turn volume I into a computer-illustrated text. The aim is to allow the reader to simulate examples arising from volume I. The examples do not have to be approached in numerical order; at the expense of some repetition, the examples have been made largely independent of each other although appropriate cross references are made.

Each example is further subdivided into five subsections as follows.

Reference

This subsection refers to the appropriate section of volume I, and allows the examples of volume II to be executed in conjunction with the relevant sections of volume I.

Description

This subsection sets the background to the example and explains its significance.

Programme interaction

A copy of the screen output generated by **CSTC** is given for comparison with the output from the modified examples which the reader is encouraged to investigate.

Discussion

The result of the simulation as displayed in the corresponding figure (and, hopefully, on the reader's computer display) is discussed in connection with volume I.

Further investigations.

The user is not constrained to use the given examples as they stand, but rather is encouraged to use them as a starting point for further investigations. Some ideas are given in this subsection.

0.2. USER GUIDE

0.2.1. PC CONFIGURATION

1. To run the software you will need an IBM PC, or compatible, with either 3.5" or 5.25" discs and a maths coprocessor.

2. To display the results you will need a graphics package capable of displaying columns of data from an ASCII file. The recommended package is PC-MATLAB.

0.2.2. INSTALLING THE PROGRAMME ON A PC

1. Boot your PC.

2. Create a directory called CSTC:

   md cstc

3. Move to directory CSTC:

   cd cstc

4. Insert the distribution diskette into drive A: of your PC.

5. Install the software by typing:

    a:install

0.2.3. RUNNING THE PROGRAMME ON A PC

1. Decide which example that you wish to run (say example 3 of chapter 6) and execute it by typing 'runex' followed by the chapter followed by the example number followed by the return key.

    runex 6 3

2. The computer should reply with the example name followed by the **CSTC** heading, for example:

    Using a setpoint filter
    ======== C S T C *Version 5.3* ========
    Enter all variables (y/n)?

    Continued pressing of return will step though the programme input phase, leaving the defaults as displayed. These may be changed - see the next section. The output should correspond to that given in the appropriate section.

3. Plot the results using your favourite graphics package with the facility for plotting ASCII data files (columns of numbers). If you are lucky enough to have MATLAB, then the distributed .m files will help. For example, plot6.m plots data pertaining to the examples of chapter 6. If you don't have MATLAB, then you will have to read section 5 which describes the file format. (In this case, you can run CSTC from MATLAB using !run or !runex commands).

4. If you wish to rerun the same example, retaining whatever changes that you made, type

    run

0.2.4. USER INTERACTION

The programme, CSTC, is equipped with a simple, but quite powerful, user interface. The user is presented with a **variable name,** its **current value** and a **prompt** asking for a new value. For example, the real variable 'Sample interval' may be presented as:

    Sample Interval   =   0.050000 :=

The user may then type in a new value (and then press the 'return' key) or retain the default (0.05) by pressing the 'return' key. There are four types of variables:

1. **Integers**

2. **Reals**

3. **Booleans**

4. **Polynomials**

   Integers are entered in the usual format. For example

   Approximation Order   =   5 :=
   2

changes the integer variable 'Approximation Order' from 5 to 2.

   Reals are also entered in the usual format. Each of the following examples changes the real variable 'Sample Interval' to 0.1.

   Sample Interval   =   0.500000 :=
   0.1

   Sample Interval   =   0.500000 :=
   1e-1

   Booleans can be either 'TRUE' or 'FALSE'. The boolean variable 'Constant between samples' can be set to false by any of the following:

   Constant between samples = TRUE :=
   FALSE

   Constant between samples = TRUE :=
   F

   Constant between samples = TRUE :=
   f

   Polynomials are entered in terms of their coefficients, highest order first. Thus the polynomial variable $A(s) = s^2 + 1$ can be changed to the value $A(s) = s^2 + 3s + 2$ by either of the following:

A (system denominator)   =   1.000000   0.000000   1.000000 :=

1 3 2

A (system denominator)   =   1.000000   0.000000   1.000000 :=

1.0 3.0 2.0

Alternatively, polynomials can be entered in factored form. If a polynomial entry is terminated by a '*', then another factor can be entered on the next line. Thus the polynomial

$$A(s) = s^3 + 3s^2 + 3s + 1 \qquad (0.2.4.1)$$

$$= (s+1)(s+1)(s+1)$$

$$= (s^2 + 2s + 1)(s+1)$$

can be changed from $A(s) = s^2 + 1$ by any of the following:

A (system denominator)   =   1.000000   0.000000   1.000000 :=

1 3 3 1

A (system denominator)   =   1.000000   0.000000   1.000000 :=

1 1*

1 1*

1 1

A (system denominator)   =   1.000000   0.000000   1.000000 :=

1 2 1*

1 1

WARNING. According to the usual Pascal conventions, entering **0.1** as **.1** will lead to a run time error. **ALWAYS** prefix a decimal point with a digit, even if it is 0.

0.2.5. HIDDEN VARIABLES

There are a lot of variables associated with this programme, so it is convenient to hide them from the user. The programme starts by asking

Enter all variables (y/n)?

the default response is no, and most variables are then hidden from the user.

On the other hand, a yes answer reveals all variables to the user. In addition, the programme then marks all variables which are changed by the user (or unchanged by default by typing a space). All other variables are hidden when a subsequent 'run' is invoked.

0.2.6. INPUT FILES

There are two input files to this programme:

1. inlog.dat

2. indata.dat

Inlog.dat

Inlog.dat contains a set of default parameters and is automatically copied into the working directory by the 'runex' command. The programme checks the variable names against what it expects to find; discrepancies lead to a built in default being used, and the corresponding variable is not hidden.

For example, the inlog.dat file corresponding to example 3 of chapter 6 is:

```
    Chapter                    6
======== Data Source    ========
External data          FALSE
Last time              25.000000
Print interval              1
======== Filters        ========
Sample Interval        0.050000
Approximation Order         5
Continuous-time?       TRUE
======== Control action ========
Automatic controller mode TRUE
Integral action        FALSE
======== Assumed system ========
#A (system denominator)      1.000000    0.000000    0.000000
#B (system numerator)        1.000000    1.000000
Number of interactions       0
D (initial conditions)   0.000000    0.000000
Time delay             0.000000
======== Emulator design ========
Z has factor B         FALSE
Z-+ (Z- not including B)    1.000000
Z+ (nice model numerator)   1.000000
Linear-quadratic poles    FALSE
#P (model denominator)      0.500000    1.000000
#C (emulator denominator)   0.500000    1.000000
```

Pade approximation order   *0*
Small positive number   *0.000100*
======== STC type   ========
Explicit self-tuning   *TRUE*
Using lambda filter   *FALSE*
Identifying system   *TRUE*
#Tuning initial conditions FALSE
======== Identification ========
#Initial Variance   *100000.000000*
#Forget time   *1000.000000*
Dead band   *0.000000*
Estimator on   *TRUE*
Tune interval   *1*
#Cs (emulator denominator)   *1.000000*   *2.000000*   *1.000000*
Identifying rational part TRUE
Identifying delay   *FALSE*
======== Controller   ========
Q numerator   *0.000000*
Q denominator   *1.000000*
#R numerator   *0.500000*   *1.000000*
#R denominator   *1.000000*   *1.414000*   *1.000000*
#Maximum control signal   *100.000000*
#Minimum control signal   *-100.000000*
Switched control signal   FALSE
======== Simulation   ========
======== Setpoint   ========
Step amplitude   *50.000000*
Square amplitude   *25.000000*
Cos amplitude   *0.000000*
Period   *20.000000*
======== In Disturbance ========
Step amplitude   *0.000000*
Square amplitude   *0.000000*
Cos amplitude   *0.000000*
Period   *20.000000*
======== Out Disturbance ========
Step amplitude   *0.000000*
Square amplitude   *0.000000*
Cos amplitude   *0.000000*
Period   *20.000000*
======== Actual system   ========
#A (system denominator)   *1.000000*   *1.000000*   *0.000000*
#B (system numerator)   *1.000000*   *0.100000*
D (initial conditions)   *0.000000*   *0.000000*
Time delay   *0.000000*
Number of lags   *0*
More time   *FALSE*

The leftmost column contains a '#' for each non-hidden variable, other variables are **not** displayed by default.

Indata.dat

Indata.dat allows external data to be read into the programme; for example, if some real system is to be identified. The columns of the file must be arranged as in the following table:

Column	Variable	Symbol
1	Time	t
2	System input	$u(t)$
3	System output	$y(t)$

Additional columns may be added for multi-input systems. Surplus columns are ignored; in particular, **outdata.dat** files can be copied and used as **indata.dat** files.

Blank rows initiate data splicing*. (See example 5.2.8)

0.2.7. OUTPUT FILES

There are three output files:

1.   outdata.dat

2.   outsyspar.dat

3.   outempar.dat

Outdata.dat

Outdata.dat contains signals arising from the simulation. For single-input single-output systems, the columns of this file are as follows:

---

* Gawthrop, P.J. (1984) "Parameter identification from non-contiguous data", Proceedings IEE, vol. 131 pt. D, No. 6, pp261-265.

Column	Variable	Symbol
1	Time	t
2	System input	$u(t)$
3	System output	$y(t)$
4	Setpoint	$w(t)$
5	Model output	$y_m(t)$
6	Emulator output	$\hat{\phi}(t)$
7	Emulated signal	$\phi(t)$

The last column is not always relevant.

If you have **MATLAB**, the following .m file will help:

```
function [t,u,y,w,ym,phih,phi] = convert
%function [t,u,y,w,ym,phih,phi] = convert;
%Converts data from 'outdata.dat' into relevant column vectors.

%File convert.m
%P.J. Gawthrop, May 1988.

load outdata.dat;
t  =   outdata(:,1);
u  =   outdata(:,2);
y  =   outdata(:,3);
w  =   outdata(:,4);
ym =   outdata(:,5);
phih = outdata(:,6);
phi = outdata(:,7);
```

For cascade, and multiple-input multiple-output systems, the situation is more complicated.

1. A column for each interaction variable is interposed immediately after the system input.

2. A new set of columns is created for each loop.

A useful .m file for two-loop cascade control (Chapter 9) is

```
function [t,u1,u2,y1,y2,w1,w2,ym1,ym2] = convert9
%function [t,u1,u2,y1,y2,w1,w2,ym1,ym2] = convert9;
%Converts data from 'outdata.dat' into relevant column vectors (Chapter 9).

%File convert9.m
```

%P.J. Gawthrop, May 1988.

load outdata.dat;
t = outdata(:,1);
u1 = outdata(:,2); u2 = outdata(:,9);
y1 = outdata(:,3); y2 = outdata(:,10);
w1 = outdata(:,5); w2 = outdata(:,11);
ym1 = outdata(:,6); ym2 = outdata(:,12);

and for two-loop multivariable control (Chapter 10):

function [t,u1,u2,y1,y2,w1,w2,ym1,ym2] = convert10
%function [t,u1,u2,y1,y2,w1,w2,ym1,ym2] = convert10;
%Converts data from 'outdata.dat' into relevant column vectors. (Chapter 10)

%File convert10.m
%P.J. Gawthrop, May 1988.

load outdata.dat;
t = outdata(:,1);
u1 = outdata(:,2); u2 = outdata(:,10);
y1 = outdata(:,3); y2 = outdata(:,11);
w1 = outdata(:,5); w2 = outdata(:,13);
ym1 = outdata(:,6); ym2 = outdata(:,14);

Outsyspar.dat

Outsyspar.dat contains estimated system polynomials arising from the simulation. For single-input single-output systems, the columns of this file are as follows:

Column	Variable	Symbol
1	Time	t
2	Estimation error	$\hat{e}(t)$
3	Sigma	σ
4	Estimated delay	T
5..	Estimated system numerator	$B(s)$
6..	Estimated system denominator	$A(s)$
7..	Estimated system initial conditions	$D(s)$

Columns labelled 5.., 6.. and 7.. are blocks of columns containing the polynomial coefficients in decreasing order. If you have **MATLAB**, the following .m file will help:

```
function [t,error,sigma,delay,A,B,D] = sysparconvert(nA,nB,nD);
%function [t,error,sigma,delay,A,B,D] = sysparconvert(nA,nB,nD);
%Gets system parameters from CSTC simulation
% nA, nB, nD:   Degrees of A, B and D
%P.J. Gawthrop, May 1988.
%File sysparconvert.m

load outsyspar.dat
t = outsyspar(:,1);
error = outsyspar(:,2);
sigma = outsyspar(:,3);
delay = outsyspar(:,4);
A = outsyspar(:,5:5+nA);
B = outsyspar(:,6+nA:6+nA+nB);
if nD>=0
      D = outsyspar(:,7+nA+nB:7+nA+nB+nD);
end;
```

For cascade, and multiple-input multiple-output systems, the situation is more complicated. A block of columns for each interaction polynomial is interposed immediately after the $B(s)$ polynomial.

Outempar.dat

Outempar.dat contains estimated emulator polynomials arising from the simulation. For single-input single-output systems, the columns of this file are as follows:

Column	Variable	Symbol
1	Time	t
2	Estimation error	$\hat{e}(t)$
3	Sigma	σ
4	Estimated delay	T
5..	Estimated emulator numerator (output)	$F(s)$
6..	Estimated emulator numerator (input)	$G(s)$
7..	Estimated emulator numerator (initial conditions)	$I(s)$

Columns labelled 5.., 6.. and 7.. are blocks of columns containing the polynomial coefficients in decreasing order. If you have **MATLAB**, the following .m file will help:

```
[t,error,sigma,F,G,I] = emparconvert(nF,nG,nI);
%[t,error,sigma,F,G,I] = emparconvert(nF,nG,nI);
%Gets emulator parameters from CSTC simulation
% nF, nG, nI:   Degrees of F, G and I

%P.J. Gawthrop, May 1988.

%File emparconvert.m

load outempar.dat

t=outempar(:,1);
error=outempar(:,2);
sigma=outempar(:,3);
F=outempar(:,4:nF+3);
G=outempar(:,nF+4:nF+4+nG);
if nI>0
      I=outempar(:,nF+5+nG:nF+5+nG+nI);
end;
```

For cascade, and multiple-input multiple-output systems, the situation is more complicated. A block of columns for each interaction polynomial is interposed immediately after the $G(s)$ polynomial.

0.2.8. PLOTTING RESULTS

All result files are in the form of columns of ASCII numbers as discussed in the previous section. Thus many plotting packages will be able to display them graphically. The figures in this book were obtained using **MATLAB.** The corresponding .m files are included with the distribution diskette as indicated in Table 0.1:

| Table 0.1: MATLAB plotting commands |||
Chapter	Example	Command
1	1	plot1_1
1	2	plot1_2
1	3	plot1_3
3	All	plot3
4	All	plot4
5	All (parameters)	plot5p
5	All (data)	plot5
6	All	plot6
7	All	plot7
8	All	plot8
9	All	plot9
10	All	plot10

Note that when using **plot5** and **plot5p** the variables: **nA, nB** and **nI** must be set within **MATLAB** to correspond to the degrees of A, B and D respectively.

0.2.9. CREATING NEW EXAMPLES

It may be that you will not find a suitable starting example for the problem that you wish to simulate. If so, a new example may be created. There are three levels at which this may be done:

1. Same structure, same hidden variables

2. Same structure, new hidden variables

3. New structure

These possibilities are considered in turn. In each case, you can save your examples for later use by copying **inlog.dat** to a safe place. It can then be reused by copying back again. You may care to create your own version of **runex** for this purpose.

Same structure, same hidden variables

After using the **runex** command, a file **inlog.dat** is created containing the the values of the variables that have been changed by the user, together with those that have not been changed. Hidden variables remain hidden. Using **run**, in place of **runex**, uses this modified file. Thus repeated use of **run** allows *incremental* changes to be made to the exposed variables.

Same structure, new hidden variables

Answering **yes** to the initial question "Enter all variables (y/n)?" exposes *all* variables. The resultant **inlog.dat** contains not only modified values, but also a new list of hidden variables. Variables are marked as exposed in the inlog.dat file if

a)   A value is changed

b)   A value is left at default, but a <space> is inserted before the <return>.

Subsequent invocation of the **run** command uses this new file with the corresponding hidden variables.

Similar effects can be obtained by editing **inlog.dat.** Hidden variables are exposed by replacing the space forming the first character in a line by #; exposed variables may be hidden by replacing the '#' forming the first character in a line by a space.

New structure

If none of the supplied examples is appropriate, a completely new file can be created. Start by creating an empty file called **inlog.dat.** Execute the **run** command and Answer **yes** to the initial question "Enter all variables (y/n)?". No variables are hidden, and each defaults to an internal value. The first variable corresponds to the appropriate chapter of the book. Take particular care to choose the appropriate polynomial orders; there is no checking here, and unpredictable effects can occur if choices are made incorrectly. So it is important to think carefully before creating a new example.

CHAPTER 1

Continuous-Time Systems

Aims. To consider the representation of polynomials and transfer functions. To illustrate the properties of the continuous-time state-variable filter and to investigate the approximations involved in its discrete-time implementation.

1.1. IMPLEMENTATION DETAILS

1.1.1. [1.2] TRANSFER FUNCTIONS

The rational transfer functions considered in Vol. 1 are ratios of polynomials. Therefore the polynomial is a key data structure in the implementation of the corresponding algorithms in CSTC. In particular, the type **Polynomial** is defined as:

Polynomial =
RECORD
    Deg: Degree;
    Coeff: ARRAY [0..MaxDegree] OF REAL
    END;

and the type **Degree** as

Degree = - 1..MaxDegree;

The two components of the record are **Deg** which is the degree of the polynomial, and **Coeff** the corresponding coefficients. It is convenient to allow a degree of -1 to indicate the absence of a particular polynomial.

CSTC includes a library of polynomial manipulation routines as indicated in the Table 1.1. The simpler routines are self explanatory, the more complex ones are as described in this volume. The source code for each algorithm is provided as part of CSTC to provide an executable description of the key algorithms of Vol 1.

Table 1.1: POLYNOMIAL MANIPULATION ROUTINES	
Name	Function
PROCEDURE PolWrite	Writes a polynomial
PROCEDURE PolLineWrite	Writes a polynomial and appends newline
FUNCTION PolNorm	Finds the absolute value of the largest coefficient
PROCEDURE PolRemove	Removes unwanted coefficients
PROCEDURE PolTruncate	Removes small coefficients
PROCEDURE PolZero	Generates the zero polynomial of degree zero
PROCEDURE PolUnity	Generates the unit polynomial of degree zero
PROCEDURE PolEquate	Equates two polynomials
PROCEDURE PolOfMinusS	Generates polynomial with -s replacing s
PROCEDURE PolAdd	Adds two polynomials
PROCEDURE PolMinus	Subtracts two polynomials
PROCEDURE PolWeightedAdd	Adds two polynomials with weighting scalars
PROCEDURE PolScalarMultiply	Multiplies a polynomial by a scalar
PROCEDURE PolsMultiply	Multiplies a polynomial by s
PROCEDURE PolsDivide	Divides a polynomial by s
PROCEDURE PolMultiply	Multiplies two polynomials
PROCEDURE PolSquare	Given $P(s)$ computes $P(s)P(-s)$
PROCEDURE PolSqrt	Given $P(s)P(-s)$ computes $P(s)$
PROCEDURE PolNormalise	Normalises a pair of polynomials
FUNCTION PolGain	Steady-state gain of system represented by a polynomial
FUNCTION PolHFGain	High frequency transfer function gain
PROCEDURE PolUnitGain	Forces polynomail to have unit steady-state gain
PROCEDURE PolMarkovRecursion	Markov recursion algorithm
PROCEDURE PolDerivativeEmulator	Derivative emulator design
PROCEDURE PolDivide	Polynomial long division - gives quotient and remainder
PROCEDURE PolEuclid	Euclids algorithm for GCD of two polynomials
PROCEDURE PolDioRecursion	The diophantine recursion algorithm
PROCEDURE PolDiophantine	Solves the diophantine equation
PROCEDURE PolZeroCancellingEmulator	Zero cancelling emulator design
PROCEDURE PolInitialConditions	Emulator initial conditions
PROCEDURE PolEmulator	General emulator design
PROCEDURE PolPade	Pade polynomials
PROCEDURE PolDelayEmulator	General emulator design with time-delay

1.1.2. [1.4] THE MARKOV RECURSION ALGORITHM

This algorithm is implemented using procedure **PolMarkovRecursion**. Firstly, the algorithm checks whether

$$deg\,(F\,) < deg\,(A\,)-1 \qquad\qquad (1.1.2.1)$$

If so, then the corresponding Markov parameter is zero, and $F\,(s)$ is multiplied by s. The transfer function $F\,(s)/A\,(s)$ has the relative degree reduced by one, but, because of inequality 1 is still strictly proper.

If inequality 1 is not satisfied, then the three equations I-2 are implemented. The first equation is labelled 2a in the listing, the second 2b and the third 2c. In step 2b, E is multiplied by s. The zero degree coefficient is then made equal to the Markov parameter. In step 2c, F is multiplied by s and then added to - $hkA\,(s)$

1.1.3. [1.6] THE STATE-VARIABLE FILTER

A key algorithm in CSTC is the numerical solution of the state-variable filter given by the differential equation

$$\frac{d}{dt}\underline{X}(t) = A\,\underline{X}(t) + Uu \qquad\qquad (1.1.3.1)$$

where the superscript c has been dropped for convenience. The algorithm given here is based on one given by Gawthrop and Roberts*. In our discrete-time implementation, values of $\underline{X}(t)$ are only required at the discrete time points

$$t = i\,\Delta \qquad\qquad (1.1.3.2)$$

With this in mind, the differential equation equation can be integrated between two consecutive time point to yield

$$\underline{X}(i\,\Delta + \Delta) = e^{A\,\Delta}\underline{X}(i\,\Delta) + \int_{i\Delta}^{(i+1)\Delta} e^{A\,\Delta(t-\tau)}Uu\,(\tau)d\tau \qquad\qquad (1.1.3.3)$$

At this stage, two *approximations* are made:

---

* Gawthrop, P.J. (1984): ' Parameter identification from non-contiguous data', Proceedings IEE, Vol 131 pt. D, No 6, pp261-265; Gawthrop, P.J., Kountzeris, A. and Roberts, J.B.(1988):' Parametric identification of non-linear roll motion from forced roll data' Journal of ship research, Vol. 32, No 2, pp101-111.

1. $e^{A\Delta}$ is expanded in a truncated Maclaurin series

$$e^{A\Delta} \cong \sum_{j=0}^{N} \frac{(A\,\Delta)^j}{j!} \qquad (1.1.3.4)$$

2. $u(\tau)$ is expanded in a truncated Maclaurin series

$$u(\tau) \cong \sum_{j=0}^{M} u^{[j]}\frac{\tau^j}{j!} \qquad (1.1.3.5)$$

where

$$u^{[j]} = \frac{d^j}{dt^j} u(\tau) \qquad (1.1.3.6)$$

Substituting these two expressions into 1.1.3.3 gives the following recursive scheme

$$\underline{X}(i\Delta + \Delta) = \sum_{k=0}^{N} \underline{\tilde{X}}_k \qquad (1.1.3.7)$$

where

$$\underline{\tilde{X}}_k = \frac{\Delta}{k}\left[\underline{A}\,\underline{\tilde{X}}_{k-1} + \frac{\Delta^{k-1}}{(k-1)!}\underline{U}u^{[k-1]}\right] \quad 1 \le i \le M+1 \qquad (1.1.3.8)$$

$$= \frac{\Delta}{k}\underline{A}\,\underline{\tilde{X}}_{k-1}\, i > M+1 \qquad (1.1.3.9)$$

and

$$\underline{\tilde{X}}_0 = \underline{X}(i\Delta) \qquad (1.1.3.10)$$

This algorithm is implemented within procedure **cStateVariableFilter**. The Maclaurin series for $u(t)$ is truncated at M=2; thus the control signal is approximated by a ramp function joining two adjacent samples

$$u((i-1)\Delta + \tau) \cong u((i-1)\Delta) + u(i\Delta) - u((i-1)\Delta)\,\frac{\tau}{\Delta} \qquad (1.1.3.11)$$

The current filter input $u(i\Delta)$ is held in variable **u**; the previous filter input $u((i-1)\Delta)$ is held in variable **FilterState.Old**. The variable **ApproximationOrder** corresponds to N, and the loop starting

FOR k := 1 TO ApproximationOrder DO

implements the recursive expressions 1.1.4.8&9. Variable **Increment** contains $\underline{\tilde{X}}$ and **FilterState.State** contains $\underline{X}$ The special cases k=1 and k=2 are handled by IF statements. The matrix multiplication is performed within the loops indicated in the listing; the sparseness of the matrix in I-1.6.3 is used to simplify the calculation.

1.1.4. IMPLEMENTATION OF THE DISCRETE-TIME STATE-VARIABLE FILTER

CSTC is primarily designed to implement the *continuous-time* algorithms to be found in Volume 1. However, only minor modifications are required to give a purely discrete-time implementation. The switch between the two domains is accomplished via the Boolean variable **ContinuousTime.**

Procedure **StateVariableFilter** encapsulates two versions of the state-variable filter algorithm: **cStateVariableFilter** for the continuous-time version and **dStateVariableFilter** for the discrete-time version. The choice between them is made in the statement

IF ContinuousTime THEN

appearing in procedure **StateVariableFilter.**

Procedure **dStateVariableFilter** has the same argument list as **cStateVariableFilter,** but the interpretation of the polynomial **A** is different: it contains the coefficients of

$$A(z) = a_0 z^n + a_1 z^{n-1} + \cdots + a_n \tag{1.1.4.1}$$

in place of the coefficients of

$$A(s) = a_0 s^n + a_1 s^{n-1} + \cdots + a_n \tag{1.1.4.2}$$

The corresponding state vector is given in the z-domain by

$$\underline{X} = \frac{1}{A(z)} \begin{bmatrix} z^n \\ z^{n-1} \\ \cdots \\ 1 \end{bmatrix} \tag{1.1.4.3}$$

The algorithm has two parts:

1. The components of the state are shifted (z corresponds to the forward shift operator),

2. The zeroth component (corresponding to z^n) is computed in terms of the other states and the filter input **u.**

The algorithm in **dStateVariableFilter** is simpler than that in **cStateVariableFilter**; this is a consequence of the algorithm domain matching the implementation domain. However, it is argued in volume 1 that the advantages of the continuous-time approach outweigh this disadvantage.

1.2. EXAMPLES

1.2.1. TRANSIENT RESPONSE OF OSCILLATOR.

Reference: Section 1.6; page 1-10

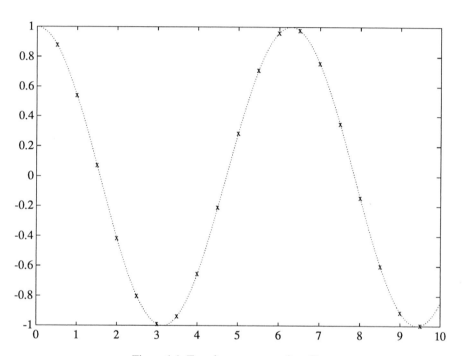

Figure 1.1. Transient response of oscillator.

Description

The state-variable filter provides a discrete-time approximation to a continuous-time transfer function. There are two ways of changing the accuracy of the approximation: the sample interval and the approximation order. There are two approximations involved in the the implementation: the series approximation to the state transition matrix and approximation of the input signal by a straight-line joining the samples. As the input is zero here, the latter approximation has no effect.

The simulated transfer function is:

$$\frac{1}{s^2 + 1}$$ (1.2.1.1)

and the initial 'position' is 1. Thus

$$D(s)=1$$ (1.2.1.2)

The corresponding transient response is

$$\cos t$$ (1.2.1.3)

Programme interaction

runex 1 1
Example 1 of chapter 1: Transient response of oscillator.

======== C S T C Version 6.0 ========

Enter all variables (y/n, default n)?

======== Data Source   ========
======== Filters   ========
Sample Interval   =   0.500000 :=
Approximation Order   =   5 :=
======== Control action ========
======== Assumed system ========
A (system denominator) =   1.000000   0.000000   1.000000 :=
B (system numerator)   =   1.000000 :=
D (initial conditions) =   1.000000   0.000000 :=
======== Simulation   ========
======== Setpoint   ========
Step amplitude   =   0.000000 :=
======== In Disturbance ========
======== Out Disturbance ========
Simulation running:
*   25% complete*
*   50% complete*
*   75% complete*
*   100% complete*
Time now is   10.000000

Discussion

The simulated step response, marked by 'x', is superimposed on the exact solution : $\cos t$. The approximation is quite good. Note that the simulated output at t=0 (the initial condition) is not generated by the simulation programme.

Further investigations

1   Try the effect of varying the approximation order and the sample interval. As there is no input approximation, it should be possible to choose a large enough approximation order to work well for an arbitrarily large sample interval. What is the minimum acceptable value of the approximation order for sample intervals of: 0.1, 0.5, 1.0 and 2.0?

1.2.2. STEP RESPONSE OF OSCILLATOR.

Reference: Section 1.6; page 1-10

Description

This example is identical to example 1.2.1 except that the initial condition is zero and a step input is applied. Although the straight-line approximation is exact for t>0, it is incorrect during the initial timestep when the input changes from 0 to 1. For this reason, an alternative approximation is used where the input is deemed to be *constant* at the value measured at the current sample for the previous timestep. This gives an exact approximation for a step input, except that the output is delayed by one sample.

Programme interaction

runex 1 2
Example 1 of chapter 2: Step response of oscillator.

  ======== *C S T C Version 6.0* ========

Enter all variables (y/n, default n)?

  ======== *Data Source*   ========
  ======== *Filters*   ========
Sample Interval   =   *0.500000* :=
Approximation Order =   *5* :=

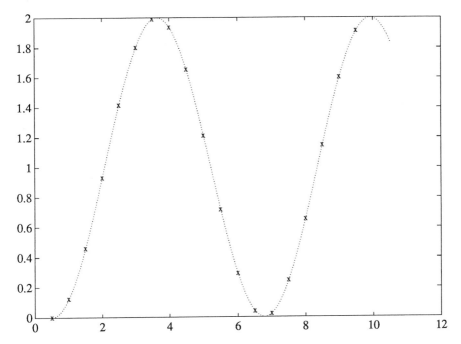

Figure 1.2. Step response of oscillator.

```
======= Control action ========
======= Assumed system ========
A (system denominator)   =    1.000000    0.000000    1.000000  :=
B (system numerator)     =    1.000000  :=
D (initial conditions)   =    0.000000    0.000000  :=
======= Simulation       ========
======= Setpoint         ========
Step amplitude           =    1.000000  :=
======= In Disturbance  ========
======= Out Disturbance ========
Constant between samples = TRUE  :=
Simulation running:
    25% complete
    50% complete
    75% complete
    100% complete
Time now is    10.000000
```

Discussion

The simulated step response, marked by 'x', is superimposed on the exact solution : 1 - cos t. The approximation is quite good.

Further investigations

1   Try the effect of varying the approximation order and the sample interval. As there is no input approximation, it should be possible to choose a large enough approximation order to work well for an arbitrarily large sample interval. What is the minimum acceptable value of the approximation order for sample intervals of: 0.1, 0.5, 1.0 and 2.0? Does this result correspond to that of example 1.2.1?

2   Set 'Constant between samples' to FALSE. This gives the straight-line approximation which is poor for the initial timestep. How does this affect the response? Is it possible to reduce the error by increasing the approximation order? Is it possible to reduce the error by decreasing the sample interval?

1.2.3. SINUSOIDAL RESPONSE OF OSCILLATOR.

Reference: Section 1.6; page 1-10

Description

This example is identical to example 1.2.1 except that the initial condition is zero and a sinusoidal sin t input is applied. The straight-line approximation is not exact in this case, but it is certainly better than the constant between samples approximation.

Unlike the previous two examples, then, the sample interval must be chosen so that the straight-line approximation is valid, and the approximation order then chosen appropriately.

The corresponding response is then:

0.5(sin t - t cos t)   (1.2.3.1)

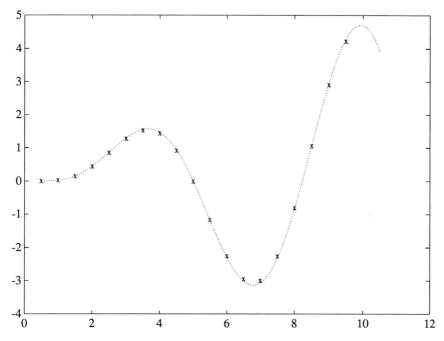

Figure 1.3. Sinusoidal response of oscillator.

Programme interaction

runex 1 3
Example 1 of chapter 3: Sinusoidal response of oscillator.

======== C S T C Version 6.0 ========

Enter all variables (y/n, default n)?

======== Data Source   ========
======== Filters   ========
Sample Interval   =   0.500000 :=
Approximation Order   =   5 :=
======== Control action ========
======== Assumed system ========
A (system denominator) =   1.000000   0.000000   1.000000 :=

B (system numerator) = *1.000000* :=
D (initial conditions) = *0.000000   0.000000* :=
 ======== *Simulation*   ========
 ======== *Setpoint*   ========
Cos amplitude = *1.000000* :=
Period = *6.283185* :=
 ======== *In Disturbance* ========
 ======== *Out Disturbance* ========
Constant between samples = *FALSE* :=
Simulation running:
  25% complete
  50% complete
  75% complete
  100% complete
Time now is   10.000000

Discussion

The simulated step response, marked by 'x', is superimposed on the exact solution : 1 - cos *t*. The approximation is quite good.

Further investigations

1. Try the effect of varying the approximation order and the sample interval. As there is an input approximation, the approximation order cannot be increased to overcome inaccuracies due to a long sample interval. Choose a large approximation order (20), and find the longest acceptable sample interval. Using this interval, what is then the minimum acceptable approximation order?

2. Set 'Constant between samples' to TRUE. This gives the constant approximation which is poor for a sinusoidal input. How does this affect the response? Is it possible to reduce the error by increasing the approximation order? Is it possible to reduce the error by decreasing the sample interval?

CHAPTER 2
Emulators

Aims. To describe some implementation details of the emulator design methods of chapter I-2. To illustrate the emulator design methods of chapter I-2 by numerical examples.

2.1. IMPLEMENTATION DETAILS

2.1.1. [2.2] OUTPUT DERIVATIVES

The procedure **PolMarkovRecursion** for evaluating equation I-2.2.2 and I-2.2.5 is described in section 1.1.3. The polynomials $E_1(s)$ and $F_1(s)$ in equation I-2.2.19 are evaluated using equations I-2.2.23 and I-2.2.25 in conjunction with the Markov recursion algorithm in procedure **PolDerivativeEmulator.**

If A is zero degree (and assumed to be unity), then the solution is trivial

$$E(s) = P(s)C(s); F(s) = 0 \tag{2.1.1.1}$$

Otherwise the Markov recursion algorithm is initialised as in equation I-1.5.3. That is

$$E_0(s) = 0; F_0(s) = 1 \tag{2.1.1.2}$$

The Markov recursion algorithm is then used to recursively generate the $F_{1k}(s)$ and $E_{1k}(s)$ polynomials and take the weighted sum to form $E_1(s)$ and $F_1(s)$ as in equations I-2.2.23 and I-2.2.25.

It is important to note that

$$deg\,(C\,(s)) < deg\,(A\,(s))$$ (2.1.1.3)

for this algorithm to work correctly.

Procedure **PolDerivativeEmulator** can be thought of as a way of performing **polynomial long division** as in equation I-2.2.26. This operation is needed later on, so the procedure **PolDivide** is defined exploiting this property. In general, the equation

$$\frac{B'(s)}{A'(s)} = E'(s) + \frac{F'(s)}{A'(s)}$$ (2.1.1.4)

can be solved by using procedure **PolDerivativeEmulator** with

$$P\,(s) = B'(s);\ C\,(s) = 1$$ (2.1.1.5)

This is the method used in procedure **PolDivide**.

Procedure **PolDerivativeEmulator** is embedded in procedure **PolEmulator**. It is invoked if $Z(s)$ is a zero degree polynomial; it is assumed that, in this case

$$Z(s) = Z^{-}(s) = Z^{+}(s) = 1$$ (2.1.1.6)

The emulator numerator polynomial

$$G_1(s) = E_1(s)B\,(s) = E_1(s)B^{+}(s)$$ (2.1.1.7)

is computed in procedure **PolEmulator,** together with the corresponding denominator polynomials GFilter and FFilter which are both equal to $C(s)$ in this case.

Procedure **PolInitialConditions** is used to compute the initial condition terms. The first step is to compute the polynomial $E^{D}{}_1(s)$. The expression for $E^{D}{}_1(s)$ (equations I-2.2.14 and I-2.2.24) is the same as that for $E_1(s)$ but with $D\,(s)$ (the initial condition numerator) replacing $C\,(s)$ (the disturbance numerator). Hence $E^{D}{}_1(s)$ can be computed using procedure **PolDerivativeEmulator** but with the argument C replaced by D. The initial condition term is then calculated from equation I-2.2.21. In this case, $B^{-}(s) = 1$ so the statement

PolDivide(InitialCondition, Rem, InitialCondition,
          BMinus);

has no effect here. Finally, procedure **PolTruncate** is applied to clean up the initial condition polynomial.

2.1.2. [2.3] ZERO CANCELLING AND OTHER FILTERS

The algorithms required for the design of emulators corresponding to section I-2.4 are more complicated than those required for the previous section due to the additional design parameter $Z(s)$. There are many possible choices for $Z(s)$, but these must always obey the two design rules on page I-2-12. Here, $Z(s)$ is generated, in terms of user-chosen polynomials, by procedure **SetDesignKnobs**. The user supplies two polynomials **ZMinusPlus** ($Z^{-+}(s)$) and **ZPlus** ($Z^{+}(s)$), and two Boolean variables **ZHasFactorB** and **IntegralAction**. It is assumed that both polynomials ($Z^{-+}(s)$ and $Z^{+}(s)$) are stable.

Procedure **SetDesignKnobs** then generates Z, and decomposes B, as follows. There are three possibilities dependent on the two Boolean variables.

1. ZHasFactorB = FALSE

$B(s)$ is decomposed as

$$B^{+}(s) = B(s); \, B^{-}(s) = 1 \tag{2.1.2.1}$$

2. ZHasFactorB = TRUE, IntegralAction=FALSE

It is assumed that $B(0) \neq 0$. $B(s)$ is decomposed as

$$B^{+}(s) = 1; \, B^{-}(s) = B(s) \tag{2.1.2.2}$$

3. ZHasFactorB = TRUE, IntegralAction=TRUE

It is assumed that $B(s) = sB's$, $B'(0) \neq 0$. $B(s)$ is decomposed as

$$B^{+}(s) = s; \, B^{-}(s) = B'(s) \tag{2.1.2.3}$$

In each case, $B^{-}(s)$ is normalised so that $B^{-}(0) = 1$ and $B^{+}(s)$ adjusted accordingly. This is always possible as $B^{-}(0) \neq 0$.

$Z(s)$ and $Z^{-}(s)$ are generated as

$$Z^{-}(s) = Z^{-+}(s)B^{-}(s); \, Z(s) = Z^{+}(s)Z^{-}(s) \tag{2.1.2.4}$$

The emulator polynomials $E_2(s)$ and $F_2(s)$ are generated by procedure **PolZeroCancellingEmulator.**

Firstly, as discussed in section I-2.4 (page I-2-17), any common factors between $A(s)$ and $Z^-(s)$ are detected using Euclid's algorithm (see the next section) and removed. To retain the same $Z(s)$, this factor is then put into $Z^+(s)$. This latter step will only be useful if the factor is stable.

The Diophantine equation I-2.3.23 is solved for $E_2(s)$ and $F_2(s)$ using the procedure **PolDiophantine** described in the next section.

As with procedure **PolDerivativeEmulator**, procedure **PolZeroCancellingEmulator** is embedded in procedure **PolEmulator** to generate the remaining emulator polynomials. It is invoked if $Z(s)$ has degree greater than zero. It is assumed that this polynomial has been correctly generated (for example using **SetDesignKnobs**) to obey the two design rules on page I-2-12.

The emulator numerator polynomial

$$G_1(s) = E_1(s)B^+(s) \tag{2.1.2.5}$$

is computed in procedure **PolEmulator**, together with the corresponding denominator polynomials GFilter and FFilter which are both equal to $C(s)$ in this case.

If a common factor $g(s)$ of $A(s)Z^+(s)$ and $Z^-(s)$ is found, the resultant emulator parameters are not relevant - essentially the Diophantine equation has been solved with $g(s)P(s)$ replacing $P(s)$. The solution to the difficulty used here is to *remove* the factor $g(s)$ from $Z^-(s)$ and append it to $Z^+(s)$. This removes the common factor whilst retaining the same $Z(s) = Z^+(s)Z^-(s)$ as before. However, this method will not be useful if $g(s)$ is not stable.

Procedure **PolInitialConditions** is used to compute the initial condition terms. The first step is to compute the polynomial $E^D{}_2(s)$. The expression for $E^D{}_2(s)$ (equation I-2.3.7) is the same as that for $E_2(s)$ but with $D(s)$ (the initial condition numerator) replacing $C(s)$ (the disturbance numerator). Hence $E^D{}_2(s)$ can be computed using procedure **PolZeroCancellingEmulator** but with the argument C replaced by D. The initial condition term is then calculated from equation I-2.3.26.

2.1.3. SOLVING DIOPHANTINE EQUATIONS

As discussed on page I-2-18, there are three steps involved in solving Diophantine equations of the form

$$P(s)C(s) = E_2(s)A(s)Z^+(s) + F_2(s)Z^-(s) \tag{2.1.3.1}$$

for $E_2(s)$ and $F_2(s)$.

A   Find the greatest common divisor of $Z^-(s)$ and $A(s)Z^+(s)$ using Euclid's algorithm.

B   Solve

$$1 = e(s)A(s)Z^+(s) + f(s)Z^-(s) \tag{2.1.3.2}$$

for e(s) and f(s).

C   Use e(s) and f(s) to solve equation 1 recursively.

Steps A and B are implemented in procedure **PolEuclid**; step C is implemented in procedure **PolDioRecursion.**

Procedure **PolEuclid** has three main sections.

1.   Procedure **FindGCD** which implements step A,

2.   Procedure **DeduceEandF** which implements step B and

3.   procedures to clean up E and F and to normalise the GCD.

Equations I-2.4.5&6 of the recursive algorithm are implemented in procedure **FindGCD**. The initialisation step of equation I-2.4.1 occurs implicitly in the parameter passing mechanism when

FindGCD(AlphaIminus1{A},AlphaI{B} : Polynomial);

is called within procedure **PolEuclid as**

FindGCD(a,b);

The corresponding quotients q_i are saved in an array for use in procedure **DeduceEandF.**

The equations for finding the polynomials e(s) and f(s) solving the Diophantine equation 2.1.4.2 are given on pages I-2-21&22. They are implemented in procedure **DeduceEandF**. The quotients q_i are always preceded by a minus sign in these equations, so as a first step in the algorithm, the quotients are all multiplied by -1. In the trivial case where the a(s) =a is scalar (N=0) then the particular solution

$$e = 1/a \,;\, f = 0 \text{ is chosen,} \tag{2.1.3.3}$$

otherwise, β and γ are initialised as in the equations following I-2.4.9.

Equations I.2.4.14 are recursively implemented in a FOR loop from N-1 down to 1.

The **Diophantine recursion algorithm** is summarised on page I-2-21. In the following discussion, we shall assume that $Z^-(s)$ has been adjusted to avoid factors in common with $A(s)Z^+(s)$ (see the previous section). The basic idea is that given $E_{2k}(s)$ and $F_{2k}(s)$ solving

$$\frac{s^k}{a(s)b(s)} = \frac{E_{2k}(s)}{b(s)} + \frac{F_{2k}(s)}{a(s)}$$ (2.1.3.4)

where

$$a(s) = A(s)Z^+(s); \ b(s) = Z^-(s)$$ (2.1.3.5)

It follows that

$$\frac{s^{k+1}}{a(s)b(s)} = \frac{sE_{2k}(s)}{b(s)} + \frac{sF_{2k}(s)}{a(s)}$$ (2.1.3.6)

$$= \frac{E_{2k+1}(s)}{b(s)} + \frac{F_{2k+1}(s)}{a(s)}$$ (2.1.3.7)

where $E_{2k+1}(s)$ and $F_{2k+1}(s)$ are defined by

$$E_{2k+1}(s) = sE_{2k}(s) + hkb(s); \ F_{2k+1}(s) = sF_{2k}(s) - hka(s)$$ (2.1.3.8)

If h_k is chosen as the first Markov parameter of $\dfrac{F_{2k}(s)}{a(s)}$, then $\dfrac{F_{2k+1}(s)}{a(s)}$ will be proper as required. As the solution for k=0 has been found using Euclid's algorithm as described above, this **Diophantine recursion algorithm** provides a means of solution for all k *without* needing to solve further Diophantine equations.

The recursive equations 2.1.4.6-8 are implemented in procedure **PolDioRecursion**. There are two cases. Firstly, if $deg(a(s)) < deg(sF(s))$, then the corresponding Markov parameter is zero and both $E_{2k}(s)$ and $F_{2k}(s)$ are multiplied by s. Otherwise, equations 2.1.4.6-8 are implemented.

The whole solution of the Diophantine equation is brought together in procedure **PolDiophantine**. Firstly, the Diophantine equation

$$1 = E0sA(s)Z^+(s) + F0sZ^-(s)$$ (2.1.3.9)

is solved using procedure **PolEuclid**. (If a common factor is found, then 1 is replaced by such a factor, but this situation is always avoided as described in section I-2.3.) Then the polynomials *Eks* and *Fks* solving

$$s^k = EksA(s)Z^+(s) + FksZ^-(s)$$ (2.1.3.10)

are computed recursively using procedure **PolDioRecursion** and these are summed, weighted by the corresponding coefficients of $P(s)C(s)$, to form $E_2(s)$ and $F_2(s)$.

Note

There is an inconsistency in notation between sections I-2.3 and I-2.4. The former defines the polynomials *Eks* and *Fks* by

$$s^k C(s) = EksA(s)Z^+(s) + FksZ^-(s) \tag{2.1.3.11}$$

and the latter by

$$s^k = EksA(s)Z^+(s) + FksZ^-(s) \tag{2.1.3.12}$$

It is the latter definition that is used here. If the former had been used then *Eks* and *Fks* would have been weighted by the coefficients of $P(s)$ (as in equations I-2.3.20&22), not by the coefficients of $P(s)C(s)$.

2.1.4. [2.6] APPROXIMATE TIME-DELAYS

The **Pade polynomial** of order N is computed by procedure **PolPade**. This recursively computes the coefficients using the formula I-2.6.7.

The emulator coefficients corresponding to $\overline{\phi}_4(s)$ are computed in procedure **PolDelayEmulator**. Firstly, procedure **PolPade** is used to find the denominator $T(s)$ of the time-delay approximation; the corresponding numerator $T(-s)$ is computed using procedure **PolOfMinusS**. The polynomials $P_T(s)$ and *Zminus* are computed according to equations I-2.6.8&9. Notice that this change is local to the procedure as **DesignKnobs** is passed by value. Procedure **PolEmulator** is then used to calculate the emulator coefficients based on the modified polynomials.

2.1.5. [2.7] LINEAR-IN-THE PARAMETERS FORM

In general, the emulator equation I-2.7.1 can be combined with I-2.7.6, I-2.7.7, or I-2.7.8 and rewritten as

$$\overline{\phi}^{**}(s) = \frac{G(s)}{G_f(s)}\overline{u}(s) + \frac{F(s)}{F_f(s)}\overline{y}(s) + \frac{I(s)Z^{-+}(s)}{G_f(s)} \tag{2.1.5.1}$$

where

$$G_f(s) = C(s)TsZ^{-+}(s); \ F_f(s) = C(s)Z^+(s) \tag{2.1.5.2}$$

This equation is implemented as function **Emulator.**

Firstly, the local variable **Em** is set to zero. The various components formed by filtering the system input, the system output and the initial condition term are in turn added to the local variable Em. Secondly, the terms corresponding to interaction variables (see chapter 10) are added to Em. Finally, Em is assigned to the function output.

In this implementation, the equation I-2.7.9 is not explicitly implemented. But if the operation of function **Filter,** and its associated procedures **StateVariableFilter** and **StateOutput,** are considered, it can be seen that the emulator output is found by generating the data vectors $\overline{X}_u(s)$, $\overline{X}_y(s)$ and $\overline{X}_i(s)$, and then forming the inner product of these vectors with the vectors formed from the coefficients of the respective polynomials within function **StateOutput.**

2.1.6. DISCRETE-TIME IMPLEMENTATION

CSTC is primarily designed to implement the *continuous-time* algorithms to be found in Volume 1. However, it should be emphasised that *algebraicly* controller design in *discrete-time* is very similar.

The switch between the two domains is accomplished via the Boolean variable **ContinuousTime.** The minor modifications (with regard to the *design* algorithms) implied by setting this switch to FALSE can be seen from the listing of CSTC. The only place where **ContinuousTime** has any effect is in computing the steady-state gain of **BMinus,** using **PolGain** in procedure **SetDesignKnobs.** In the continuous-time case, the steady-state gain of $B^-(s)$ is $B^-(0)$; in the continuous-time case, the steady-state gain of $B^-(s)$ is $B^-(1)$. This is reflected in procedure **PolGain.**

2.2. EXAMPLES

2.2.1. OUTPUT DERIVATIVES

Reference: Section 2.2; pp 2-9 - 2-11.

Description

The example refers to the system:

$$\frac{B(s)}{A(s)} = \frac{0.1s+1}{s(s+1)}$$

(2.2.1.1)

with initial conditions defined by:

$$D(s) = 0.1s + 1$$

(2.2.1.2)

The design is based on the output derivative approach with:

$$P(s) = C(s) = 0.5s+1$$

(2.2.1.3)

Programme interaction

runex 2 1
Example 2 of chapter 1: Output derivatives

======== C S T C Version 6.0 ========

Enter all variables (y/n, default n)?

======== Assumed system ========
A (system denominator)   =   1.000000   1.000000   0.000000 :=
B (system numerator)   =   0.100000   1.000000 :=
D (initial conditions)   =   0.100000   1.000000 :=
======== Emulator design ========
P (model denominator)   =   0.500000   1.000000 :=
C (emulator denominator) =   0.500000   1.000000 :=
----
*   System polynomials*

A   1.000000   1.000000   0.000000
B   0.100000   1.000000
D   0.100000   1.000000

Design polynomials

```
------------------------------------
B+          0.100000      1.000000
B-          1.000000
C           0.500000      1.000000
P           0.500000      1.000000
Z+          1.000000
Z-          1.000000
Z-+         1.000000
------------------------------------
F           0.750000      1.000000
F filter    0.500000      1.000000
G           0.025000      0.250000
G filter    0.500000      1.000000
I           0.200000
E           0.250000
ED          0.050000
------------------------------------
```

Discussion

The emulator parameters agree with those given in volume I. $G(s)$ has one root at s=10 corresponding to the system zero.

Further investigations

1. Try the effect of varying P, A and B. Take careful note of the degrees of the various polynomials. Check that $G(s)$ contains $B(s)$ as a factor.

2.2.2. ZERO CANCELLATION

   Reference: Sections 2.4, pp I-22 - I-26

Description

This example illustrates the design of an emulator for multiple derivatives with zero cancellation: that is, multiple derivatives of the partial state. The first example on page I-2-25 is used, the second example appears under further investigation. Note that the Boolean variable 'Z has factor B' is now TRUE; this gives the zero cancellation effect.

Programme interaction

runex 2 2
Example 2 of chapter 2: Zero cancellation

======== C S T C Version 6.0 ========

Enter all variables (y/n, default n)?

======== Assumed system ========
A (system denominator)   =   1.000000   1.000000   0.000000 :=
B (system numerator)   =   0.100000   1.000000 :=
D (initial conditions)   =   0.100000   1.000000 :=
======== Emulator design ========
Z has factor B   = TRUE :=
P (model denominator)   =   0.250000   1.000000   1.000000 :=
C (emulator denominator) =   0.500000   1.000000 :=
Small positive number   =   0.000100 :=

       System polynomials

A   1.000000   1.000000   0.000000
B   0.100000   1.000000
D   0.100000   1.000000

       Design polynomials

B+   1.000000
B-   0.100000   1.000000
C   0.500000   1.000000
P   0.250000   1.000000   1.000000
Z+   1.000000
Z-   0.100000   1.000000
Z-+   1.000000

F   0.861111   1.000000
F filter 0.500000 1.000000
G   0.125000   0.538889
G filter 0.500000 1.000000
I   0.288889
E   0.125000   0.538889
ED   0.025000   0.250000

Discussion

Note that the emulator parameters agree with those of volume I. This emulator should be compared with that of the previous example; in particular, note that G does not contain $B(s)$ as a factor. What is the root of $G(s)$?

Further investigations

1. Try changing $B(s)$ to give a non-minimum phase system.

$$B(s) = 1-s$$

The resultant emulator should correspond to equation 47 on page I-2-25.

2. Try the effect of varying P, A and B. Take careful note of the degrees of the various poynomials.

3. Try setting the Boolean variable 'Z contains factor B' to FALSE. The resultant emulator then corresponds to the multiple derivative emulator of the previous example.

4. Try using the following system which has a pole/zero cancellation:

$$\frac{B(s)}{A(s)} = \frac{s+1}{s^2 + s} = \frac{1}{s} \qquad (2.2.2.1)$$

Notice that the algorithm finds the GCD of $Z^-(s)$ and $A(s)$.

5. Try using the following system which has an approximate pole/zero cancellation:

$$\frac{B(s)}{A(s)} = \frac{0.99s+1}{s^2 + s} \cong \frac{1}{s} \qquad (2.2.2.2)$$

Notice that the emulator now has rather strange coefficients due to this approximate cancellation. Try the effect of changing the 'Small positive number' to 0.1. The algorithm now finds the approximate cancellation.

2.2.3. PREDICTORS

Reference: Section 2.6; pp 2-33 - 2-36.

Description

This example illustrates emulator design for a system with a time delay using the Pade approximation. Essentially, as discussed in section I-2.5, the time delay translates into a rational non-minimum phase transfer function, and the zero-cancelling algorithm is applied.

The system has a first order rational part with unit time constant together with a unit delay

$$e^{-sT} \frac{B(s)}{A(s)} = e^{-s} \frac{1}{1+s} \qquad (2.2.3.1)$$

Programme interaction

runex 2 3
Example 2 of chapter 3: Predictors

======== C S T C Version 6.0 ========

Enter all variables (y/n, default n)?

======== Assumed system ========
A (system denominator) =   1.000000   1.000000 :=
B (system numerator)   =   1.000000 :=
Time delay   =   1.000000 :=
======== Emulator design ========
Z has factor B   = TRUE :=
P (model denominator)   =   1.000000 :=
C (emulator denominator) =   1.000000 :=
Pade approximation order =   4 :=
----
*   System polynomials*

A   1.000000   1.000000
B   1.000000
D   0.000000
----
*   Design polynomials*

B+   1.000000
B-   1.000000
C   1.000000
P   1.000000
Z+   1.000000
Z-   1.000000
Z-+   1.000000
Pade   0.000595   0.011905   0.107143   0.500000   1.000000

F   0.367879
F filter 1.000000
G   0.000376   0.015908   0.051819   0.632121
G filter 0.000595   0.011905   0.107143   0.500000   1.000000
I

| E | 0.000376 | 0.015908 | 0.051819 | 0.632121 |
| ED | 0.000000 | 0.000000 | 0.000000 | 0.000000 |

Discussion

Note that the degree of $F(s)$ is the same as that of $C(s)$ but the degree of G is increased by the degree of the Pade approximation.

Further investigations

1. Try varying the order of the Pade approximation.

2. Try varying the time delay. Note that the gain of the emulator transfer function multiplying y decreases with delay; this is because the future becomes less dependent on the present for large delays.

3. Try including multiple derivatives by using P.

CHAPTER 3
Emulator-Based Control

Aims. To describe the implementation of the controller. To illustrate the behaviour of the various control algorithms when the system is precisely known.

3.1. IMPLEMENTATION DETAILS

3.1.1. [3.2] THE CONTROL LAW

On page I-3-2, the control law is written in two forms. As equation I-3.2.1 appears to give an explicit expression for the control signal, whereas equation I-3.2.2 gives an implicit expression for the control signal, we will refer to equation I-3.2.1 as the **explicit form** and to equation I-3.2.2 as the **implicit form.**

Both forms are implemented in CSTC within procedure **Control:** the implicit form is implemented in procedure **ImplicitSolution;** the explicit form appears directly in procedure **Control.** The choice between the two method is made on the basis of the relative degree of $Q(s)$. Now, as stated in section I3.2, $\dfrac{1}{Q(s)}$ must be proper, so there are two possibilities: either

1. $\dfrac{1}{Q(s)}$ is *strictly* proper or

2. $\dfrac{1}{Q(s)}$ has numerator and denominator of equal degrees.

In the former case, the **explicit form** of the control equation is appropriate as the right-hand side of
I-3.2.1 does not depend instantaneously on the the control signal u. In the latter case, $Q(s)$ is also
proper, and so I-3.2.2 contains proper transfer functions. This decision is made at the IF statement in
Control.

Explicit solution

   The explicit solution is straightforward, the error signal **w - PhiHat** is fed into a filter implementing the transfer function $\dfrac{1}{Q(s)}$. **PhiHat** itself is generated using procedure **Emulator** within the body
of procedure **SelfTuningControl.**

Implicit solution

   The implicit solution is more complex. Essentially, the equation has to decomposed into two
terms: one independent on the current control signal, and the remainder. In principle, this can be done
by considering the instantaneous gains other various transfer-functions involved, but a more direct
approach is used here. Within function **ImplicitSolution,** the term

$$\overline{\phi}^*(s) + Q(s)\hat{u}(s) \qquad\qquad\qquad (3.1.1.1)$$

is evaluated twice using the the state from the previous time step: firstly with the current value of
control equal to zero; and secondly with the current value of control equal to unity. These values are
stored in **PhiQ0Hat** and in **PhiQ1Hat** respectively. It is important to realise that two copies of the
past states of the emulator and the $Q(s)$ filter are made for this purpose by passing **Em0State,**
Em0State, Q0State, and **Q1State** by value. The term independent of the *current* control signal is
then **PhiQ0Hat - w;** the remaining term is then the product of the current control signal **u** with
PhiQ1Hat - PhiQ0Hat. The control signal can then be directly computed.

   This approach has the disadvantage of requiring a lot of computation; procedure **Emulator** is
executed an additional two times. But this approach has the merit of solving the equation *exactly* for
the discrete-time approximation of the actual continuous-time control law. This has found to be more
effective numerically than computing the two components of the control equation directly.

Limiting the control signal

As emphasised in section I-3.2, it is essential that all filters comprising the emulator-based control act on the actual control signal sent to the process - including the effect of any limiting - rather than the computed control signal. This is achieved in CSTC by implementing the procedure **Emulator** *after* the control signal limiting in **PutData** within the body of **SelfTuningControl**. In addition, when the implicit control law calculation is used, the filter corresponding to $Q(s)$ is updated immediately following the emulator.

PutData implements two forms of control signal modification dependent on the value of the Boolean variable **Switched**. If **Switched** is false then the control signal is truncated if greater than **Max** or less than **Min**. If, on the other hand, **Switched** is true then the the control signal is set to **Max** or to **Min** depending on which value is closest. This thus implements an elementary form of switched control; more advanced versions appear in a recent paper*.

3.1.2. INTEGRAL ACTION [3.10]

The PID design rule 1 (page I-3-23) requires that $A(s)$ and $B(s)$ have a common root s=0. This is achieved in CSTC via the Boolean variable **IntegralAction.** If this variable is 'TRUE' then the factor s is appended to $A(s)$ and $B(s)$ in procedure **SystemInitialise** using procedure **SystemInitialise**. In the multi-loop case, the interaction polynomials **BInteraction[i]** are also multiplied by s. The initial condition term is similarly treated.

PID design rule 2 (page I-3-23) requires that the factor s is put into $B^+(s)$. This is taken care of in procedure **SetDesignKnobs.**

3.2. EXAMPLES

3.2.1. MODEL REFERENCE CONTROL

Reference: Section 3.4; page 3-12.

---

* Demircioglu, H. and Gawthrop, P.J. (1988):" Continuous-time relay self-tuning control", Int. J. Control. **47**, pp. 1061-1080.

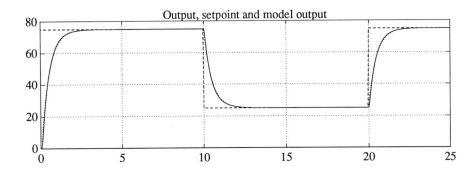

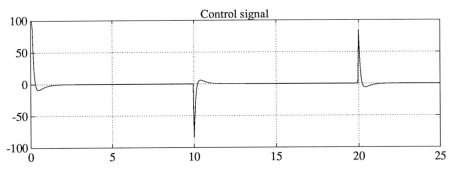

Figure 3.1. Model reference control

Description

As discussed in volume I, the emulator designed in example 2.2.1 may be embedded in a feed-back loop to give model reference control. The system numerator has been multiplied by 10 for the purposes of this example.

The aim of the controller is to make the system output follow the model:

$$\bar{y}(s) = \frac{Z(s)}{P(s)} \bar{w}(s) \tag{3.2.1.1}$$

where, in this case, $Z(s)=1$ and $P(s) = 1+Ts$, where the model time-constant $T = 0.5$.

Programme interaction

runex 3 1
Example 3 of chapter 1: Model reference control

======== C S T C Version 6.0 ========

Enter all variables (y/n, default n)?

======== Data Source   ========
======== Filters   ========
Sample Interval   =   0.050000 :=
======== Control action ========
======== Assumed system ========
A (system denominator)   =   1.000000   1.000000   0.000000 :=
B (system numerator)   =   1.000000   10.000000 :=
D (initial conditions)   =   0.000000   0.000000 :=
======== Emulator design ========
P (model denominator)   =   0.500000   1.000000 :=
C (emulator denominator) =   0.500000   1.000000 :=

      System polynomials

A	1.000000	1.000000	0.000000
B	1.000000	10.000000	
D	0.000000	0.000000	

      Design polynomials

B+	1.000000	10.000000
B-	1.000000	
C	0.500000	1.000000
P	0.500000	1.000000
Z+	1.000000	
Z-	1.000000	
Z-+	1.000000	

F	0.750000	1.000000
F filter	0.500000	1.000000
G	0.250000	2.500000
G filter	0.500000	1.000000
I		
E	0.250000	
ED	0.000000	

======== Controller   ========
Maximum control signal   =   100.000000 :=

Minimum control signal = *-100.000000* :=
Switched control signal = *FALSE* :=
  ======== *Simulation* ========
  ======== *Setpoint* ========
  ======== *In Disturbance* ========
  ======== *Out Disturbance* ========
Simulation running:
    25% complete
    50% complete
    75% complete
    100% complete
Time now is *25.000000*

Discussion

The upper graph displays three signals: the system output $y(t)$, the setpoint $w(t)$ and the ideal model output $y_m(t)$ where $\overline{y}_m(s) = \dfrac{Z(s)}{P(s)}\overline{w}(s)$.

As expected, $y(t) \cong y_m(t)$. Any discrepancy is due to numerical inaccuracy.

Further investigations

1. Try the effect of varying the time constant T of the inverse model P. How does this affect the system output and the control signal?

2. The emulator denominator $C(s)$ is also of the form 1+Ts. Try the effect of varying the time constant T of the emulator denominator C. How does this affect the system output and the control signal?

3. Try changing the limits of the control signal so that it is clipped; for example choose 'Maximum control signal' as 10 and 'Minimum control signal' as -10. How does this affect the system output and the control signal?

4. The controller and simulation are implemented as discrete-time systems. Try the effect of varying the sample interval on closed-loop performance.

5. Try using a switched controller by setting 'Switched control signal' to TRUE. How does the performance depend on:

   a) Sample interval

   b) The maximum and minimum control limits.

3.2.2. POLE-PLACEMENT CONTROL

Reference: Section 3.4; page 3-13.

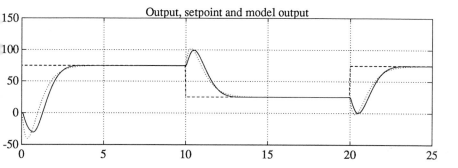

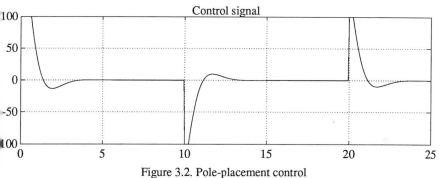

Figure 3.2. Pole-placement control

Description

As discussed in volume I, the emulator designed in the second example of section I-2.4 may be embedded in a feedback loop to give pole-placement control.

The aim of the controller is to make the system output follow the model:

$$\bar{y}(s) = \frac{Z(s)}{P(s)}\bar{w}(s) \qquad\qquad (3.2.2.1)$$

where, in this case, $Z(s) = B(s)$ and $P(s) = (1+Ts)^2$ where the model time-constant $T = 0.5$.

Programme interaction

runex 3 2
Example 3 of chapter 2: Pole-placement control

======== C S T C Version 6.0 ========

Enter all variables (y/n, default n)?

======== Data Source   ========
======== Filters   ========
Continuous-time?   = TRUE :=
======== Control action ========
======== Assumed system ========
A (system denominator) =   1.000000   1.000000   0.000000 :=
B (system numerator)   = -1.000000   1.000000 :=
======== Emulator design ========
Z has factor B   = TRUE :=
P (model denominator)   =   0.250000   1.000000   1.000000 :=
C (emulator denominator) =   0.500000   1.000000 :=

    System polynomials

A   1.000000   1.000000   0.000000
B   -1.000000   1.000000
D   0.000000   0.000000

    Design polynomials

B+   1.000000
B-   -1.000000   1.000000
C   0.500000   1.000000
P   0.250000   1.000000   1.000000
Z+   1.000000
Z-   -1.000000   1.000000
Z-+   1.000000

F   0.937500   1.000000
F filter 0.500000   1.000000
G   0.125000   1.562500
G filter 0.500000   1.000000
I
E   0.125000   1.562500
ED   0.000000   0.000000

======== Controller   ========
Maximum control signal = 100.000000 :=

Minimum control signal   = -100.000000 :=
Switched control signal = FALSE :=
======== Simulation   ========
======== Setpoint   ========
======== In Disturbance ========
======== Out Disturbance ========
Simulation running:
*   25% complete*
*   50% complete*
*   75% complete*
*   100% complete*
Time now is   25.000000

Discussion

The upper graph displays three signals: the system output $y(t)$, the setpoint $w(t)$ and the ideal model output $y_m(t)$ where $\bar{y}_m(s) = \dfrac{Z(s)}{P(s)} \bar{w}(s)$.

In this case, note the typical behaviour of a system with right-hand plane zeros: the output initially goes the wrong way in response to a step change.

Further investigations

1. Try the effect of varying the time constant T of the inverse model P. How does this affect the system output and the control signal?

2. Try repeating this example using the same system as the previous section ($B(s) = 10+s$). How does the closed-loop response when using pole-placement differ from that when using model-reference control?

3. Try using a switched controller by setting 'Switched control signal' to TRUE. How does the performance depend on:

    a) Sample interval

    b) The maximum and minimum control limits.

3.2.3. USING A SETPOINT FILTER

Reference: Section 3.5; page 3-15.

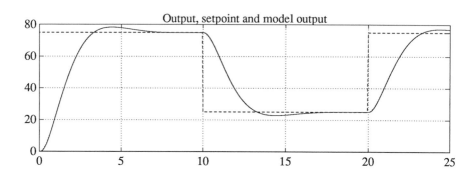

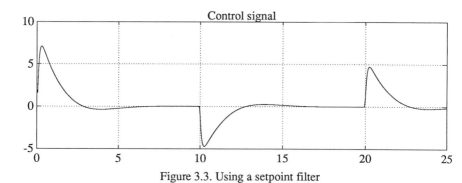

Figure 3.3. Using a setpoint filter

Description

This example is identical to example 3.2.1 except that a setpoint filter is added:

$$\overline{w}_R(s) = R(s)\overline{w}(s); \; R(s) = \frac{0.5s+1}{s^2 + \sqrt{2}s + 1} \tag{3.2.3.1}$$

The closed loop response is thus:

$$\overline{y}(s) = \frac{Z(s)}{P(s)}R(s)\overline{w}(s) = \frac{1}{0.5s+1} \frac{0.5s+1}{s^2 + \sqrt{2}s + 1}\overline{w}(s) \tag{3.2.3.2}$$

$$= \frac{1}{s^2 + \sqrt{2}s + 1}\overline{w}(s)$$

Programme interaction

runex 3 3
Example 3 of chapter 3: Using a setpoint filter

    ======== C S T C Version 6.0 ========

Enter all variables (y/n, default n)?

    ======== Data Source   ========
    ======== Filters   ========
Sample Interval   =   0.050000 :=
    ======== Control action ========
    ======== Assumed system ========
A (system denominator)   =   1.000000   1.000000   0.000000 :=
B (system numerator)   =   1.000000   10.000000 :=
D (initial conditions)   =   0.000000   0.000000 :=
    ======== Emulator design ========
P (model denominator)   =   0.500000   1.000000 :=
C (emulator denominator) =   0.500000   1.000000 :=

        System polynomials

A   1.000000   1.000000   0.000000
B   1.000000   10.000000
D   0.000000   0.000000

        Design polynomials

B+   1.000000   10.000000
B-   1.000000
C   0.500000   1.000000
P   0.500000   1.000000
Z+   1.000000
Z-   1.000000
Z-+   1.000000

F   0.750000   1.000000
F filter 0.500000   1.000000
G   0.250000   2.500000
G filter 0.500000   1.000000
I
E   0.250000
ED   0.000000

    ======== Controller   ========
R numerator   =   0.500000   1.000000 :=

R denominator = *1.000000 1.414000 1.000000* :=
Maximum control signal = *100.000000* :=
Minimum control signal = *-100.000000* :=
======== *Simulation* ========
======== *Setpoint* ========
======== *In Disturbance* ========
======== *Out Disturbance* ========
Simulation running:
   25% complete
   50% complete
   75% complete
   100% complete
Time now is *25.000000*
More time = *FALSE* :=

Discussion

The upper graph displays three signals: the system output $y(t)$, the setpoint $w(t)$ and the ideal model output $y_m(t)$ where $\bar{y}_m(s) = \dfrac{Z(s)}{P(s)}\bar{w}(s)$.

Note that the control signal is considerably reduced, and that the output is smoother.

Further investigations

1. Try the effect of different choices of $R(s)$ and $P(s)$ on the system input and output if $\dfrac{R(s)}{P(s)}$ does not change.

2. Try the effect of different choices of $R(s)$ and $P(s)$ on the system input and output if $\dfrac{R(s)}{P(s)}$ does change.

3. Choose $R(s)$ to give a critically damped response, for example:

$$R(s) = \frac{0.5s+1}{s^2 + 2s + 1} \qquad (3.2.3.3)$$

3.2.4. CONTROL-WEIGHTED MODEL REFERENCE

Reference: Section 3.6; page 3-16.

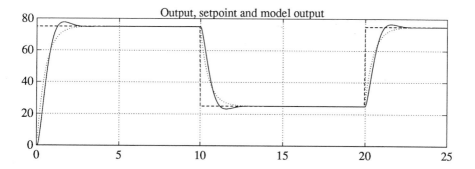

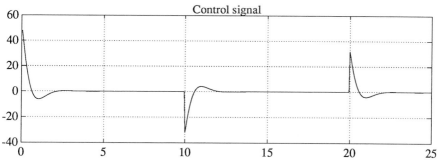

Figure 3.4. Control-weighted model reference

Description

In example 3.2.1, exact model-reference control was achieved by setting $Q(s)=0$. For this example, $Q(s)$ is chosen as

$$Q(s) = \frac{0.1s}{s+1} \qquad\qquad (3.2.4.1)$$

this satifies the $Q(s)$ design rule on page I-3-17: $Q(0) = 0$.

Programme interaction

runex 3 4
Example 3 of chapter 4: Control-weighted model reference

```
======== C S T C Version 6.0 ========

Enter all variables (y/n, default n)?

======== Data Source    ========
======== Filters        ========
Sample Interval       =    0.050000  :=
Continuous-time?         = TRUE  :=
======== Control action ========
Automatic controller mode = TRUE  :=
======== Assumed system ========
A (system denominator)  =    1.000000    1.000000    0.000000  :=
B (system numerator)    =    1.000000   10.000000  :=
D (initial conditions)  =    0.000000    0.000000  :=
======== Emulator design ========
P (model denominator)    =    0.500000    1.000000  :=
C (emulator denominator) =    0.500000    1.000000  :=
-----------------------------------
        System polynomials
-----------------------------------
A         1.000000    1.000000    0.000000
B         1.000000   10.000000
D         0.000000    0.000000
-----------------------------------
        Design polynomials
-----------------------------------
B+         1.000000   10.000000
B-         1.000000
C          0.500000    1.000000
P          0.500000    1.000000
Z+         1.000000
Z-         1.000000
Z-+        1.000000
-----------------------------------
F          0.750000    1.000000
F filter   0.500000    1.000000
G          0.250000    2.500000
G filter   0.500000    1.000000
I
E          0.250000
ED         0.000000
-----------------------------------
======== Controller     ========
Q numerator           =    1.000000    0.000000  :=
Q denominator         =    1.000000    1.000000  :=
Maximum control signal  =    100.000000  :=
Minimum control signal  =   -100.000000  :=
======== Simulation     ========
======== Setpoint       ========
```

======== *In Disturbance* ========
======== *Out Disturbance* ========
Simulation running:
    25% complete
    50% complete
    75% complete
    100% complete
Time now is   25.000000
More time   = FALSE :=

Discussion

The upper graph displays three signals: the system output $y(t)$, the setpoint $w(t)$ and the ideal model output $y_m(t)$ where $\bar{y}_m(s) = \dfrac{Z(s)}{P(s)}\bar{w}(s)$.

Notice that the control signal is reduced with respect to that of example 3.2.1. The model following is no longer exact, but the use of the $Q(s)$ design rule ensures that there is no steady-state offset.

Further investigations

1.   Try the effect of varying q in:

$$Q(s) = \frac{qs}{1+s} \qquad\qquad (3.2.4.2)$$

2.   Try the effect of varying T in:

$$Q(s) = \frac{s}{1+Ts} \qquad\qquad (3.2.4.3)$$

3.   Replace $Q(s)$ by:

$$Q(s) = q \qquad\qquad (3.2.4.4)$$

There is still no offset as, in this case, the system contains an integrator and so the control signal is zero in the steady-state.

4.   Replace $Q(s)$ by:

$$Q(s) = q \qquad\qquad (3.2.4.5)$$

and $A(s)$ by:

$$A(s) = s^2 + 2s + 1 \qquad (3.2.4.6)$$

Note that there is now an offset dependent on q.

5. Use the default value of $Q(s)$ but replace $A(s)$ by:

$$A(s) = s^2 + 2s + 1 \qquad (3.2.4.7)$$

Note that the offset disappears.

3.2.5. CONTROL-WEIGHTED POLE-PLACEMENT

Reference: Section 3.6; page 3-16.

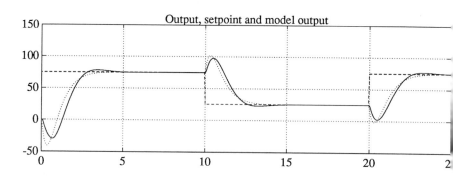

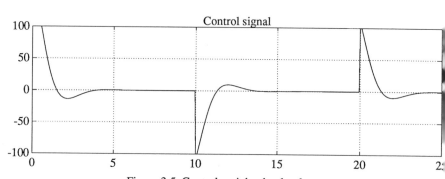

Figure 3.5. Control-weighted pole-placement

Description

In example 2, exact pole-placement control was achieved by setting $Q(s)=0$. For this example, $Q(s)$ is chosen as

$$Q(s) = \frac{s}{s+1} \tag{3.2.5.1}$$

As $Q(0)=0$, this satifies the $Q(s)$ design rule on page 3-17 of vol. 1.

Programme interaction

runex 3 5
Example 3 of chapter 5: Control-weighted pole-placement

======== C S T C Version 6.0 ========

Enter all variables (y/n, default n)?

======== Data Source   ========
======== Filters   ========
======== Control action ========
======== Assumed system ========
A (system denominator) =   1.000000   1.000000   0.000000 :=
B (system numerator)   =   -1.000000   1.000000 :=
======== Emulator design ========
Z has factor B   = TRUE :=
P (model denominator)   =   0.250000   1.000000   1.000000 :=
C (emulator denominator) =   0.500000   1.000000 :=

    System polynomials

A	*1.000000*	*1.000000*	*0.000000*
B	*-1.000000*	*1.000000*	
D	*0.000000*	*0.000000*	

    Design polynomials

B+	*1.000000*		
B-	*-1.000000*	*1.000000*	
C	*0.500000*	*1.000000*	
P	*0.250000*	*1.000000*	*1.000000*
Z+	*1.000000*		
Z-	*-1.000000*	*1.000000*	
Z-+	*1.000000*		

F	*0.937500*	*1.000000*
F filter	*0.500000*	*1.000000*
G	*0.125000*	*1.562500*
G filter	*0.500000*	*1.000000*
I		
E	*0.125000*	*1.562500*
ED	*0.000000*	*0.000000*

======== Controller   ========
Q numerator   =   0.100000   0.000000 :=
Q denominator   =   1.000000   1.000000 :=
Maximum control signal =   100.000000 :=
Minimum control signal = -100.000000 :=
======== Simulation   ========
======== Setpoint   ========
======== In Disturbance ========
======== Out Disturbance ========
Simulation running:
*   25% complete*
*   50% complete*
*   75% complete*
*   100% complete*
Time now is   25.000000

Discussion

The upper graph displays three signals: the system output $y(t)$, the setpoint $w(t)$ and the ideal model output $y_m(t)$ where $\bar{y}_m(s) = \dfrac{Z(s)}{P(s)}\bar{w}(s)$.

Notice that the control signal is reduced with respect to that of example 3.2.2. The model following is no longer exact, but the use of the $Q(s)$ design rule ensures that there is no steady-state offset.

Further investigations

1. Try the effect of varying q in:

$$Q(s) = \frac{qs}{1+s} \tag{3.2.5.2}$$

2. Try the effect of varying T in:

$$Q(s) = \frac{s}{1+Ts} \tag{3.2.5.3}$$

3. Replace $Q(s)$ by:

$$Q(s) = q \qquad (3.2.5.4)$$

There is still no offset as, in this case, the system contains an integrator and so the control signal is zero in the steady-state.

4. Replace $Q(s)$ by:

$$Q(s) = q \qquad (3.2.5.5)$$

and $A(s)$ by:

$$A(s) = s^2 + 2s + 1 \qquad (3.2.5.6)$$

Note that there is now an offset dependent on q.

5. Use the default value of $Q(s)$ but replace $A(s)$ by:

$$A(s) = s^2 + 2s + 1 \qquad (3.2.5.7)$$

Note that the offset disappears.

3.2.6. TIME-DELAY SYSTEM

Reference: Section 3.7; page 3-18.

Description

This example corresponds to example 3.2.1, except that the system now is first order and has a time delay of one unit.

$$\frac{B(s)}{A(s)} = e^{-s} \frac{1}{s} \qquad (3.2.6.1)$$

The corresponding emulator is based on the Pade approximation approach discussed in section I-2.6. But note that the simulation of the system uses an exact time-delay algorithm.

Programme interaction

runex 3 6
Example 3 of chapter 6: Time-delay system

======== C S T C Version 6.0 ========

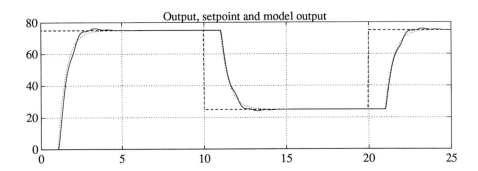

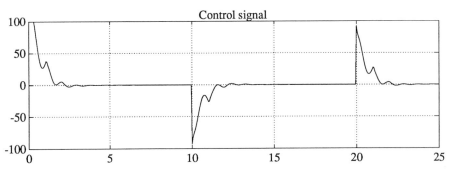

Figure 3.6. Time-delay system

Enter all variables (y/n, default n)?

```
======= Data Source    =======
======= Filters        =======
Sample Interval      =    0.050000  :=
======= Control action =======
======= Assumed system =======
A (system denominator)  =    1.000000   0.000000  :=
B (system numerator)    =    1.000000  :=
D (initial conditions)  =    0.000000  :=
======= Emulator design =======
P (model denominator)   =    0.500000   1.000000  :=
C (emulator denominator) =    1.000000  :=
Pade approximation order =       3  :=
------------------------------------
    System polynomials
------------------------------------
```

A	1.000000	0.000000
B	1.000000	
D	0.000000	

Design polynomials

B+	1.000000			
B-	1.000000			
C	1.000000			
P	0.500000	1.000000		
Z+	1.000000			
Z-	1.000000			
Z-+	1.000000			
Pade	0.008333	0.100000	0.500000	1.000000

F	1.000000			
F filter	1.000000			
G	0.004167	0.066667	0.250000	1.500000
G filter	0.008333	0.100000	0.500000	1.000000
I				
E	0.004167	0.066667	0.250000	1.500000
ED	0.000000	0.000000	0.000000	0.000000

```
======== Controller    ========
Maximum control signal  =  100.000000  :=
Minimum control signal  = -100.000000  :=
======== Simulation    ========
======== Setpoint      ========
======== In Disturbance ========
======== Out Disturbance ========
Simulation running:
    25% complete
    50% complete
    75% complete
    100% complete
Time now is   25.000000
More time          = FALSE  :=
```

Discussion

The upper graph displays three signals: the system output $y(t)$, the setpoint $w(t)$ and the ideal model output $y_m(t)$ where $\overline{y}_m(s) = \dfrac{Z(s)}{P(s)}\overline{w}(s)$.

Despite the approximation involved, the model following is close. Note that the system output is delayed by one time unit.

Further investigations

1. Try the effect of using a lower order (for example 1) approximation to a time delay in the emulator calculation.

2. Try the effect of using a higher order (for example 5) approximation to a time delay in the emulator calculation.

Note that 5 is the largest permissible value for the Pade approximation order in this implementation.

3.2.7. MODEL REFERENCE - DISTURBANCES

Reference: Section 3.9; page 3-20.

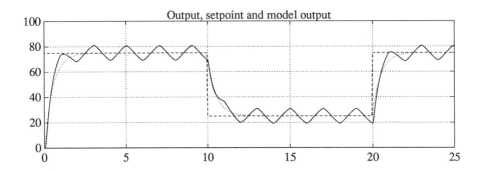

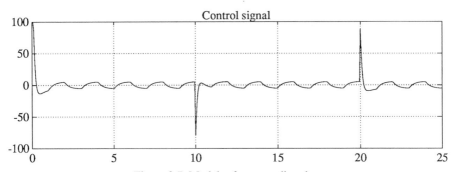

Figure 3.7. Model reference - disturbances

Description

This example is identical to example 3.2.1, except that a square wave disturbance of amplitude 5 units and period two units is added to the system input. The purpose of the example is to illustrate the role of the polynomial $C(s)$ in determining closed-loop disturbance rejection. Initially, $C(s)=0.5s+1$.

Programme interaction

runex 3 7
Example 3 of chapter 7: Model reference - disturbances

$======== C\ S\ T\ C\ Version\ 6.0\ ========$

Enter all variables (y/n, default n)?

$======== Data\ Source\ =======$
$======== Filters\ =======$
Sample Interval   =   0.050000 :=
$======== Control\ action\ =======$
Automatic controller mode = TRUE :=
$======== Assumed\ system\ =======$
A (system denominator)   =   1.000000   1.000000   0.000000 :=
B (system numerator)   :=   1.000000   10.000000 :=
D (initial conditions)   =   0.000000   0.000000 :=
$======== Emulator\ design\ =======$
P (model denominator)   =   0.500000   1.000000 :=
C (emulator denominator) =   0.500000   1.000000 :=

     System polynomials

A   1.000000   1.000000   0.000000
B   1.000000   10.000000
D   0.000000   0.000000

     Design polynomials

B+   1.000000   10.000000
B-   1.000000
C   0.500000   1.000000
P   0.500000   1.000000
Z+   1.000000
Z-   1.000000
Z-+   1.000000

F	0.750000	1.000000
F filter	0.500000	1.000000
G	0.250000	2.500000
G filter	0.500000	1.000000
I		
E	0.250000	
ED	0.000000	

======== Controller   ========
Maximum control signal   =   100.000000 :=
Minimum control signal   = -100.000000 :=
======== Simulation   ========
======== Setpoint   ========
======== In Disturbance ========
Square amplitude   =   5.000000 :=
Period   =   2.000000 :=
======== Out Disturbance ========
Square amplitude   =   0.000000 :=
Period   =   20.000000 :=
Simulation running:
    25% complete
    50% complete
    75% complete
    100% complete
Time now is   25.000000
More time   = FALSE :=

Discussion

The upper graph displays three signals: the system output $y(t)$, the setpoint $w(t)$ and the ideal model output $y_m(t)$ where $\bar{y}_m(s) = \dfrac{Z(s)}{P(s)}\bar{w}(s)$.

The effect of the disturbance is to perturb the system output; the control signal reacts to some extent to counteract this effect.

Further investigations

1. The emulator denominator $C(s)$ is of the form 1+Ts. Try the effect of varying the time constant T (try, for example, T=0.1) of the emulator denominator C. How does this affect the system output and the control signal?

2. Investigate the effect of an <u>output</u> disturbance on the control system.

3.2.8. MODEL REFERENCE PID

Reference: Section 3.10; page 3-24.

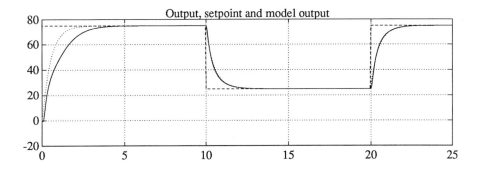

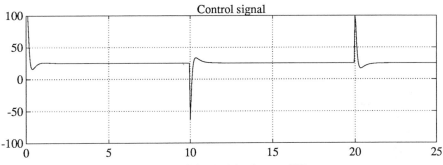

Figure 3.8. Model reference PID

Description

This example is identical to example 3.2.1 except that:

a) A constant of value -25 is added to the system input.

b) The assumption that there is a constant offset is built in by setting "Integral action" to "TRUE".

c) The degree of $C(s)$ is increased by one: $C(s) = (1+0.5s)^2$.

Programme interaction

runex 3 8
Example 3 of chapter 8: Model reference PID

======== C S T C Version 6.0 ========

Enter all variables (y/n, default n)?

======== Data Source   ========
======== Filters   ========
Sample Interval   =   0.050000 :=
======== Control action ========
Integral action   = TRUE :=
======== Assumed system ========
A (system denominator) =   1.000000   1.000000   0.000000 :=
B (system numerator)   =   1.000000   10.000000 :=
D (initial conditions)   =   0.000000   0.000000 :=
======== Emulator design ========
P (model denominator)   =   0.500000   1.000000 :=
*C (emulator denominator) =   0.500000   1.000000 * :=*
Next factor ...
C (emulator denominator) =   0.500000   1.000000 :=

    System polynomials

A	*1.000000*	*1.000000*	*0.000000*	*0.000000*
B	*1.000000*	*10.000000*	*0.000000*	
D	*0.000000*	*0.000000*	*0.000000*	

    Design polynomials

B+	*1.000000*	*10.000000*	*0.000000*
B-	*1.000000*		
C	*0.250000*	*1.000000*	*1.000000*
P	*0.500000*	*1.000000*	
Z+	*1.000000*		
Z-	*1.000000*		
Z-+	*1.000000*		

F	*0.625000*	*1.500000*	*1.000000*
F filter	*0.250000*	*1.000000*	*1.000000*
G	*0.125000*	*1.250000*	*0.000000*
G filter	*0.250000*	*1.000000*	*1.000000*
I			
E	*0.125000*		
ED	*0.000000*		

```
------------------------------------
======== Controller    ========
Maximum control signal   =   100.000000  :=
Minimum control signal   =  -100.000000  :=
======== Simulation    ========
======== Setpoint      ========
======== In Disturbance ========
Step amplitude          =   -25.000000  :=
======== Out Disturbance ========
Step amplitude          =    0.000000  :=
Simulation running:
    25% complete
    50% complete
    75% complete
    100% complete
Time now is    25.000000
More time              = FALSE  :=
```

Discussion

The upper graph displays three signals: the system output $y(t)$, the setpoint $w(t)$ and the ideal model output $y_m(t)$ where $\bar{y}_m(s) = \dfrac{Z(s)}{P(s)} \bar{w}(s)$.

The effect of the disturbance is, in the short term, to spoil the closed-loop response; but, in the long term, the response is not affected. Note that the steady-state control signal has a value of +25 to compensate for the disturbance. The controller has integral action.

Further investigations

1. Try the controller of example 1, but with the disturbance. (Set integral action to FALSE and set $C(s) = 0.5s+1$ by setting the second factor =1). What is the effect of the input disturbance?

2. Repeat step 1, but with an output disturbance in place of an input distubance. Explain what you observe.

3.2.9. POLE-PLACEMENT PID

Reference: Section 3.10; page 3-25.

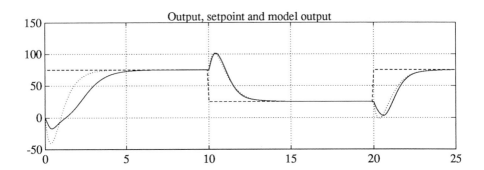

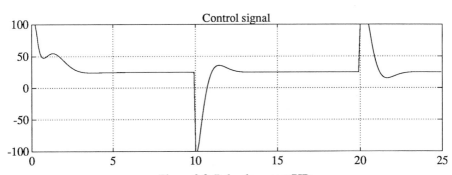

Figure 3.9. Pole-placement PID

Description

This example is identical to example 3.2.2 except that:

a)   A constant of value -25 is added to the system input.

b)   The assumption that there is a constant offset is built in by setting "Integral" action to "TRUE".

c)   The degree of $C(s)$ is increased by one: $C(s) = (1+0.5s)^2$.

d)   The sample interval is decreased to 0.01 to give a satisfactory approximation.

Programme interaction

runex 3 9
Example 3 of chapter 9:   Pole-placement PID

======== *C S T C Version 6.0* ========

Enter all variables (y/n, default n)?

======== *Data Source* ========
======== *Filters* ========
Sample Interval = 0.010000 :=
======== *Control action* ========
Integral action = TRUE :=
======== *Assumed system* ========
A (system denominator) = 1.000000   1.000000   0.000000 :=
B (system numerator) = -1.000000   1.000000 :=
======== *Emulator design* ========
Z has factor B = TRUE :=
P (model denominator) = 0.250000   1.000000   1.000000 :=
C (emulator denominator) = 0.500000   1.000000 * :=
Next factor ...
C (emulator denominator) = 0.500000   1.000000 :=

   System polynomials

A   1.000000   1.000000   0.000000   0.000000
B   -1.000000   1.000000   0.000000
D   0.000000   0.000000   0.000000

   Design polynomials

B+   1.000000   0.000000
B-   -1.000000   1.000000
C   0.250000   1.000000   1.000000
P   0.250000   1.000000   1.000000
Z+   1.000000
Z-   -1.000000   1.000000
Z-+   1.000000

F   2.031250   3.000000   1.000000
F filter   0.250000   1.000000   1.000000
G   0.062500   2.468750   0.000000
G filter   0.250000   1.000000   1.000000
I
E   0.062500   2.468750
ED   0.000000   0.000000

======== *Controller* ========
Maximum control signal = 100.000000 :=
Minimum control signal = -100.000000 :=
======== *Simulation* ========
======== *Setpoint* ========
======== *In Disturbance* ========

Step amplitude   =   -25.000000 :=
======== Out Disturbance ========
Step amplitude   =   0.000000 :=
Simulation running:
  25% complete
  50% complete
  75% complete
  100% complete
Time now is   25.000000
More time   = FALSE :=

Discussion

The upper graph displays three signals: the system output $y(t)$, the setpoint $w(t)$ and the ideal model output $y_m(t)$ where $\overline{y}_m(s) = \dfrac{Z(s)}{P(s)}\overline{w}(s)$.

The effect of the disturbance is, in the short term, to spoil the closed-loop response; but, in the long term, the response is not affected. Note that the steady-state control signal has a value of +25 to compensate for the disturbance: the controller has integral action.

Further investigations

1. Try the controller of example 3.2.1, but with the disturbance. (Set integral action to FALSE and set $C(s) = 0.5s+1$ by setting the second factor =1). What is the effect of the input disturbance?

2. Repeat step 1, but with an output disturbance in place of an input distubance. Explain what you observe.

3.2.10. DETUNED MODEL-REFERENCE

Reference: Section 3.11; page 3-28.

Description

The example on page I-3-28 illustrates the use of a reference model with one pole and one zero:

$$\frac{Z(s)}{P(s)} = \frac{0.03s+1}{0.3s+1} \tag{3.2.10.1}$$

together with control weighting:

$$Q(s) = \frac{qs}{0.03s+1} \tag{3.2.10.2}$$

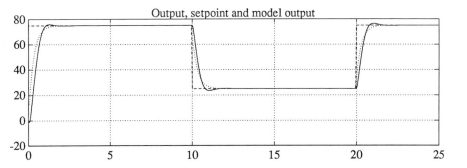

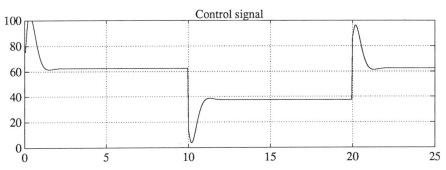

Figure 3.10. Detuned model-reference

In this example q=0.05 is used initially.

Programme interaction

runex 3 10
Example 3 of chapter 10: Detuned model-reference

======== C S T C Version 6.0 ========

Enter all variables (y/n, default n)?

======== Data Source   ========
======== Filters   ========
Sample Interval   =   0.050000 :=
======== Control action ========

```
======== Assumed system  ========
A (system denominator)  =    1.000000    1.000000  :=
B (system numerator)    =    2.000000  :=
======== Emulator design ========
Z-+ (Z- not including B) =   0.030000    1.000000  :=
P (model denominator)    =   0.300000    1.000000  :=
C (emulator denominator) =   0.300000    1.000000  :=
```

    System polynomials

```
A       1.000000    1.000000    0.000000
B       2.000000    0.000000
D       0.000000
```

    Design polynomials

```
B+       2.000000    0.000000
B-       1.000000
C        0.300000    1.000000
P        0.300000    1.000000
Z+       1.000000
Z-       0.030000    1.000000
Z-+      0.030000    1.000000
```

```
F        0.494845    1.000000
F filter 0.300000    1.000000
G        0.150309    0.000000
G filter 0.009000    0.330000    1.000000
I
E        0.075155
ED
```

```
======== Controller   ========
Q numerator      =    0.100000    0.000000  :=
Q denominator    =    0.100000    1.000000  :=
======== Simulation   ========
======== Setpoint     ========
======== In Disturbance ========
Step amplitude   =   -25.000000  :=
======== Out Disturbance ========
Simulation running:
    25% complete
    50% complete
    75% complete
    100% complete
Time now is   25.000000
```

Discussion

The model following is not exact due to the presence of the control weighting; but note that exact model following is not possible anyway as system with relative order $\rho=1$ cannot follow a model with relative order $\rho=0$.

Further investigations

1. Examine the effect of varying the parameter q.

3.2.11. PREDICTIVE CONTROL

Reference: Sections 3.7&8; page 3-18.

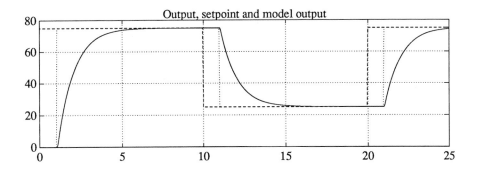

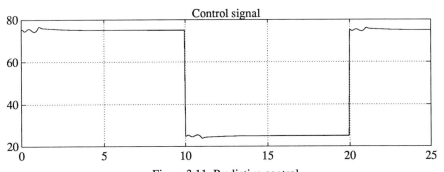

Figure 3.11. Predictive control

Description

A predictive emulator was designed in example 2.2.3. In this example, the emulator is embedded in a feedback loop to give predictive control. As discussed in section I-3.7, this is related to Smith's method.

The open loop system has a first order rational part with unit time constant ,together with a unit delay

$$e^{-sT} \frac{B(s)}{A(s)} = e^{-s} \frac{1}{1+s} \tag{3.2.11.1}$$

$Q(s)$ is chosen to be an inverse PI controller:

$$\frac{1}{Q(s)} = 1 + \frac{1}{s} \tag{3.2.11.2}$$

When the predictor is used, the nominal loop gain is:

$$L(s) = e^{s} \frac{1+s}{s} e^{-s} \frac{1}{1+s} = \frac{1}{s} \tag{3.2.11.3}$$

giving a closed loop system setpoint response with the delay removed from the denominator:

$$\bar{y}(s) = e^{-s} \frac{1}{1+s} \bar{w}(s) \tag{3.2.11.4}$$

Without the predictor, however, the nominal loop gain is

$$L(s) = e^{-s} \frac{1}{s} \tag{3.2.11.5}$$

giving a closed loop system setpoint response:

$$\bar{y}(s) = e^{-s} \frac{1}{e^{-s}+s} \bar{w}(s) \tag{3.2.11.6}$$

Programme interaction

runex 3 11
Example 3 of chapter 11: Predictive control

$======== C\ S\ T\ C\ Version\ 6.0 ========$

Enter all variables (y/n, default n)?

```
======== Data Source    ========
======== Filters        ========
======== Control action ========
Integral action        = FALSE  :=
======== Assumed system ========
A (system denominator)  =    1.000000   1.000000  :=
B (system numerator)    =    1.000000  :=
Time delay              =    1.000000  :=
======== Emulator design ========
Z has factor B          = TRUE  :=
P (model denominator)   =    1.000000  :=
C (emulator denominator) =   1.000000  :=
Pade approximation order =       4  :=
-----------------------------------
    System polynomials
-----------------------------------
A        1.000000    1.000000
B        1.000000
D        0.000000    0.000000
-----------------------------------
    Design polynomials
-----------------------------------
B+       1.000000
B-       1.000000
C        1.000000
P        1.000000
Z+       1.000000
Z-       1.000000
Z-+      1.000000
Pade     0.000595    0.011905    0.107143    0.500000    1.000000
-----------------------------------
F        0.367879
F filter 1.000000
G        0.000376    0.015908    0.051819    0.632121
G filter 0.000595    0.011905    0.107143    0.500000    1.000000
I
E        0.000376    0.015908    0.051819    0.632121
ED       0.000000    0.000000    0.000000    0.000000
-----------------------------------
======== Controller     ========
Q numerator            =    1.000000   0.000000  :=
Q denominator          =    1.000000   1.000000  :=
======== Simulation     ========
======== Setpoint       ========
======== In Disturbance ========
======== Out Disturbance ========
Step amplitude         =    0.000000  :=
```

Cos amplitude   =   0.000000 :=
Simulation running:
  25% complete
  50% complete
  75% complete
  100% complete
Time now is   25.000000

Discussion

The upper graph displays three signals: the system output $y(t)$,the setpoint $w(t)$ and the ideal model output $y_m(t) = y(t-1)$.

Note that the response is as predicted: a delayed first-order response delayed by one unit.

Further investigations

1. Try the effect of varying the order of the Pade approximation. Note that zero corresponds to having no predictor, and the response is not good. What is the smallest satisfactory order?

2. Try varying the system time delay. For each value of delay, find the minimum satisfactory Pade order. Note that for larger Pade orders, you may need to reduce the sample interval for numerical reasons.

3. Try putting integral action into the predictor (Integral action = TRUE, C = s+1) and use a Pade order of 3. Observe the performance with an output step disturbance, and compare to the integral-free case.

4. Add a sinusoidal disturbance to the system output; how does the performance depend on the amplitude of this signal and the system time-delay?

3.2.12. LINEAR-QUADRATIC POLE-PLACEMENT

Reference: Section 3.4; page 3-14.

Description

This example is identical to example 3.2.2, except that the closed-loop poles are chosen to solve equation I-3.4.23:

$$P(s)P(-s) = B(s)B(-s) + \lambda A(s)A(-s)$$

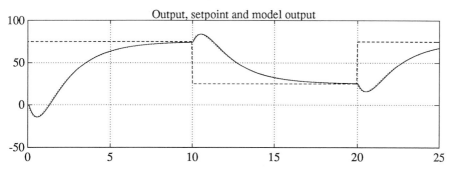

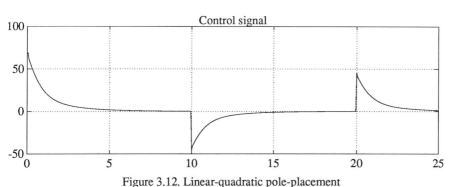

Figure 3.12. Linear-quadratic pole-placement

That is, the poles are chosen to correspond to those given by linear-quadratic optimisation theory where λ is the linear-quadratic weighting.

Programme interaction

runex 3 12
Example 3 of chapter 12: Linear-quadratic pole-placement

======== C S T C Version 6.0 ========

Enter all variables (y/n, default n)?

======== Data Source   ========

```
======== Filters        ========
======== Control action ========
======== Assumed system  ========
A (system denominator)  =    1.000000    1.000000    0.000000  :=
B (system numerator)    =   -1.000000    1.000000  :=
======== Emulator design ========
Z has factor B          = TRUE  :=
Linear-quadratic poles   = TRUE  :=
Linear-quadratic weight  =    1.000000  :=
C (emulator denominator) =    0.500000    1.000000  :=
-------------------------------------
      System polynomials
-------------------------------------
A          1.000000    1.000000    0.000000
B         -1.000000    1.000000
D          0.000000    0.000000
-------------------------------------
      Design polynomials
-------------------------------------
B+         1.000000
B-        -1.000000    1.000000
C          0.500000    1.000000
P          1.000000    2.449490    1.000000
Z+         1.000000
Z-        -1.000000    1.000000
Z-+        1.000000
-------------------------------------
F          1.112372    1.000000
F filter   0.500000    1.000000
G          0.500000    2.837117
G filter   0.500000    1.000000
I
E          0.500000    2.837117
ED         0.000000    0.000000
-------------------------------------
======== Controller     ========
Maximum control signal  =    100.000000  :=
Minimum control signal  =   -100.000000  :=
======== Simulation     ========
======== Setpoint       ========
======== In Disturbance ========
======== Out Disturbance ========
Simulation running:
    25% complete
    50% complete
    75% complete
    100% complete
Time now is    25.000000
```

Discussion

The upper graph displays three signals: the system output $y(t)$, the setpoint $w(t)$ and the ideal model output $y_m(t)$ where $\bar{y}_m(s) = \dfrac{Z(s)}{P(s)}\bar{w}(s)$.

As in example 3.2.2 ,note the typical behaviour of a system with right-hand plane zeros: the output initially goes the wrong way in response to a step change.

The desired closed loop zeros are the same as in example 3.2.2, that is, the system zeros are unchanged, but the poles, and the step rise-time, now depend on $A(s)$, $B(s)$ and λ.

Further investigations

1. Try the effect of varying the linear-quadratic weighting λ. How does this affect the system output and the control signal?

2. Try repeating this example using the same system as example 3.2.1 $(B(s) = 10+s)$. How does the closed-loop response when using linear-quadratic control differ from that when using model-reference control?

3.2.13. LINEAR-QUADRATIC PID

Reference: Section 3.4; page 3-14 and section 3.10; page 3-25.

Description

This example is identical to example 12 except that:

a) A constant of value -25 is added to the system input.

b) The assumption that there is a constant offset is built in by setting "Integral action" to "TRUE".

c) The degree of $C(s)$ is increased by one: $C(s) = (1+0.5s)^2$.

d) The sample interval is decreased to 0.01 to give a satisfactory approximation.

Programme interaction

runex 3 13
Example 3 of chapter 13: Linear-quadratic PID

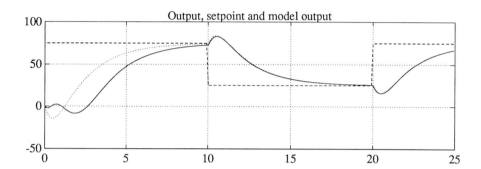

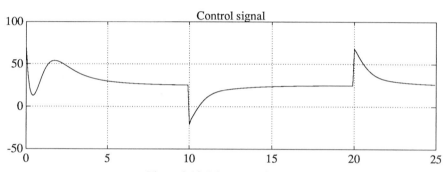

Figure 3.13. Linear-quadratic PID

```
======== C S T C Version 6.0 ========

Enter all variables (y/n, default n)?

======== Data Source    ========
======== Filters        ========
Sample Interval      =    0.010000  :=
======== Control action ========
Integral action      = TRUE  :=
======== Assumed system ========
A (system denominator)  =    1.000000   1.000000   0.000000  :=
B (system numerator)    =   -1.000000   1.000000  :=
======== Emulator design ========
Z has factor B       = TRUE  :=
Linear-quadratic poles  = TRUE  :=
Linear-quadratic weight  =    1.000000  :=
C (emulator denominator) =    0.500000   1.000000 *  :=
```

Next factor ...
C (emulator denominator) =   0.500000   1.000000   :=

    System polynomials

A	1.000000	1.000000	0.000000	0.000000
B	-1.000000	1.000000	0.000000	
D	0.000000	0.000000	0.000000	

    Design polynomials

B+	1.000000	0.000000	
B-	-1.000000	1.000000	
C	0.250000	1.000000	1.000000
P	1.000000	2.449490	1.000000
Z+	1.000000		
Z-	-1.000000	1.000000	
Z-+	1.000000		

F	3.393304	4.449490	1.000000
F filter	0.250000	1.000000	1.000000
G	0.250000	4.755676	0.000000
G filter	0.250000	1.000000	1.000000
I			
E	0.250000	4.755676	
ED	0.000000	0.000000	

======== *Controller*   ========
Maximum control signal   =   100.000000   :=
Minimum control signal   =   -100.000000   :=
======== *Simulation*   ========
======== *Setpoint*   ========
======== *In Disturbance* ========
Step amplitude   =   -25.000000   :=
======== *Out Disturbance* ========
Step amplitude   =   0.000000   :=
Simulation running:
    25% complete
    50% complete
    75% complete
    100% complete
Time now is   25.000000

Discussion

The upper graph displays three signals: the system output $y(t)$, the setpoint $w(t)$ and the ideal model output $y_m(t)$ where $\bar{y}_m(s) = \dfrac{Z(s)}{P(s)}\bar{w}(s)$.

The effect of the disturbance is, in the short term, to spoil the closed-loop response; but, in the long term, the response is not affected. Note that the steady-state control signal has a value of +25 to compensate for the disturbance: the controller has integral action.

Further investigations

1. Try the controller of example 3.2.12, but with the disturbance. (Set integral action to FALSE and set $C(s) = 0.5s+1$ by setting the second factor =1). What is the effect of the input disturbance?

2. Repeat step 1, but with an output disturbance in place of an input distubance. Explain what you observe.

3.2.14. DISCRETE-TIME MODEL-REFERENCE CONTROL

   Reference:

Description

Cstc can be used for simulation of discrete-time as well as continuous-time systems. This example considers the discrete-time time-delay system:

$$\frac{1}{z^4 - 2z^3 + z^2} = \frac{z^{-4}}{1 - 2z^{-1} + z^{-2}} \tag{3.2.14.1}$$

A minimum-variance type control stategy is used where the desired closed-loop model is:

$$\frac{Z}{P} = z^{-4} = \frac{1}{z^4} \tag{3.2.14.2}$$

Choosing the degree of C to one less than A (i.e.3) with all roots at the origin:

$$C = z^3 \tag{3.2.14.3}$$

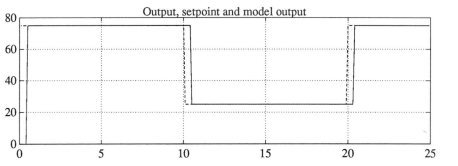

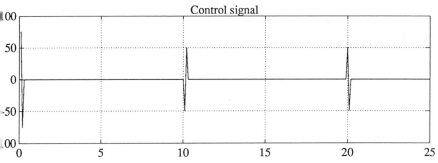

Figure 3.14. Discrete-time model-reference control

Programme interaction

runex 3 14
Example 3 of chapter 14: Discrete-time model-reference control

======== C S T C Version 6.0 ========

Enter all variables (y/n, default n)?

======== Data Source   ========
======== Filters   ========
======== Control action ========
======== Assumed system ========
A (system denominator) =   1.000000 -2.000000   1.000000   0.000000   0.000000 :=
B (system numerator)   =   1.000000 :=
======== Emulator design ========

Z+ *(nice model numerator)* =   *1.000000*   :=
P *(model denominator)*   =   *1.000000*   *0.000000*   *0.000000*   *0.000000*   *0.000000* :=
C *(emulator denominator)* =   *1.000000*   *0.000000*   *0.000000*   *0.000000* :=

      System polynomials

A   *1.000000*   *-2.000000*   *1.000000*   *0.000000*   *0.000000*
B   *1.000000*
D   *0.000000*   *0.000000*

      Design polynomials

B+   *1.000000*
B-   *1.000000*
C   *1.000000*   *0.000000*   *0.000000*   *0.000000*
P   *1.000000*   *0.000000*   *0.000000*   *0.000000*   *0.000000*
Z+   *1.000000*
Z-   *1.000000*
Z-+   *1.000000*

F   *5.000000*   *-4.000000*   *0.000000*   *0.000000*
F *filter* *1.000000*   *0.000000*   *0.000000*   *0.000000*
G   *1.000000*   *2.000000*   *3.000000*   *4.000000*
G *filter* *1.000000*   *0.000000*   *0.000000*   *0.000000*
I
E   *1.000000*   *2.000000*   *3.000000*   *4.000000*
ED   *0.000000*   *0.000000*

======== *Controller*   ========
======== *Simulation*   ========
======== *Setpoint*   ========
======== *In Disturbance* ========
======== *Out Disturbance* ========
Simulation running:
    25% complete
    50% complete
    75% complete
    100% complete
Time now is   25.000000

Discussion

The upper graph displays three signals: the system output y_i and the setpoint w_i.

As requested, the system output follows the setpoint after a delay of four samples.

Further investigations

1.   Try modifying the system to have a zero at z=-0.9:

$B = z+0.9$ (3.2.14.4)

Because the realtive order has now been reduced to 3, change P to z^{-3}. What is the effect on the output and the control signal?

2.   Investigate the effect of moving two of the closed-loop poles to z=-0.9:

$P = z^4 - 1.8z^3 + 0.81z^2$ (3.2.14.5)

and set Z + = 0.01 to give unit steady-state gain. What is the effect on the output and the control signal?

3.2.15. DISCRETE-TIME POLE-PLACEMENT CONTROL

Reference:

Description

Cstc can be used for simulation of discrete-time as well as continuous-time systems. This example considers the discrete-time time-delay system:

$$\frac{z+0.9}{z^4 - 2z^3 + z^2} = \frac{z^{-4}}{1 - 2z^{-1} + z^{-2}}$$ (3.2.15.1)

A pole-placement type control stategy is used where the desired closed-loop model is:

$$\frac{Z}{P} = z^{-4}B = \frac{z+0.9}{z^4}$$ (3.2.15.2)

Choosing the degree of C to one less than A (i.e.3) with all roots at the origin:

$C = z^3$ (3.2.15.3)

Programme interaction

runex 3 15
Example 3 of chapter 15: Discrete-time pole-placement control

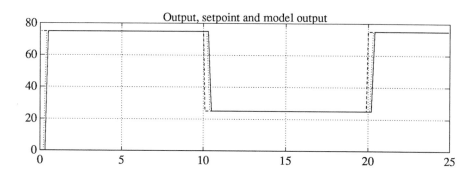

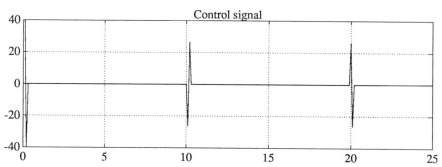

Figure 3.15. Discrete-time pole-placement control

======== *C S T C Version 6.0* ========

Enter all variables (y/n, default n)?

    ======== *Data Source* ========
    ======== *Filters* ========
    ======== *Control action* ========
    ======== *Assumed system* ========
A (system denominator) = *1.000000 -2.000000 1.000000 0.000000 0.000000 :=*
B (system numerator) = *1.000000 0.900000 :=*
    ======== *Emulator design* ========
Z has factor B = *TRUE :=*
Z+ (nice model numerator) = *1.000000 :=*
P (model denominator) = *1.000000 0.000000 0.000000 0.000000 0.000000 :=*
C (emulator denominator) = *1.000000 0.000000 0.000000 0.000000 :=*

    System polynomials

```
-------------------------------------
A        1.000000   -2.000000   1.000000   0.000000   0.000000
B        1.000000    0.900000
D        0.000000    0.000000
-------------------------------------
         Design polynomials
-------------------------------------
B+       1.900000
B-       0.526316    0.473684
C        1.000000    0.000000   0.000000   0.000000
P        1.000000    0.000000   0.000000   0.000000   0.000000
Z+       1.000000
Z-       0.526316    0.473684
Z-+      1.000000
-------------------------------------
F        4.473684   -3.473684   0.000000   0.000000
F filter 1.000000    0.000000   0.000000   0.000000
G        1.900000    3.800000   5.700000   3.126316
G filter 1.000000    0.000000   0.000000   0.000000
I
E        1.000000    2.000000   3.000000   1.645429
ED       0.000000    0.000000
-------------------------------------
======= Controller    =======
======= Simulation    =======
======= Setpoint      =======
======= In Disturbance  =======
======= Out Disturbance =======
Simulation running:
    25% complete
    50% complete
    75% complete
    100% complete
Time now is   25.000000
```

Discussion

The upper graph displays three signals: the system output y_i and the setpoint w_i.

Compared with further example 1 of the previous example, the control signal is not oscillatory: the zero at z=0.9 has not been cancelled.

Further investigations

1. Try modifying the system to have a zero at $z=+0.9$:

$$B = z-0.9 \qquad\qquad (3.2.15.4)$$

Why is the output now rather horrible? Recall that $z^{-4}10(z-0.9)$ was asked for.

CHAPTER 4

Non-Adaptive Robustness

Aims. To examine by simulation the effect of neglected dynamics on the performance of emulator based control.

4.1. IMPLEMENTATION DETAILS

The implementation is identical to that described in chapter 3. The neglected dynamics are introduced into the simulated system by including additional factors in the system polynomials. This approach is not very satisfactory from the numerical point of view and high precision floating point arithmetic is required.

4.2. EXAMPLES

4.2.1. DETUNED MODEL-REFERENCE CONTROL - NEGLECTED DYNAMICS

Reference: Section 4.7; page 4-11.

Description

This example is identical to example 3.2.10 except that neglected dynamics are included. As discussed in volume I, the system then corresponds to that of Rohrs. That is, the system is *assumed* to be

$$\frac{B(s)}{A(s)} = \frac{2b}{1+s} \qquad (4.2.1.1)$$

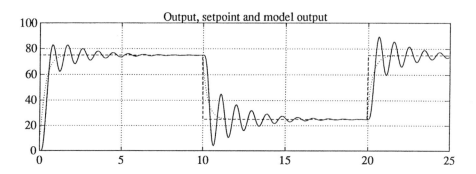

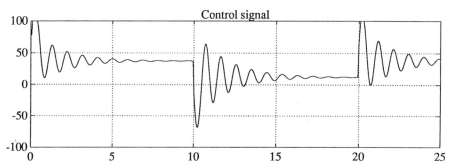

Figure 4.1. Detuned model-reference control - neglected dynamics

but is *actually* given by

$$N(s)\frac{B(s)}{A(s)} = \frac{100}{s^2 + 8s + 100} \frac{2}{1+s} = \frac{200}{s^3 + 9s^2 + 108s + 100} \qquad (4.2.1.2)$$

In this example, b=1 and the control weighting is

$$Q(s) = \frac{qs}{0.03s+1} \qquad (4.2.1.3)$$

with q = 0.05. This corresponds to the first row of the table on page I-4-16.

Programme interaction

runex 4 1
Example 4 of chapter 1:   Detuned model-reference control - neglected dynamics

$========= C\ S\ T\ C\ Version\ 6.0\ =========$

Enter all variables (y/n, default n)?

```
======== Data Source   ========
======== Filters       ========
Sample Interval       =    0.050000  :=
======== Control action ========
======== Assumed system ========
A (system denominator)  =    1.000000   1.000000  :=
B (system numerator)    =    2.000000  :=
======== Emulator design ========
P (model denominator)   =    0.300000   1.000000  :=
C (emulator denominator) =    0.300000   1.000000  :=
```

   System polynomials

A	1.000000	1.000000	0.000000
B	2.000000	0.000000	
D	0.000000		

   Design polynomials

B+	2.000000	0.000000	
B-	1.000000		
C	0.300000	1.000000	
P	0.300000	1.000000	
Z+	1.000000		
Z-	0.030000	1.000000	
Z-+	0.030000	1.000000	

F	0.494845	1.000000	
F filter	0.300000	1.000000	
G	0.150309	0.000000	
G filter	0.009000	0.330000	1.000000
I			
E	0.075155		
ED			

```
======== Controller    ========
Q numerator        =    0.050000   0.000000  :=
Q denominator      =    0.030000   1.000000  :=
```

```
======== Simulation      ========
======== Setpoint        ========
======== In Disturbance  ========
======== Out Disturbance ========
======== Actual system   ========
```
Next factor ...
Next factor ...
Simulation running:
    25% complete
    50% complete
    75% complete
    100% complete
Time now is   25.000000

Discussion

The effect of the neglected dynamics is to give a rather nasty oscillatory closed-loop response; but, as predicted, the closed-loop system is stable. Note that, in this case, the notional feedback system is unstable, so the error term due to the emulator has a stabilising effect. See volume I for more discussions.

The adaptive case is more interesting, and is considered in chapter 7.

Further investigations

1. Try changing q to 0.2 as in the second row of the table on page I-4-16.

2. Try changing b to 0.5 ($B(s) = 1.0$) as in the third row of the table on page 4I--16. Does the closed-loop system verify the instability prediction? Note that the control signal is limited to the range -100 to +100.

3. Try changing b to 0.5 and q to 0.2 as in the fourth row of the table on page I-4-16.

CHAPTER 5

Least-Squares Identification

Aims. To describe the implementation of least-squares parameter estimation routines. To illustrate the behaviour of least-squares parameter estimation algorithms. To investigate, using a simple example, how least squares parameter estimation is affected by disturbance signals.

5.1. IMPLEMENTATION DETAILS

5.1.1. [5.2 & 6.3] LINEAR IN THE PARAMETERS SYSTEMS

As discussed in Vol. I, section 5.2, the standard linear in the parameters model to be used in this book is

$$\psi(t) = \underline{X}^T(t)\underline{\theta} + e(t) \qquad (5.1.1.1)$$

where $\psi(t)$ is the scalar system output, $\underline{X}(t)$ is a column vector of measured variables and $\underline{\theta}$ a column vector of parameters and $e(t)$ the error.

As discussed Vol. I, section 6.3, for the purposes of system identification the special case:

$$y(t) = \underline{X}_s^T(t)\underline{\theta}_s + e_s(t) \qquad (5.1.1.2)$$

where the **data vector** $\underline{X}_s(t)$ and the **parameter vector** $\underline{\theta}_s$ are given, in Laplace transform terms by

$$\underline{\overline{X}}_s(s) \triangleq \begin{bmatrix} \underline{\overline{X}}_i(s) \\ \underline{\overline{X}}_u(s) \\ \underline{\overline{X}}_y(s) \end{bmatrix}; \ \underline{\theta}_s = \begin{bmatrix} \underline{\theta}_i \\ \underline{\theta}_u \\ \underline{\theta}_y \end{bmatrix} \qquad (5.1.1.3)$$

Where

$$\underline{X}_u(s) = \frac{1}{C_s(s)} \begin{bmatrix} s^{n-1} \\ s^{n-2} \\ \vdots \\ 1 \end{bmatrix} e^{-sT} \; \overline{u}(s); \; \underline{X}_y(s) = \frac{1}{C_s(s)} \begin{bmatrix} s^{n-1} \\ s^{n-2} \\ \vdots \\ 1 \end{bmatrix} \overline{y}(s) \qquad (5.1.1.4)$$

$$\underline{X}_i(s) = \frac{1}{C_s(s)} \begin{bmatrix} s^{n-1} \\ s^{n-2} \\ \vdots \\ 1 \end{bmatrix} \qquad (5.1.1.5)$$

Note that the data vector has been reordered in CSTC as compared with that in Vol. I.

The data vector $\overline{X}(s)$ is created in two stages with procedure **IdentifySystem**:

1.   The data are filtered within procedure **Emulator** (which also gives $\hat{y}(t)$ based on the system parameters) and

2.   the data are loaded into $\overline{X}(s)$ using procedure **SetData**.

(There are also experimental procedures invoked when **IdentifyingDelay** is set to TRUE, but this is beyond the scope of this book).

Procedure **SetData** takes data from its input argument **State**. In this case, **SetData** is called with **State** replaced by **SysEmState**, of type **TypeEmState**. Amongst other things, this record contains: **ICState**, **uState** and **yState**. These three states contain the corresponding filtered data vectors: $\overline{X}_i(s)$, $\overline{X}_u(s)$ and $\overline{X}_y(s)$. The purpose of **SetData** is to load the appropriate elements into the output argument **DataVector**. It does this by simply extracting the appropriate elements, incrementing the counter **j**, and loading into **DataVector**.

The integer variable **Integrating** is set to 1 if **IntegralAction** is set to TRUE, otherwise it is set to 0.

5.1.2. [5.7] DISCRETE-TIME PARAMETER ESTIMATION

CSTC does *not* use the continuous-time algorithm, but rather the discrete-time algorithm presented in section 5.7. But it is emphasised that *continuous-time* parameters are estimated; and that the discrete-time algorithm can be regarded as an approximation to the continuous-time algorithm.

Given the data vector discussed in the previous section, there are three stages to the algorithm within **IdentifySystem**.

1. The variable **EstimationError** is computed in the statement:

    EstimationError := yHat - y;

2. The least squares gain vector $\underline{S}_d^{-1})_m \underline{X}_m$ is updated in procedure **UpdateLeastSquaresGain.**

3. The parameters are updated in procedure **TuneEmulator.** Rather than update a parameter vector and then transfer the elements to the appropriate polynomials, the polynomial coefficients are updated directly. These polynomials are encapsulated in the record **Knobs** of type **TypeEmKnobs.**

5.2. EXAMPLES

5.2.1. ESTIMATION OF A 1ST ORDER SYSTEM

Reference: Section 5.2; pages 5-2 - 5-3.

Description

This example provides a simple introduction to parameter estimation with the noise-free system of the example on page I-5-2. with the following values:

$$a = 2; b = 3; c = 1; d = 4. \qquad (5.2.1.1)$$

The effects of initial variance, forgetting time and sample interval are investigated.

Programme interaction

runex 5 1
Example 5 of chapter 1: Estimation of a 1st order system

======== C S T C Version 6.0 ========

Enter all variables (y/n, default n)?
Chapter   =   5 :=

======== Data Source   =======
======== Filters   =======
Sample Interval   =   0.100000 :=
======== Control action ========
Automatic controller mode = FALSE :=

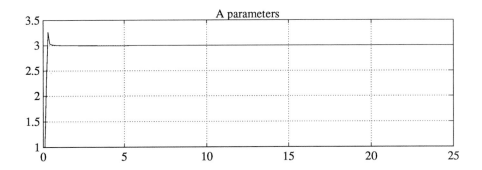

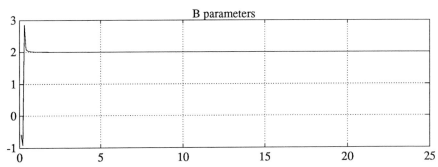

Figure 5.1. Estimation of a 1st order system

```
Integral action        = FALSE  :=
======== Assumed system ========
A (system denominator)    =    1.000000    0.000000  :=
B (system numerator)      =    1.000000  :=
D (initial conditions)    =    0.000000  :=
Tuning initial conditions = TRUE  :=
======== Identification ========
Initial Variance        = 100000.000000  :=
Forget time             = 1000.000000  :=
Dead band               =    0.000000  :=
Cs (emulator denominator) =    1.000000    1.000000  :=
======== Simulation     ========
======== Setpoint       ========
Step amplitude          =   25.000000  :=
Square amplitude        =   25.000000  :=
Period                  =   10.000000  :=
======== In Disturbance ========
```

```
======== Out Disturbance ========
======== Actual system  ========
A (system denominator)   =    1.000000   2.000000  :=
B (system numerator)     =    3.000000  :=
D (initial conditions)   =    4.000000  :=
Simulation running:
    25% complete
    50% complete
    75% complete
    100% complete
Time now is    25.000000
-----------------------------------
    System polynomials
-----------------------------------
A          1.000000    2.000017
B          2.999816
D          3.846844
```

Discussion

The three system parameters rapidly converge to the correct values. This is because there is no noise and the initial variance is large. The initial condition parameter does not converge to as accurate a value; usually we are not interested in its value, it is just there to improve estimation of the system parameters. The statements can be examined by following the "further investigations".

The estimation error is non-zero; this is due to numerical innaccuracies in the implementation of the state-variable filter when step changes occur.

Further investigations

1. Try setting the Boolean variable 'Tuning initial conditions' to FALSE. How is the estimation of the other parameters affected?

2. Try using a smaller initial variance; for example use 1 instead of 100000. What happens to the rate of parameter convergence? Repeat for variance values of 0.1 and 10.0.

3. While using a small initial variance (for example 1.0) try the effect of using a small forget time (for example 10.0). What effect does this have on the rate of convergence? Repeat for forget times of 50 and 100. Note that the effect of noise is examined in a later example.

4. Try using a different sample interval (for example 0.5). How does this affect the estimation? Try some other values as well.

5. Repeat 2 but with different initial parameters. How does the choice of initial parameters affect the estimates for each value of initial variance?

6. Try setting the system emulator denominator $C(s)$ to be the same as the system denominator. Why is the estimation error now virtually zero?

5.2.2. THE EFFECT OF OUTPUT NOISE

Reference: Section 5.2; pages 5-2 - 5-3.

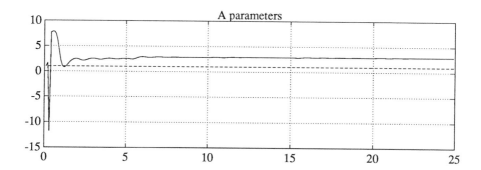

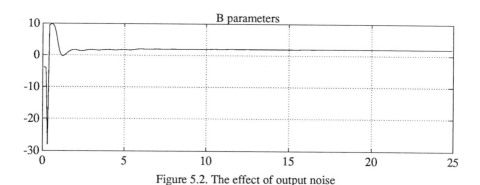

Figure 5.2. The effect of output noise

Description

This example is the same as example 5.2.1 except that a sinusoidal signal $0.25\sin 2\pi t$ is added to the output of the system; this may be thought of as measurement noise.

Programme interaction

runex 5 2
Example 5 of chapter 2: The effect of output noise

======== C S T C Version 6.0 ========

Enter all variables (y/n, default n)?

======== Data Source   ========
======== Filters   ========
Sample Interval   =   0.100000   :=
======== Control action ========
======== Assumed system ========
A (system denominator)   =   1.000000   0.000000   :=
B (system numerator)   =   1.000000   :=
D (initial conditions)   =   0.000000   :=
Tuning initial conditions = TRUE   :=
======== Identification ========
Initial Variance   = 100000.000000   :=
Forget time   = 1000.000000   :=
Dead band   =   0.000000   :=
Cs (emulator denominator) =   1.000000   1.000000   :=
======== Simulation   ========
======== Setpoint   ========
======== In Disturbance ========
======== Out Disturbance ========
Cos amplitude   =   10.000000   :=
Period   =   1.000000   :=
======== Actual system ========
A (system denominator)   =   1.000000   2.000000   :=
B (system numerator)   =   3.000000   :=
D (initial conditions)   =   4.000000   :=
Simulation running:
*   25% complete*
*   50% complete*
*   75% complete*
*   100% complete*
Time now is   25.000000
----
*   System polynomials*

A   1.000000   1.959012
B   2.935745
D   9.797439

Discussion

The parameter estimates corresponding to $A(s)$ and $B(s)$ take longer to settle down as compared to the previous example; but they end up near to the correct values. The initial condition estimate is, however, completely spoiled by the noise.

Further investigations

1. Try increasing the amplitude of the sinusoidal measurement noise. What effect does this have on parameter convergence?

2. Try using a shorter forgetting time and/or a smaller initial variance. What effect does this have on parameter convergence?

5.2.3. THE EFFECT OF INPUT NOISE

Reference: Section 5.2; pages 5-2 - 5-3.

Description

This example is the same as example 5.2.1 except that a sinusoidal signal $0.25\sin 2\pi t$ is added to the input of the system; this may be thought of as a load disturbance.

Programme interaction

runex 5 3
Example 5 of chapter 3: The effect of input noise

   ======== C S T C Version 6.0 ========

Enter all variables (y/n, default n)?

   ======== *Data Source*   ========
   ======== *Filters*   ========
Sample Interval   =   *0.100000*   :=

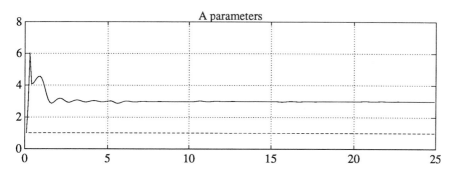

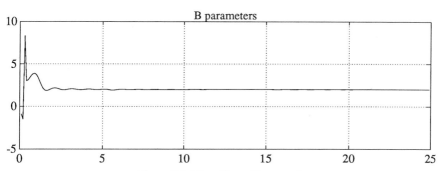

Figure 5.3. The effect of input noise

```
======== Control action  ========
======== Assumed system  ========
A (system denominator)   =    1.000000   0.000000  :=
B (system numerator)     =    1.000000  :=
D (initial conditions)   =    0.000000  :=
Tuning initial conditions = TRUE  :=
======== Identification  ========
Initial Variance         = 100000.000000  :=
Forget time              = 1000.000000  :=
Dead band                =    0.000000  :=
Cs (emulator denominator) =   1.000000   1.000000  :=
======== Simulation      ========
======== Setpoint        ========
======== In Disturbance  ========
Cos amplitude            =   10.000000  :=
Period                   =    1.000000  :=
======== Out Disturbance ========
```

```
======== Actual system  ========
A (system denominator)   =    1.000000   2.000000  :=
B (system numerator)     =    3.000000  :=
D (initial conditions)   =    4.000000  :=
Simulation running:
      25% complete
      50% complete
      75% complete
     100% complete
Time now is    25.000000
-----------------------------------
      System polynomials
-----------------------------------
A          1.000000    1.995478
B          2.993337
D          8.910800
```

Discussion

The parameter estimates vary in a similar fashion to those of the previous example.

Further investigations

1. Try increasing the amplitude of the sinusoidal load disturbance. What effect does this have on parameter convergence?

2. Try using a shorter forgetting time and/or a smaller initial variance. What effect does this have on parameter convergence?

5.2.4. THE EFFECT OF AN OUTPUT OFFSET

Reference: Section 5.5; I-5-11&12

Description

This example is the same as example 5.2.1 except that a constant value of 0.5 is added to the output of the system; this may be thought of as an offset due to scaling of variables or to linearisation about an operating point.

The idea of modelling a such an offset as the output of an integrator is discussed in section I-5.2 and section I-1.9. This is incorporated in this programme using the Boolean variable 'Integral action'; but note that, as on I-5-3, the order of $C(s)$ must be increased by 1.

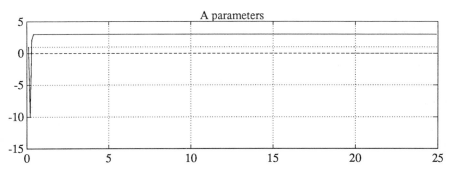

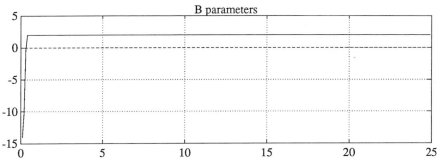

Figure 5.4. The effect of an output offset

Programme interaction

runex 5 4
Example 5 of chapter 4: The effect of an output offset

======== C S T C Version 6.0 ========

Enter all variables (y/n, default n)?
Chapter   =   5 :=

======== Data Source   ========
======== Filters   ========
Sample Interval   =   0.100000 :=
======== Control action ========
Automatic controller mode = FALSE :=
Integral action   = TRUE :=

```
======== Assumed system ========
A (system denominator)  =    1.000000   0.000000  :=
B (system numerator)    =    1.000000  :=
D (initial conditions)  =    0.000000  :=
Tuning initial conditions = TRUE  :=
======== Identification ========
Initial Variance        = 100000.000000  :=
Forget time             = 1000.000000  :=
Dead band               =    0.000000  :=
Cs (emulator denominator) =   1.000000   1.000000 *  :=
Next factor ...
Cs (emulator denominator) =   1.000000   1.000000  :=
======== Simulation    ========
======== Setpoint      ========
Step amplitude          =   25.000000  :=
Square amplitude        =   25.000000  :=
Period                  =   10.000000  :=
======== In Disturbance ========
======== Out Disturbance ========
Step amplitude          =   25.000000  :=
======== Actual system ========
A (system denominator)  =    1.000000   2.000000  :=
B (system numerator)    =    3.000000  :=
D (initial conditions)  =    4.000000  :=
Simulation running:
    25% complete
    50% complete
    75% complete
    100% complete
Time now is   25.000000
-----------------------------------
    System polynomials
-----------------------------------
A       1.000000   1.998333   0.000000
B       2.997501   0.000000
D      28.951583   51.400217
```

Discussion

The parameter estimates converge rapidly. Note that there are now two initial condition terms as:

$$\frac{D(s)}{(s+2)} = \frac{4}{s+2} + \frac{25}{s} \qquad (5.2.4.1)$$

giving

$$D(s) = 4s + 25(s+2) = 29s + 50 \qquad (5.2.4.2)$$

Further investigations

1. Try the effect of not accounting for the offset. Do this by setting 'Integral action' to FALSE and changing $C(s)$ to 1+s. What is the effect on the parameter estimates?

2. Repeat 1 but with a shorter forgetting time. Why does this improve matters?

5.2.5. ESTIMATION OF A 4TH ORDER SYSTEM

Reference: Section 5.2; pages 5-2 - 5-3.

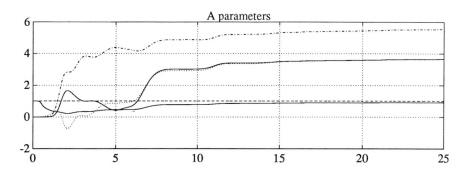

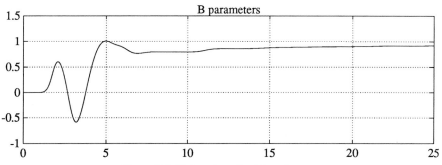

Figure 5.5. Estimation of a 4th order system

Description

This example corresponds to the 4th order system:

$$\frac{1}{(s+1)^4} = \frac{1}{s^4 + 4s^3 + 6s^2 + 4s + 1}$$

(5.2.5.1)

Programme interaction

runex 5 5
Example 5 of chapter 5: Estimation of a 4th order system

======== C S T C Version 6.0 ========

Enter all variables (y/n, default n)?
Chapter   =   5 :=

======== Data Source   ========
======== Filters   ========
Sample Interval   =   0.020000 :=
======== Control action ========
Automatic controller mode = FALSE :=
Integral action   = FALSE :=
======== Assumed system ========
A (system denominator)   =   1.000000   0.000000   0.000000   0.000000   0.000000 :=
B (system numerator)   =   1.000000 :=
D (initial conditions)   =   0.000000 :=
Tuning initial conditions = FALSE :=
======== Identification ========
Initial Variance   =   100.000000 :=
Forget time   =   1000.000000 :=
Dead band   =   0.000000 :=
*Cs (emulator denominator) =   0.500000   1.000000 * :=*
Next factor ...
*Cs (emulator denominator) =   0.500000   1.000000 * :=*
Next factor ...
*Cs (emulator denominator) =   0.500000   1.000000 * :=*
Next factor ...
Cs (emulator denominator) =   0.500000   1.000000 :=
Normalising Cs so that c0 = 1
Cs   1.000000   8.000000   24.000000   32.000000   16.000000
======== Simulation   ========
======== Setpoint   ========
Step amplitude   =   25.000000 :=

Square amplitude　　　=　　*25.000000 :=*
Period　　　　　　=　　*10.000000 :=*
======== In Disturbance ========
======== Out Disturbance ========
======== Actual system　========
A (system denominator)　=　　*1.000000　　1.000000 *　:=*
Next factor ...
A (system denominator)　=　　*1.000000　　1.000000 *　:=*
Next factor ...
A (system denominator)　=　　*1.000000　　1.000000 *　:=*
Next factor ...
A (system denominator)　=　　*1.000000　　1.000000 :=*
B (system numerator)　　=　　*1.000000 :=*
D (initial conditions)　=　　*0.000000 :=*
Simulation running:
　　25% complete
　　50% complete
　　75% complete
　100% complete
Time now is　　25.020000

　　System polynomials

A　　　1.000000　　3.656695　　5.542385　　3.666092　　0.918106
B　　　0.917702
D　　　0.000000

Discussion

The parameters all converge to their correct values, but this takes rather longer than for a first order system.

Further investigations

1. The assumed system denominator $B(s)$ is zero order. Repeat the estimation with $B(s) = s^3$ so that a third order numerator is estimated. What is the estimated $B(s)$ polynomial? How acccurate are the estimates now that the knowledge of the order of $B(s)$ has been removed? How small is the estimation error compared with the the previous case?

2. Try using a smaller initial variance; for example use 1 instead of 100000. What happens to the rate of parameter convergence? Repeat for variance values of 0.1 and 10.0.

3. While using a small initial variance (for example 1.0) try the effect of using a small forget time (for example 10.0). What effect does this have on the rate of convergence? Repeat for forget

times of 50 and 100.

4. Try using a different sample interval (for example 0.5). How does this affect the estimation? Try some other values as well.

5. Repeat 2 but with different initial parameters. How does the choice of initial parameters affect the estimates for each value of initial variance?

6. Try setting the system emulator denominator $C(s)$ to be the same as the system denominator. Why is the estimation error now virtually zero?

5.2.6. ESTIMATION OF A 5TH ORDER SYSTEM

Reference: Chapter 5.

Description

This example corresponds to the system:

$$\frac{0.0233s^4-0.1860s^3+0.6696s^2-1.2500s+1}{(0.0233s^4+0.1860s^3+0.6696s^2+1.2500s + 1)(s+1)} \qquad (5.2.6.1)$$

$$= \frac{0.0233s^4-0.1860s^3+0.6696s^2-1.2500s+1}{0.0233s^5 + 0.2093s^4 + 0.8556s^3 + 1.9196s^2 + 2.2500s + 1}$$

$$= \frac{1.0000s^4 - 7.9828s^3 + 28.7382s^2 - 53.6481s + 42.9185}{s^5 + 8.9828s^4 + 36.7210s^3 + 82.3863s^2 + 96.5665s + 42.9185}$$

This is, in fact, a Pade approximation to the system:

$$\frac{e^{-2.5s}}{s+1} \qquad (5.2.6.2)$$

Programme interaction

runex 5 6
Example 5 of chapter 6: Estimation of a 5th order system

   ======== C S T C Version 6.0 ========

Enter all variables (y/n, default n)?

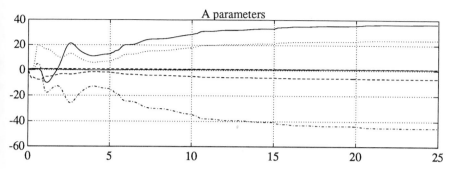

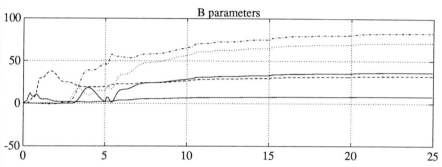

Figure 5.6. Estimation of a 5th order system

Chapter   =   5 :=

======== Data Source   ========
======== Filters   ========
Sample Interval   =   0.010000 :=
======== Control action ========
Automatic controller mode = FALSE :=
Integral action   = FALSE :=
======== Assumed system ========
A (system denominator)   =   1.000000   0.000000   0.000000   0.000000   0.000000   0.000000 :=
B (system numerator)   =   1.000000   0.000000   0.000000   0.000000   0.000000 :=
D (initial conditions)   =   0.000000 :=
Tuning initial conditions = FALSE :=
======== Identification ========
Initial Variance   =   100.000000 :=
Forget time   =   1000.000000 :=
Dead band   =   0.000000 :=

Cs (emulator denominator) =   1.000000   1.000000 * :=
Next factor ...
Cs (emulator denominator) =   1.000000   1.000000 * :=
Next factor ...
Cs (emulator denominator) =   1.000000   1.000000 * :=
Next factor ...
Cs (emulator denominator) =   1.000000   1.000000 * :=
Next factor ...
Cs (emulator denominator) =   1.000000   1.000000 :=
======== Simulation   ========
======== Setpoint   ========
Step amplitude   =   25.000000 :=
Square amplitude   =   25.000000 :=
Period   =   10.000000 :=
======== In Disturbance ========
======== Out Disturbance ========
======== Actual system ========
A (system denominator)   =   0.023300   0.186000   0.669600   1.250000   1.000000 * :=
Next factor ...
A (system denominator)   =   1.000000   1.000000 :=
B (system numerator)   =   0.023300   -0.186000   0.669600   -1.250000   1.000000 :=
D (initial conditions)   =   0.000000 :=
Simulation running:
    25% complete
    50% complete
    75% complete
   100% complete
Time now is   25.000000

        System polynomials

A   1.000000   8.007624   32.328589   71.309420   82.859892   36.619263
B   0.771162   -6.564503   23.979724   -45.324281   36.620029
D   0.000000

Discussion

To interpret the parameter estimates from this programme, it is important to realise that the estimates are *normalised* so that $A(s)$ is monic; that is, all coefficients are divided by the highest degree A coefficient: $a_0 = 0.0213$.

The parameters are not accurate, and the estimation error is not small. This is due to the poor approximation of a high order system by state-variable filter algorithm.

Further investigations

1. Try using a smaller initial covariance; for example use 1 instead of 100000. What happens to the rate of parameter convergence? What happens to the rate of estimation error convergence? Repeat for covariance values of 0.1 and 10.0.

2. While using a small initial variance (for example 1.0) try the effect of using a small forget time (for example 10.0). What effect does this have on the rate of convergence? Repeat for forget times of 50 and 100. Note that the effect of noise is examined in a later example.

3. Try using a different sample interval (for example 0.05). How does this affect the estimation? Try some other values as well.

4. Try setting the system emulator denominator $C(s)$ to be the same as the system denominator. Why is the estimation error now virtually zero?

5.2.7. ESTIMATION OF A TIME-VARYING SYSTEM

Reference: Section 5.2; pages 5-2 - 5-3.

Description

For the first 7.5 time units, the identified system is identical to that of example 1:

$$a = 2; b = 3; c = 1; d = 4. \qquad (5.2.7.1)$$

For the rest of the time, the system is given by:

$$a = 3; b = 4; c = 1 \qquad (5.2.7.2)$$

Thus an abrupt change in system parameters occurs at time 7.5.

The purpose of this example is to observe the behaviour of the least-squares algorithm when faced with time varying systems. In particular, the effect of the forgetting factor is investigated.

Programme interaction

runex 5 7
Example 5 of chapter 7: Estimation of a time-varying system

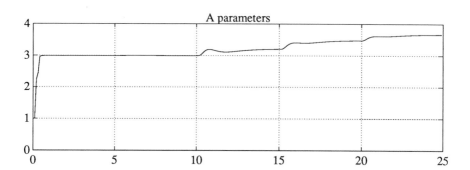

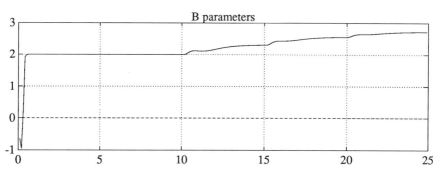

Figure 5.7. Estimation of a time-varying system

======== *C S T C Version 6.0* ========

Enter all variables (y/n, default n)?
Chapter   =   *5* :=

======== *Data Source*   ========
======== *Filters*   ========
Sample Interval   =   *0.100000* :=
======== *Control action* ========
Automatic controller mode = *FALSE* :=
Integral action   = *TRUE* :=
======== *Assumed system* ========
A (system denominator)   =   *1.000000   0.000000* :=
B (system numerator)   =   *1.000000* :=
D (initial conditions)   =   *0.000000* :=
Tuning initial conditions = *TRUE* :=
======== *Identification* ========

Initial Variance   =   *100.000000   :=*
Forget time   =   *10.000000   :=*
Dead band   =   *0.000000   :=*
Cs (emulator denominator) =   *1.000000   2.000000   1.000000   :=*
========= *Simulation*   ========
========= *Setpoint*   ========
Step amplitude   =   *25.000000   :=*
Square amplitude   =   *25.000000   :=*
Period   =   *10.000000   :=*
======== *In Disturbance* ========
======== *Out Disturbance* ========
Cos amplitude   =   *0.000000   :=*
Period   =   *0.123000   :=*
======== *Actual system*   ========
A (system denominator)   =   *1.000000   2.000000   :=*
B (system numerator)   =   *3.000000   :=*
D (initial conditions)   =   *4.000000   :=*
Simulation running:
    25% complete
    50% complete
    75% complete
    100% complete
Time now is   7.600000
Extra time   =   *17.500000   :=*
======== *Actual system*   ========
A (system denominator)   =   *1.000000   3.000000   :=*
B (system numerator)   =   *4.000000   :=*
Simulation running:
    25% complete
    50% complete
    75% complete
    100% complete
Time now is   25.000000

    System polynomials

A   *1.000000   2.717764   0.000000*
B   *3.670209   0.000000*
D   *-9.043300   13.593639*

Discussion

Initially, the three system parameters rapidly converge to the correct values. This is because there is no noise and the initial variance is large. After time 7.5, the estimates begin to move towards their new values. This is a slow process as the estimator is assuming a time invariant system.

Further investigations

1. Try using a smaller initial variance; for example,

    use 1. What happens to the rate of parameter convergence after the step parameter change? Repeat for variance values of 0.1 and 10.0.

2. Try using different forget times. How does the rate of parameter convergence after the step parameter change depend on the forget time?

3. As discussed in examples 2 and 3, noise adversely affects parameter convergence, particularly with small forget times. Investigate the effect of noise in this case.

5.2.8. DATA SPLICING

Reference: Chapter 5*

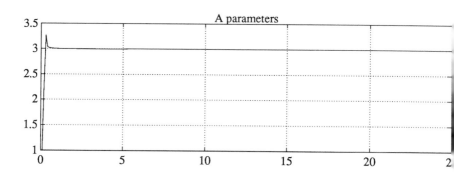

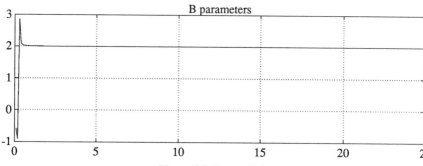

Figure 5.8. Data splicing

Description

There are a number of situations in which a number of data sets are available which, though arising from the same physical system, are not contiguous in time. Such data sets can be treated using the method of *data splicing**.

This example uses the 'outlog.dat' file from example 5.2.1, copied into 'indata.dat', and edited to remove all data from time 7.0 to time 12.0. This file is on the distribution disc as **indata.dat**. A blank line in this file marks the missing data, and the splicing procedure is invoked at this point.

Programme interaction

runex 5 8
Example 5 of chapter 8: Data splicing

======== C S T C Version 6.0 ========

Enter all variables (y/n, default n)?

======== Data Source ========
External data = TRUE :=
======== Real data ========
======== Filters ========
======== Control action ========
Automatic controller mode = FALSE :=
Integral action = FALSE :=
======== Assumed system ========
A (system denominator) = 1.000000 0.000000 :=
B (system numerator) = 1.000000 :=
Tuning initial conditions = TRUE :=
======== Identification ========
Initial Variance = 100000.000000 :=
Forget time = 1000.000000 :=
Cs (emulator denominator) = 1.000000 1.000000 :=
Processing data in file ...
Splicing data

System polynomials

---

*Gawthrop, P.J. (1984) "Parameter identification from non-contiguous data", Proceedings IEE, vol. 131 pt. D, No. 6, pp261-265.

A	1.000000	1.999926
B	2.999672	
D	74.600965	

Discussion

The graph is of the same format as for example 5.2.1. Data are missing beween times 7 and 12, and the plotting method used just joins up the graphs between these points.

Notice that the parameter estimates corresponding to $A(s)$ and $B(s)$ are entirely unaffected by the missing data; the values correspond to those in example 5.2.1. However, the initial condition estimate is quite different, as it is used in the data splicing procedure.

Further investigations

1   Investigate the effect of using the same data, but without the data splicing step. To do this, first put a copy of the **indata.dat** file in a safe place for later use. Then edit **indata.dat** and delete the blank line (just before the 12.0000 in the first column). Rerun the programme and observe the resultant parameter estimates - they are spoiled by the missing data.

2   Try out data splicing on some of the other examples. Run the relevant example, copy **outdata.dat** to **indata.dat** and delete one or more chunks of data. Leave a blank line to mark each block of missing data. Don't forget to make a safe copy of the original **indata.dat**.

5.2.9. ESTIMATION OF A DISCRETE-TIME SYSTEM

Reference: Section I-5.7; pages I-5-19&20

Description

This example is similar to example 1 except that the system is described in discrete-time. Note that all polynomials are now described in terms of z rather than s so that, in this example:

$$A(z) = z - 0.9; \ B(z) = 0.3; \ C_s(z) = z - 0.8$$

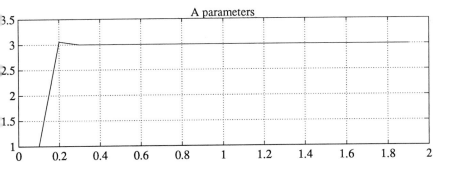

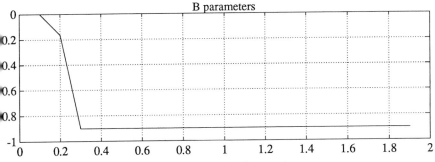

Figure 5.9. Estimation of a discrete-time system

Programme interaction

runex 5 9
Example 5 of chapter 9: Estimation of a discrete-time system

  ======== C S T C Version 6.0 ========

Enter all variables (y/n, default n)?
Chapter   =   5 :=

======== Data Source   ========
======== Filters   ========
Sample Interval   =   0.100000 :=
Continuous-time?   = FALSE :=
======== Control action ========
Automatic controller mode = FALSE :=

Integral action   = FALSE :=
======== Assumed system ========
A (system denominator)   =   1.000000   0.000000 :=
B (system numerator)   =   1.000000 :=
D (initial conditions)   =   0.000000 :=
Tuning initial conditions = TRUE :=
======== Identification ========
Initial Variance   = 100000.000000 :=
Forget time   = 1000.000000 :=
Dead band   =   0.000000 :=
Cs (emulator denominator) =   1.000000   -0.800000 :=
======== Simulation   ========
======== Setpoint   ========
Step amplitude   =   25.000000 :=
Square amplitude   =   25.000000 :=
Period   =   10.000000 :=
======== In Disturbance ========
======== Out Disturbance ========
======== Actual system   ========
A (system denominator)   =   1.000000   -0.900000 :=
B (system numerator)   =   3.000000 :=
D (initial conditions)   =   4.000000 :=
Simulation running:
*   25% complete*
*   50% complete*
*   75% complete*
*   100% complete*
Time now is   2.000000
----
*   System polynomials*

A   1.000000   -0.900000
B   3.000000
D   3.999976

Discussion

The three estimated parameters converge to the correct value in three time steps. This is not surprising as the three simultaneous equations arising from the three sets of measurements are sufficient to derive the three unknown parameters.

Further investigations

1. Try changing the value of $C_s(z)$ to z. Does this make any difference? What is the effect of $C_s(z)$ on the filtered system input and output in this case?

2. Try discrete-time analogues of all the other continuous-time examples. The simplest way to do this is to run the appropriate continuous-time example and then edit the inlof.dat file to expose the 'Continuous-time' variable.

CHAPTER 6
Self-Tuning Control

Aims. To describe the implementation of the various self-tuning control algorithms in a unified manner. To provide a number of detailed examples comparing and contrasting the performance of the various algorithms.

6.1. IMPLEMENTATION DETAILS

6.1.1. [6.2] FEEDBACK CONTROL

As in chapter 3, the feedback controller is implemented by function **Control**. As discussed in that section, the control signal is computed by function **ImplicitSolution** if the transfer function $Q(s)$ has relative order zero, and by direct filtering if $\dfrac{1}{Q(s)}$ is strictly proper. In contrast to chapter 3, function **emulator** uses the *estimated* emulator parameters in place of the correct emulator parameters; thus the self-tuning controller is implemented as a self-tuning emulator in a feedback loop.

6.1.2. [6.4] EXPLICIT SELF-TUNING CONTROL

6.1.2.1. Off-line design

The off-line (a-priori) design phase

The emulator design parameters are chosen by the user during the preliminary interaction with CSTC. It is the user that makes the decision about the values of these polynomials. For example, $P(s)$ may be chosen to give a desired closed-loop response at low frequencies, and $Q(s)$ chosen to roll off the high-frequency gain. The choice of these parameters is discussed in detail in Volume I chapter 3.

The initial values of the polynomials $A(s)$ and $B(s)$ are set by the user in procedure **SystemInitialise** making use of procedure **EnterPolynomial**. This sets two things: the values of the coefficients of the polynomials used as initial values in the parameter estimator, and the degrees of the two polynomials.

The on-line tuning phase

This is accomplished within procedure **SelfTuningControl**, with **IdentifyingSystem** and **Explicit** both set to TRUE. Steps 1 and 2 (page I-6-12) are implemented within procedure **IdentifySystem** as discussed in chapter 5. Procedure **SetDesignKnobs** has no effect in this case.

Step 3 is implemented within procedure **DesignEmulator** using the procedures discussed in chapter 2.

Steps 4, 5 and 6 are implemented within procedure **Control**. Procedure **PutData** provides additional control signal modification. The corresponding parameters are contained within the record **PutDataKnobs** of type **TypePutDataKnobs**. The control signal is limited to be between **Max** and **Min**. If **Switched** is TRUE then a relay-type control is implemented.

The emulated signal **PhiHat** ($\hat{\phi}(t)$) is then generated using this modified control signal. This not only provides $\hat{\phi}(t)$ for control and identification at the next time instant, but also updates the corresponding emulator states.

Finally, if $Q(s)$ is of zero relative order, then **qState** is updated using **StateVariableFilter**. This is because, in a copy of **qState** , not the state itself, is updated within control procedure **ImplicitCon-**

trol.

6.1.2.2. On-line design

The off-line (a-priori) design phase

With reference to step 1, page I-6-13, two algorithms involving on-line design are implemented: pole-placement control and linear-quadratic control. In each case, **ZHasFactorB** is set to TRUE, and so $Z(s)$ depends on the estimated system numerator $B(s)$. If, in addition **LQ** is TRUE, then $P(s)$ is chosen on-line to satisfy equation 23 of section 3.4 of Volume I. The corresponding weight λ is set at this stage.

With reference to steps 2 and 3, page I-6-13, on line design of $Q(s)$ and $R(s)$ is not implemented in CSTC; these transfer functions are set to fixed values during the initialisation phase.

Step 4 is implemented during the initialisation phase when the $A(s)$ and $B(s)$ are set.

The on-line tuning phase

This is identical to that corresponding to the off-line design algorithm, except that step 3a is implemented within procedure **SetDesignKnobs**. **BMinus** is set equal to the estimated system numerator $B(s)$ except that if **ZeroAtOrigin** is TRUE, the corresponding term is transferred in to $B^+(s)$ as discussed in section 2.3 of Volume I.

If **LQ** is TRUE, $P(s)$ is designed using procedure **DesignP**. This calls the rather simple minded procedures **PolSquare** and **PolSqrt**. These compute $A(s)A(-s)$ from $A(s)$ and vice versa. They are only defined for first and second order polynomials.

6.1.3. [6.5] IMPLICIT SELF-TUNING CONTROL

As discussed in volume I, *implicit* self-tuning control involves direct tuning of the emulator parameters, thus avoiding the design phase taking estimated system parameters and deriving corresponding emulator parameters. As discussed in section I-6.5, the distinction between **off-line** and **on-line** design algorithms is made. The former class gives the simplest algorithms with straightforward implementation, the latter class gives rise to more complex algorithms.

6.1.3.1. Off-line design

The off-line (a-priori) design phase

Steps 1-4 (page I-6-17) are identical to those described in section 6.1.2.1 insofar as emulator design parameters are chosen by the user during the preliminary interaction with CSTC. There are two possibilities implemented for step 5: if the Boolean variable **UsingLambda** is TRUE then $\Lambda(s)$ is chosen according to equation I-6.5.1

$$\Lambda(s) = e^{-sT} \frac{Z(s)}{P(s)} \qquad\qquad\qquad (6.1.3.1.1)$$

Otherwise $\Lambda(s) = 1$.

The on-line tuning phase

This is accomplished within procedure **SelfTuningControl,** with **IdentifyingSystem** and **Explicit** both set to FALSE.

If **UsingLambda** is TRUE then steps 1-3 are implemented within procedure **TuneLambdaEmulator.** Step 1 is implemented using the statement beginning:

PhiLambda := Filter(y, PLambda, ZLambda,

As **TuneLambdaEmulator** is with both **PLambda** and **ZLambda** equal to unit polynomials, this is equivalent to setting **PhiLambda** to **y.** The more general form is implemented to allow further research. Step 2 is implemented by the two statements beginning:

uLambda := DelayFilter(u, LambdaNumerator,

yLambda := DelayFilter(y, LambdaNumerator,

where **uLambda** and **yLambda** are the filtered versions of $u(t)$ and $y(t)$. Step 3 is implemented using the statement beginning:

PhiLamHat := Emulator(yLambda, uLambda,

where **PhiLamHat** is the corresponding emulator output and the emulator state vector is updated and saved in **LambdaEmState.** This information is extracted and put into **DataVector** $(\underline{X}_\Lambda(t))$ using the statement:

Step 4, the least-squares estimation, is accomplished using the statements

> EstimationError := PhiLamHat - PhiLambda;
>
> UpdateLeastSquaresGain(TunerState, TunerKnobs,
>
> > DataVector);
>
> TuneEmulator(EmKnobs, TunerState);

See chapter II-5 for more details. Steps 5 and 6 are implemented as described in section 6.1.2.

If, on the other hand, **UsingLambda** is FALSE then step 1 is implemented within procedure **TunePhiEmulator.** As $\Lambda(s) = 1$, $\phi_\Lambda(t) = \phi(t)$ and is generated by the statement

> Phi := Filter(y, P, Z, FilterKnobs, PhicState);

Step 2 is not relevant here. Step 3 is implemented by using the statement

> SetData(DataVector, EmState, EmKnobs);

to copy the information in the emulator state, **EmState** to **DataVector** $(\underline{X}_\Lambda(t))$. Step 4, the least-squares estimation, is accomplished in a similar fashion to **TuneLambdaEmulator,** and steps 5 and 6 are implemented as described in section 6.1.2.

6.1.3.2. On-line design

The off-line (a-priori) design phase

An in the explicit case, two algorithms involving on-line design are implemented: pole-placement control and linear-quadratic control. Steps 1-4 (page I-6-18&19) are implemented as for off-line design.

The design rule referred to in the additional step 5 (page I-6-19) is chosen according to equation 2 on page I-6-19:

$$\Lambda(s) = e^{-sT} \frac{Z(s)}{P(s)} \qquad\qquad (6.1.3.2.1)$$

The on-line tuning phase

This is accomplished within procedure **SelfTuningControl.** As the method is implicit, the Boolean variable **Explicit** set to FALSE. However, an estimate of the polynomial $B(s)$ is need for the on-line design so the Boolean variable **IdentifyingSystem** set to TRUE. Steps 1 and 2 (page I-6-19) are implemented within procedure **IdentifySystem** as discussed in chapter 5. Step 3 is implemented by procedure **SetDesignKnobs** as discussed in chapter 2. Steps 4 and 5 are not implemented in CSTC. Step 6 is implemented automatically as $\Lambda(s)$ is expressed directly in terms of $P(s)$ ands $Z(s)$. Steps 7-12 are then identical to steps 1-6 of the off-line design method described in section 6.1.3.1.

6.2. EXAMPLES

6.2.1. EXPLICIT MODEL REFERENCE

Reference: Section 6.4; page 6-11. Section 3.4; page 3-12.

Description

This is the self-tuning equivalent of example 3.2.1 using the explicit approach with off-line choice of emulator design parameters.

The aim of the controller is to make the system output follow the model:

$$\overline{y}(s) = \frac{Z(s)}{P(s)} \overline{w}(s) \tag{6.2.1.1}$$

where, in this case, $Z(s)=1$ and $P(s) = 1+Ts$ where the model time-constant $T = 0.5$.

The system parameters are estimated and the corresponding emulator parameters evaluated at each time step.

Programme interaction

runex 6 1
Example 6 of chapter 1: Explicit model reference

======== C S T C Version 6.0 ========

Enter all variables (y/n, default n)?

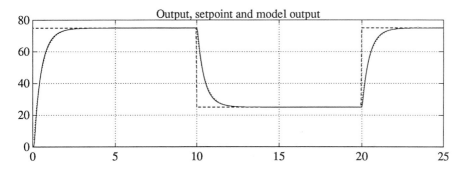

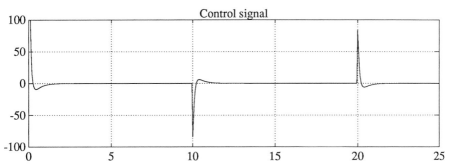

Figure 6.1. Explicit model reference

```
======== Data Source    ========
======== Filters        ========
======== Control action ========
Integral action        = FALSE :=
======== Assumed system ========
A (system denominator)  =   1.000000   0.000000   0.000000 :=
B (system numerator)    =   1.000000   1.000000 :=
======== Emulator design ========
P (model denominator)   =   0.500000   1.000000 :=
C (emulator denominator) =  0.500000   1.000000 :=

-----------------------------------
    System polynomials
-----------------------------------

A       1.000000   0.000000   0.000000
B       1.000000   1.000000
D       0.000000   0.000000
-----------------------------------
```

Design polynomials

```
-----------------------------------
B+        1.000000    1.000000
B-        1.000000
C         0.500000    1.000000
P         0.500000    1.000000
Z+        1.000000
Z-        1.000000
Z-+       1.000000
-----------------------------------
F         1.000000    1.000000
F filter  0.500000    1.000000
G         0.250000    0.250000
G filter  0.500000    1.000000
I
E         0.250000
ED        0.000000
-----------------------------------
```

```
======== STC type      ========
======== Identification ========
Initial Variance     = 100000.000000  :=
Forget time          = 1000.000000  :=
======== Controller    ========
Switched control signal  = FALSE  :=
======== Simulation    ========
======== Setpoint      ========
======== In Disturbance ========
======== Out Disturbance ========
======== Actual system  ========
A (system denominator)  =    1.000000    1.000000    0.000000  :=
B (system numerator)    =    1.000000    10.000000  :=
Simulation running:
    25% complete
    50% complete
    75% complete
    100% complete
Time now is   25.000000
```

```
-----------------------------------
```

System polynomials

```
-----------------------------------
A        1.000000    1.000132    -0.000003
B        0.997695    10.001276
D        0.000000    0.000000
-----------------------------------
```

Design polynomials

```
-----------------------------------
B+       0.997695    10.001276
B-       1.000000
C        0.500000    1.000000
```

P	0.500000	1.000000
Z+	1.000000	
Z-	1.000000	
Z-+	1.000000	

F	0.749967	1.000001
F filter	0.500000	1.000000
G	0.249424	2.500319
G filter	0.500000	1.000000
I		
E	0.250000	
ED	0.000000	

Discussion

The upper graph displays three signals: the system output $y(t)$, the setpoint $w(t)$ and the ideal model output $y_m(t)$ where $\overline{y}_m(s) = \dfrac{Z(s)}{P(s)} \overline{w}(s)$.

After a short time, the output follows the model output closely despite the initially incorrect parameters.

Further investigations

1. Try the effect of varying the time constant T of the inverse model P. How does this affect the system output and the control signal?

2. The emulator denominator $C(s)$ is also of the form 1+Ts. Try the effect of varying the time constant T of the emulator denominator C. How does this affect the system output and the control signal?

3. Try changing the limits of the control signal so that it is clipped; for example choose 'Maximum control signal' as 10 and 'Minimum control signal' as -10. How does this affect the system output and the control signal?

4. The controller and simulation are implemented as discrete-time systems. Try the effect of varying the sample interval on closed-loop performance.

5. Try using a switched controller by setting 'Switched control signal' to TRUE. How does the performance depend on:

a)   Sample interval

b)   The maximum and minimum control limits.

6.2.2. EXPLICIT POLE-PLACEMENT CONTROL

Reference: Section 6.4; page 6-11. Section 3.4; page 3-13.

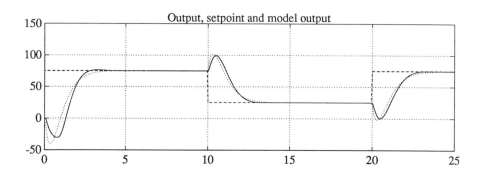

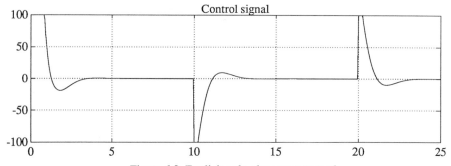

Figure 6.2. Explicit pole-placement control

Description

As discussed in volume I, the emulator designed in the second example of section I-2.4 may be embedded in a feedback loop to give pole-placement control.

The aim of the controller is to make the system output follow the model:

$$\bar{y}(s) = \frac{Z(s)}{P(s)}\bar{w}(s) \tag{6.2.2.1}$$

where, in this case, $Z(s) = B(s)$ and $P(s) = (1+Ts)^2$ where the model time-constant T = 0.5.

Programme interaction

runex 6 2
Example 6 of chapter 2: Explicit pole-placement control

======== C S T C Version 6.0 ========

Enter all variables (y/n, default n)?

```
======== Data Source   ========
======== Filters       ========
======== Control action ========
======== Assumed system ========
A (system denominator)  =   1.000000   0.000000   0.000000  :=
B (system numerator)    =   1.000000   1.000000  :=
======== Emulator design ========
Z has factor B          = TRUE  :=
P (model denominator)   =   0.500000   1.000000 *  :=
Next factor ...
P (model denominator)   =   0.500000   1.000000  :=
C (emulator denominator) =   0.500000   1.000000  :=
--------------------------------
       System polynomials
--------------------------------
A        1.000000   0.000000   0.000000
B        1.000000   1.000000
D        0.000000   0.000000
--------------------------------
       Design polynomials
--------------------------------
B+       1.000000
B-       1.000000   1.000000
C        0.500000   1.000000
P        0.250000   1.000000   1.000000
Z+       1.000000
Z-       1.000000   1.000000
Z-+      1.000000
--------------------------------
F        0.500000   1.000000
```

```
F filter    0.500000    1.000000
G           0.125000    0.250000
G filter    0.500000    1.000000
I
E           0.125000    0.250000
ED          0.000000    0.000000
```

```
======== STC type      ========
Tuning initial conditions = FALSE  :=
======== Identification ========
Initial Variance        = 100000.000000  :=
Forget time             = 1000.000000  :=
Cs (emulator denominator) =    1.000000    2.000000    1.000000  :=
======== Controller       ========
Switched control signal  = FALSE  :=
======== Simulation     ========
======== Setpoint       ========
======== In Disturbance ========
======== Out Disturbance ========
======== Actual system   ========
A (system denominator)   =    1.000000    1.000000    0.000000  :=
B (system numerator)     =   -1.000000    1.000000  :=
Simulation running:
      25% complete
      50% complete
      75% complete
      100% complete
Time now is    25.000000
```

      System polynomials

```
A          1.000000    0.999689    0.000009
B         -0.999991    0.999695
D          0.000000    0.000000
```

      Design polynomials

```
B+         0.999695
B-        -1.000297    1.000000
C          0.500000    1.000000
P          0.250000    1.000000    1.000000
Z+         1.000000
Z-        -1.000297    1.000000
Z-+        1.000000
```

```
F          0.937725    0.999985
F filter   0.500000    1.000000
G          0.124962    1.562565
G filter   0.500000    1.000000
```

```
I
E        0.125000    1.563042
ED       0.000000    0.000000
```

Discussion

The upper graph displays three signals: the system output $y(t)$, the setpoint $w(t)$ and the ideal model output $y_m(t)$ where $\bar{y}_m(s) = \dfrac{Z(s)}{P(s)}\bar{w}(s)$.

In this case, note the typical behaviour of a system with right-hand plane zeros: the output initially goes the wrong way in response to a step change. The model output $\bar{y}_m(s)$ is not exactly followed; this is because the control signal is limited.

Further investigations

1. Try the effect of varying the time constant T of the inverse model P. How does this affect the system output and the control signal?

2. Try repeating this example using the same system as the previous section ($B(s) = 10+s$). How does the closed-loop response when using pole-placement differ from that when using model-reference control?

3. Try changing the control limits. How is the response changed?

6.2.3. USING A SETPOINT FILTER

Reference: Section 6.4; page 6-11. Section 3.5; page 3-15.

Description

This example is identical to example 1 except that a setpoint filter is added:

$$wRs = R(s)\bar{w}(s); R(s) = \frac{0.5s+1}{s^2 + \sqrt{2}s + 1} \tag{6.2.3.1}$$

The closed loop response is thus:

$$\bar{y}(s) = \frac{Z(s)}{P(s)}R(s)\bar{w}(s) = \frac{1}{0.5s+1}\frac{0.5s+1}{s^2 + \sqrt{2}s + 1}\bar{w}(s) = \frac{1}{s^2 + \sqrt{2}s + 1}\bar{w}(s) \tag{6.2.3.2}$$

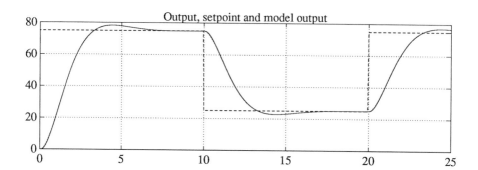

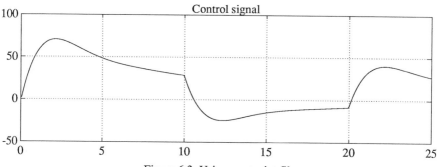

Figure 6.3. Using a setpoint filter

Programme interaction

runex 6 3
Example 6 of chapter 3: Using a setpoint filter

======== C S T C Version 6.0 ========

Enter all variables (y/n, default n)?

======== Data Source ========
======== Filters ========
======== Control action ========
======== Assumed system ========
A (system denominator) = 1.000000 0.000000 0.000000 :=
B (system numerator) = 1.000000 1.000000 :=
======== Emulator design ========

P *(model denominator)*   =   0.500000   1.000000   :=
C *(emulator denominator)* =   0.500000   1.000000   :=

    System polynomials

A   1.000000   0.000000   0.000000
B   1.000000   1.000000
D   0.000000   0.000000

    Design polynomials

B+   1.000000   1.000000
B-   1.000000
C   0.500000   1.000000
P   0.500000   1.000000
Z+   1.000000
Z-   1.000000
Z-+   1.000000

F   1.000000   1.000000
F filter 0.500000   1.000000
G   0.250000   0.250000
G filter 0.500000   1.000000
I
E   0.250000
ED   0.000000

 ========= STC type   =========
Tuning initial conditions = FALSE   :=
 ========= Identification =========
Initial Variance   = 100000.000000   :=
Forget time   = 1000.000000   :=
Cs *(emulator denominator)* =   1.000000   2.000000   1.000000   :=
 ========= Controller   =========
R numerator   =   0.500000   1.000000   :=
R denominator   =   1.000000   1.414000   1.000000   :=
Maximum control signal =   100.000000   :=
Minimum control signal =   -100.000000   :=
 ========= Simulation   =========
 ========= Setpoint   =========
 ========= In Disturbance =========
 ========= Out Disturbance =========
 ========= Actual system =========
A *(system denominator)* =   1.000000   1.000000   0.000000   :=
B *(system numerator)*   =   1.000000   0.100000   :=
Simulation running:
    25% complete
    50% complete
    75% complete

100% complete
Time now is   25.000000

   System polynomials

A	1.000000	0.999677	-0.000003
B	0.999759	0.099963	
D	0.000000	0.000000	

   Design polynomials

B+	0.999759	0.099963
B-	1.000000	
C	0.500000	1.000000
P	0.500000	1.000000
Z+	1.000000	
Z-	1.000000	
Z-+	1.000000	

F	0.750081	1.000001
F filter	0.500000	1.000000
G	0.249940	0.024991
G filter	0.500000	1.000000
I		
E	0.250000	
ED	0.000000	

Discussion

The upper graph displays three signals: the system output $y(t)$, the setpoint $w(t)$ and the ideal model output $y_m(t)$ where $\bar{y}_m(s) = \dfrac{Z(s)}{P(s)} \bar{w}(s)$.

Note that the control signal is considerably reduced.

Further investigations

1. Try the effect of different choices of $R(s)$ and $P(s)$, paying attention to the relative order ρ of $\dfrac{R(s)}{P(s)}$ and the steady-state gain $\dfrac{R(0)}{P(0)}$.

6.2.4. EXPLICIT CONTROL-WEIGHTED MODEL REFERENCE

Reference: Section 6.4; page 6-11. Section 3.6; page 3-16.

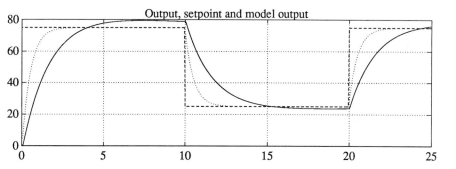

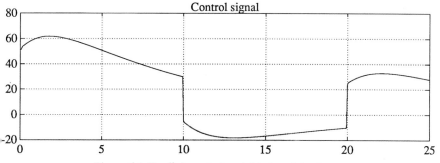

Figure 6.4. Explicit control-weighted model reference

Description

In example 6.2.1, exact model-reference control was achieved by setting $Q(s)=0$. For this example, $Q(s)$ is chosen as

$$Q(s) = \frac{s}{s+1} \tag{6.2.4.1}$$

This satifies the $Q(s)$ design rule on page I-3-17.

Programme interaction

runex 6 4
Example 6 of chapter 4: Explicit control-weighted model reference

    ======== C S T C Version 6.0 ========

Enter all variables (y/n, default n)?

    ======== Data Source   ========
    ======== Filters   ========
    ======== Control action ========
    ======== Assumed system ========
A (system denominator)   =   1.000000   0.000000   0.000000 :=
B (system numerator)   =   1.000000   1.000000 :=
    ======== Emulator design ========
P (model denominator)   =   0.500000   1.000000 :=
C (emulator denominator) =   0.500000   1.000000 :=

        System polynomials

A	*1.000000*	*0.000000*	*0.000000*
B	*1.000000*	*1.000000*	
D	*0.000000*	*0.000000*	

        Design polynomials

B+	*1.000000*	*1.000000*
B-	*1.000000*	
C	*0.500000*	*1.000000*
P	*0.500000*	*1.000000*
Z+	*1.000000*	
Z-	*1.000000*	
Z-+	*1.000000*	

F	*1.000000*	*1.000000*
F filter	*0.500000*	*1.000000*
G	*0.250000*	*0.250000*
G filter	*0.500000*	*1.000000*
I		
E	*0.250000*	
ED	*0.000000*	

    ======== STC type   ========
Tuning initial conditions = FALSE :=
    ======== Identification ========
Initial Variance   = 100000.000000 :=

Forget time   = *1000.000000* :=
Cs (emulator denominator) =   *1.000000   2.000000   1.000000* :=
======= *Controller*   =======
Q numerator   =   *1.000000   0.000000* :=
Q denominator   =   *1.000000   1.000000* :=
======= *Simulation*   =======
======= *Setpoint*   =======
======= *In Disturbance* =======
======= *Out Disturbance* =======
======= *Actual system*   =======
A (system denominator)   =   *1.000000   1.000000   0.000000* :=
B (system numerator)   =   *1.000000   0.100000* :=
Number of lags   =   *0* :=
Simulation running:
     25% complete
     50% complete
     75% complete
     100% complete
Time now is   25.000000
More time   = *FALSE* :=

     System polynomials

A   *1.000000   0.999684   -0.000003*
B   *0.999761   0.099964*
D   *0.000000   0.000000*

     Design polynomials

B+   *0.999761   0.099964*
B-   *1.000000*
C   *0.500000   1.000000*
P   *0.500000   1.000000*
Z+   *1.000000*
Z-   *1.000000*
Z-+   *1.000000*

F   *0.750079   1.000001*
F filter *0.500000   1.000000*
G   *0.249940   0.024991*
G filter *0.500000   1.000000*
I
E   *0.250000*
ED   *0.000000*

Discussion

The upper graph displays three signals: the system output $y(t)$, the setpoint $w(t)$ and the ideal model output $y_m(t)$ where $\overline{y}_m(s) = \dfrac{Z(s)}{P(s)} \overline{w}(s)$.

Notice that the control signal is reduced with respect to that of example 6.2.1. The model following is no longer exact, but the use of the $Q(s)$ design rule ensures that there is no steady-state offset.

Further investigations

1. Try the effect of varying q in:

$$Q(s) = \frac{qs}{1+s} \tag{6.2.4.2}$$

2. Try the effect of varying T in:

$$Q(s) = \frac{s}{1+Ts} \tag{6.2.4.3}$$

3. Replace $Q(s)$ by:

$$Q(s)=q \tag{6.2.4.4}$$

There is still no offset as, in this case, the system contains an integrator and so the control signal is zero in the steady-state.

4. Replace $Q(s)$ by:

$$Q(s)=q \tag{6.2.4.5}$$

and $A(s)$ by:

$$A(s) = s^2 + 2s + 1 \tag{6.2.4.6}$$

Note that there is now an offset dependent on q.

5. Use the default value of $Q(s)$ but replace $A(s)$ by:

$$A(s) = s^2 + 2s + 1 \tag{6.2.4.7}$$

Note that the offset disappears.

6.2.5. EXPLICIT CONTROL-WEIGHTED POLE-PLACEMENT

Reference: Section 6.4; page 6-11. Section 3.6; page 3-16.

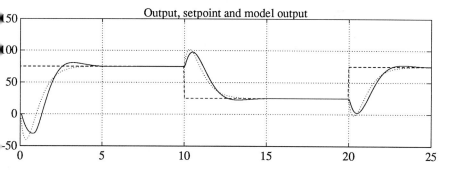

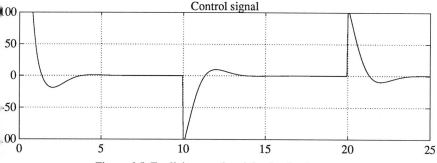

Figure 6.5. Explicit control-weighted pole-placement

Description

In example 6.2.2, exact pole-placement control was achieved by setting $Q(s)=0$. For this example, $Q(s)$ is chosen as

$$Q(s) = \frac{s}{s+1}$$ (6.2.5.1)

this satifies the $Q(s)$ design rule on page 3-17 of vol. 1.

Programme interaction

runex 6 5
Example 6 of chapter 5: Explicit control-weighted pole-placement

======== *C S T C Version 6.0* ========

Enter all variables (y/n, default n)?

======== *Data Source*   ========
======== *Filters*   ========
======== *Control action* ========
======== *Assumed system* ========
A (system denominator)   =   *1.000000   0.000000   0.000000 :=*
B (system numerator)   =   *1.000000   1.000000 :=*
======== *Emulator design* ========
Z has factor B   = *TRUE :=*
P (model denominator)   =   *0.500000   1.000000 * :=*
Next factor ...
P (model denominator)   =   *0.500000   1.000000 :=*
C (emulator denominator) =   *0.500000   1.000000 :=*

            System polynomials

A   *1.000000   0.000000   0.000000*
B   *1.000000   1.000000*
D   *0.000000   0.000000*

            Design polynomials

B+   *1.000000*
B-   *1.000000   1.000000*
C   *0.500000   1.000000*
P   *0.250000   1.000000   1.000000*
Z+   *1.000000*
Z-   *1.000000   1.000000*
Z-+   *1.000000*

F   *0.500000   1.000000*
F filter *0.500000   1.000000*
G   *0.125000   0.250000*
G filter *0.500000   1.000000*
I
E   *0.125000   0.250000*
ED   *0.000000   0.000000*

======== *STC type*   ========

```
Tuning initial conditions = FALSE  :=
======== Identification ========
Initial Variance        = 100000.000000  :=
Forget time             =   1000.000000  :=
Cs (emulator denominator) =    1.000000    2.000000    1.000000  :=
======== Controller      ========
Q numerator             =      0.100000    0.000000  :=
Q denominator           =      1.000000    1.000000  :=
======== Simulation      ========
======== Setpoint        ========
======== In Disturbance  ========
======== Out Disturbance ========
======== Actual system   ========
A (system denominator)  =      1.000000    1.000000    0.000000  :=
B (system numerator)    =     -1.000000    1.000000  :=
Number of lags          =         0  :=
Simulation running:
    25% complete
    50% complete
    75% complete
    100% complete
Time now is    25.000000
More time               = FALSE  :=
------------------------------------
    System polynomials
------------------------------------
A        1.000000    0.999703    0.000009
B       -0.999991    0.999709
D        0.000000    0.000000
------------------------------------
    Design polynomials
------------------------------------
B+       0.999709
B-      -1.000282    1.000000
C        0.500000    1.000000
P        0.250000    1.000000    1.000000
Z+       1.000000
Z-      -1.000282    1.000000
Z-+      1.000000
------------------------------------
F        0.937715    0.999986
F filter 0.500000    1.000000
G        0.124964    1.562561
G filter 0.500000    1.000000
I
E        0.125000    1.563017
ED       0.000000    0.000000
------------------------------------
```

Discussion

The upper graph displays three signals: the system output $y(t)$, the setpoint $w(t)$ and the ideal model output $y_m(t)$ where $\bar{y}_m(s) = \dfrac{Z(s)}{P(s)} \bar{w}(s)$.

Notice that the control signal is reduced with respect to that of example 6.2.2. The model following is no longer exact, but the use of the $Q(s)$ design rule ensures that there is no steady-state offset.

Further investigations

1. Try the effect of varying q (e.g. q = 0.1) in:

$$Q(s) = \frac{qs}{1+s} \tag{6.2.5.2}$$

2. Try the effect of varying T in:

$$Q(s) = \frac{s}{1+Ts} \tag{6.2.5.3}$$

3. Replace $Q(s)$ by:

$$Q(s)=q \tag{6.2.5.4}$$

There is still no offset as, in this case, the system contains an integrator and so the control signal is zero in the steady-state.

4. Replace $Q(s)$ by:

$$Q(s)=q \tag{6.2.5.5}$$

and $A(s)$ by:

$$A(s) = s^2 + 2s + 1 \tag{6.2.5.6}$$

Note that there is now an offset dependent on q.

5. Use the default value of $Q(s)$ but replace $A(s)$ by:

$$A(s) = s^2 + 2s + 1 \tag{6.2.5.7}$$

Note that the offset disappears.

6.2.6. TIME-DELAY SYSTEM (EXPLICIT)

Reference: Section 6.4; page 6-11. Section 3.7; page 3-18.

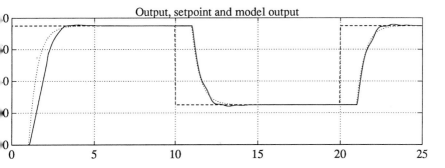

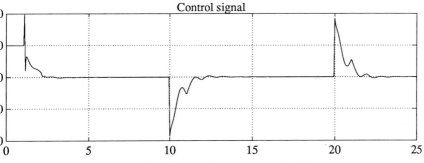

Figure 6.6. Time-delay system (explicit)

Description

This example corresponds to example 6.2.1, except that the system now is first order and has a time-delay of one unit.

$$\frac{B(s)}{A(s)} = e^{-t} \frac{1}{s} \tag{6.2.6.1}$$

The corresponding emulator is based on the Pade approximation approach discussed in section I-2.6.

But note that the simulation of the system uses an exact time-delay algorithm.

Programme interaction

runex 6 6
Example 6 of chapter 6: Time-delay system (explicit)

   ======== C S T C Version 6.0 ========

Enter all variables (y/n, default n)?

   ======== Data Source   ========
   ======== Filters   ========
   ======== Control action ========
   ======== Assumed system ========
A (system denominator)   =   1.000000   2.000000 :=
B (system numerator)   =   3.000000 :=
Time delay   =   1.000000 :=
   ======== Emulator design ========
P (model denominator)   =   0.500000   1.000000 :=
C (emulator denominator) =   1.000000 :=
Pade approximation order =   3 :=

      System polynomials

A   1.000000   2.000000
B   3.000000
D   0.000000   0.000000

      Design polynomials

B+   3.000000
B-   1.000000
C   1.000000
P   0.500000   1.000000
Z+   1.000000
Z-   1.000000
Z-+   1.000000
Pade   0.008333   0.100000   0.500000   1.000000

F   0.000000
F filter 1.000000
G   0.012500   0.150000   0.750000   1.500000
G filter 0.008333   0.100000   0.500000   1.000000
I
E   0.004167   0.050000   0.250000   0.500000

ED   0.000000   0.000000   0.000000   0.000000

\-
======== STC type   ========
Tuning initial conditions = FALSE :=
======== Identification ========
Initial Variance   = 100000.000000 :=
Forget time   = 1000.000000 :=
Cs (emulator denominator) =   1.000000   1.000000 :=
======== Controller   ========
======== Simulation   ========
======== Setpoint   ========
======== In Disturbance ========
======== Out Disturbance ========
======== Actual system   ========
A (system denominator)   =   1.000000   0.000000 :=
B (system numerator)   =   1.000000 :=
Time delay   =   1.000000 :=
Simulation running:
*   25% complete*
*   50% complete*
*   75% complete*
*   100% complete*
Time now is   25.000000
\-
*   System polynomials*
\-
A   1.000000   -0.000010
B   0.999992
D   0.000000   0.000000
\-
*   Design polynomials*
\-
B+   0.999992
B-   1.000000
C   1.000000
P   0.500000   1.000000
Z+   1.000000
Z-   1.000000
Z-+   1.000000
Pade   0.008333   0.100000   0.500000   1.000000
\-
F   1.000005
F filter   1.000000
G   0.004167   0.066667   0.249999   1.499994
G filter   0.008333   0.100000   0.500000   1.000000
I
E   0.004167   0.066667   0.250001   1.500007
ED   0.000000   0.000000   0.000000   0.000000
\-

Discussion

The upper graph displays three signals: the system output $y(t)$, the setpoint $w(t)$ and the ideal model output $y_m(t)$ where $\overline{y}_m(s) = \dfrac{Z(s)}{P(s)} \overline{w}(s)$.

Despite the approximation involved, the model following is close. Note that the system output is delayed by one time unit.

Further investigations

1.   Try the effect of using a lower order (for example 1) approximation to a time delay in the emulator calculation.

6.2.7. EXPLICIT MODEL REFERENCE - DISTURBANCES

Reference: Section 6.4; page 6-11. Section 3.9; page 3-20.

Description

This example is identical to example 6.2.1 except that a square wave disturbance of amplitude 5 units and period two units is added to the system input. The purpose of the example is to illustrate the role of the polynomial $C(s)$ in determining closed-loop disturbance rejection. Initially, $C(s)=0.5s+1$.

Programme interaction

runex 6 7
Example 6 of chapter 7: Explicit model reference - disturbances

======== C S T C Version 6.0 ========

Enter all variables (y/n, default n)?

======== Data Source   ========
======== Filters   ========
======== Control action ========
======== Assumed system ========
A (system denominator) =   1.000000   0.000000   0.000000 :=
B (system numerator)   =   1.000000   1.000000 :=
======== Emulator design ========

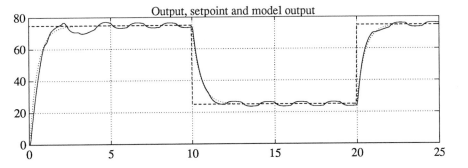

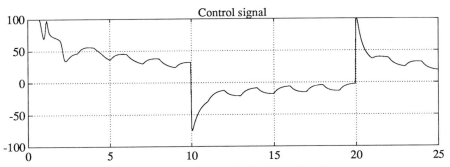

Figure 6.7. Explicit model reference - disturbances

```
P (model denominator)    =    0.500000    1.000000   :=
C (emulator denominator) =    0.500000    1.000000   :=
-------------------------------
        System polynomials
-------------------------------
A         1.000000    0.000000    0.000000
B         1.000000    1.000000
D         0.000000    0.000000
-------------------------------
        Design polynomials
-------------------------------
B+        1.000000    1.000000
B-        1.000000
C         0.500000    1.000000
P         0.500000    1.000000
Z+        1.000000
Z-        1.000000
```

```
Z-+        1.000000
-----------------------------------
F          1.000000    1.000000
F filter   0.500000    1.000000
G          0.250000    0.250000
G filter   0.500000    1.000000
I
E          0.250000
ED         0.000000
-----------------------------------
======== STC type       ========
Tuning initial conditions = FALSE  :=
======== Identification  ========
Initial Variance       = 100000.000000  :=
Forget time            = 1000.000000  :=
Cs (emulator denominator) =    1.000000    2.000000    1.000000  :=
======== Controller      ========
======== Simulation      ========
======== Setpoint        ========
======== In Disturbance  ========
Square amplitude       =    5.000000  :=
Period                 =    2.000000  :=
======== Out Disturbance ========
======== Actual system   ========
A (system denominator)  =    1.000000    1.000000    0.000000  :=
B (system numerator)    =    1.000000    0.100000  :=
Number of lags          =          0  :=
Simulation running:
    25% complete
    50% complete
    75% complete
    100% complete
Time now is    25.000000
More time              = FALSE  :=
-----------------------------------
    System polynomials
-----------------------------------
A          1.000000    0.980893    -0.001185
B          0.989023    0.094623
D          0.000000    0.000000
-----------------------------------
    Design polynomials
-----------------------------------
B+         0.989023    0.094623
B-         1.000000
C          0.500000    1.000000
P          0.500000    1.000000
Z+         1.000000
Z-         1.000000
```

```
Z-+        1.000000
------------------------------------
F          0.754777    1.000296
F filter   0.500000    1.000000
G          0.247256    0.023656
G filter   0.500000    1.000000
I
E          0.250000
ED         0.000000
------------------------------------
```

Discussion

The upper graph displays three signals: the system output $y(t)$, the setpoint $w(t)$ and the ideal model output $y_m(t)$ where $\bar{y}_m(s) = \dfrac{Z(s)}{P(s)}\bar{w}(s)$.

The effect of the disturbance is to perturb the system output; the control signal reacts to some extent to counteract this effect. The parameters do not converge to the 'correct' values, yet the control is reasonable.

Further investigations

1. The emulator denominator $C(s)$ is of the form 1+Ts. Try the effect of varying the time constant T (try, for example, T=0.1) of the emulator denominator C. How does this affect the system output and the control signal?

2. Try the effect of disturbances on example 6.2.2 - 6.2.5. (You will need to use the "Enter all variables" option to expose the disturbance variables).

6.2.8. EXPLICIT MODEL REFERENCE PID

Reference: Section 6.4; page 6-11. Section 3.10; page 3-24.

Description

This example is identical to example 6.2.1 except that:

a) A constant of value -25 is added to the system input.

b) The assumption that there is a constant offset is built in by setting "Integral action" to "TRUE".

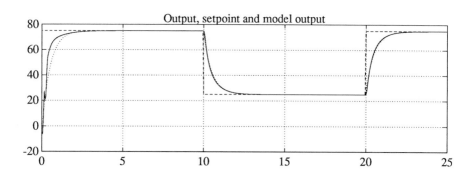

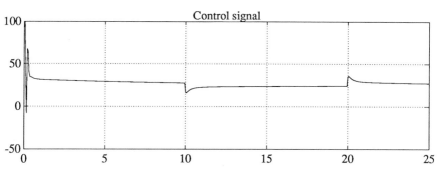

Figure 6.8. Explicit model reference PID

c)   The degree of $C(s)$ is increased by one: $C(s) = (1+0.5s)^2$.

Programme interaction

runex 6 8
Example 6 of chapter 8: Explicit model reference PID

======== C S T C Version 6.0 ========

Enter all variables (y/n, default n)?

======== Data Source   ========
======== Filters   ========
======== Control action ========
Integral action   = TRUE :=

```
B (system numerator)      =    2.000000  :=
Number of lags            =        0  :=
Simulation running:
    25% complete
    50% complete
    75% complete
    100% complete
Time now is    25.000000
More time                 = FALSE  :=
-------------------------------------
    System polynomials
-------------------------------------
A         1.000000     0.999643     0.000000
B         1.999582     0.000000
D         0.000000     0.000000     0.000000
-------------------------------------
    Design polynomials
-------------------------------------
B+        1.999582     0.000000
B-        1.000000
C         0.300000     1.000000
P         0.300000     1.000000
Z+        1.000000
Z-        0.030000     1.000000
Z-+       0.030000     1.000000
-------------------------------------
F         0.494873     1.000000
F filter  0.300000     1.000000
G         0.150276     0.000000
G filter  0.009000     0.330000     1.000000
I
E         0.075154
ED        0.000000
-------------------------------------
```

Discussion

The performance is similar to the non-adaptive case as the parameters rapidly converge to their correct values.

Further investigations

1.   Examine the effect of varying the parameter q.

2.   Examine the effect of varying the initial variance.

6.2.11. EXPLICIT PREDICTIVE CONTROL

Reference: Sections 3.7&8; page 3-18 and section 6.4 page 6-11.

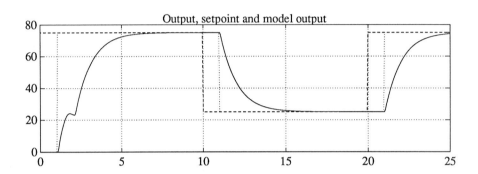

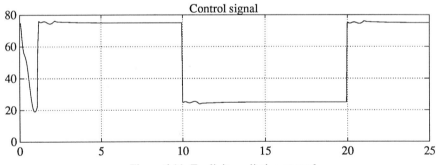

Figure 6.11. Explicit predictive control

Description

A predictive emulator in a feedback loop was discussed in example 3.2.11. In this example, the emulator is tuned using an explicit algorithm.

The open loop system has a first order rational part with unit time constant together with a unit delay

$$e^{-sT} \frac{B(s)}{A(s)} = e^{-s} \frac{1}{s+1}$$

(6.2.11.1)

$Q(s)$ is chosen to be an inverse PI controller:

$$\frac{1}{Q(s)} = 1 + \frac{1}{s} \qquad\qquad (6.2.11.2)$$

Programme interaction

runex 6 11
Example 6 of chapter 11: Explicit predictive control

======== C S T C Version 6.0 ========

Enter all variables (y/n, default n)?

======== Data Source   ========
======== Filters   ========
Sample Interval   =   0.050000 :=
======== Control action ========
Integral action   = FALSE :=
======== Assumed system ========
A (system denominator)   =   1.000000   0.000000 :=
B (system numerator)   =   2.000000 :=
Time delay   =   1.000000 :=
======== Emulator design ========
P (model denominator)   =   1.000000 :=
C (emulator denominator) =   1.000000 :=

        System polynomials

A   1.000000   0.000000
B   2.000000
D   0.000000   0.000000

        Design polynomials

B+   2.000000
B-   1.000000
C   1.000000
P   1.000000
Z+   1.000000
Z-   1.000000
Z-+   1.000000
Pade   0.000595   0.011905   0.107143   0.500000   1.000000

F   1.000000
F filter 1.000000

```
G           0.000000    0.047619    0.000000    2.000000
G filter    0.000595    0.011905    0.107143    0.500000    1.000000
I
E           0.000000    0.023810    0.000000    1.000000
ED          0.000000    0.000000    0.000000    0.000000
-------------------------------------
======= STC type        =======
Tuning initial conditions = FALSE  :=
======= Identification  =======
Initial Variance        = 100000.000000  :=
Forget time             =  1000.000000  :=
Cs (emulator denominator) =    1.000000    1.000000  :=
======= Controller      =======
Q numerator             =    1.000000    0.000000  :=
Q denominator           =    1.000000    1.000000  :=
======= Simulation      =======
======= Setpoint        =======
======= In Disturbance  =======
======= Out Disturbance =======
Step amplitude          =    0.000000  :=
Cos amplitude           =    0.000000  :=
======= Actual system   =======
A (system denominator)  =    1.000000    1.000000  :=
B (system numerator)    =    1.000000  :=
Time delay              =    1.000000  :=
Number of lags          =        0  :=
Simulation running:
    25% complete
    50% complete
    75% complete
    100% complete
Time now is    25.000000
More time               = FALSE  :=
-------------------------------------
        System polynomials
-------------------------------------
A           1.000000    1.000000
B           1.000000
D           0.000000    0.000000
-------------------------------------
        Design polynomials
-------------------------------------
B+          1.000000
B-          1.000000
C           1.000000
P           1.000000
Z+          1.000000
Z-          1.000000
Z-+         1.000000
```

Pade	0.000595	0.011905	0.107143	0.500000	1.000000
F	0.367879				
F filter	1.000000				
G	0.000376	0.015908	0.051819	0.632121	
G filter	0.000595	0.011905	0.107143	0.500000	1.000000
I					
E	0.000376	0.015908	0.051819	0.632121	
ED	0.000000	0.000000	0.000000	0.000000	

Discussion

The upper graph displays three signals: the system output $y(t)$, the setpoint $w(t)$ and the ideal model output $y_m(t) = y(t-1)$.

Note that the response is as predicted: a delayed first-order response delayed by one unit.

Further investigations

1. Try the effect of varying the order of the Pade approximation. Note that zero corresponds to having no predictor, and the response is not good. What is the smallest satisfactory order?

2. Try varying the system time delay, keeping the assumed and actual delay the same. For each value of delay, find the minimum satisfactory Pade order. Note that for larger Pade orders, you may need to reduce the sample interval for numerical reasons.

3. Try the effect of choosing an incorrect time-delay, say 0.9 in place of 1.0. Find the maximum and minimum values of the assumed delay (actual delay=1) giving satisfactory performance.

4. Try putting integral action into the predictor (Integral action = TRUE, C = s+1) and use a Pade order of 3. Observe the performance with an output step disturbance, and compare to the integral-free case.

5. Add a sinusoidal disturbance to the system output; how does the performance depend on the amplitude of this signal and the system time-delay?

6.2.12. EXPLICIT LINEAR-QUADRATIC POLE-PLACEMENT

Reference: Section 3.4; page 3-14.

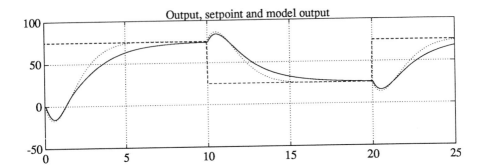

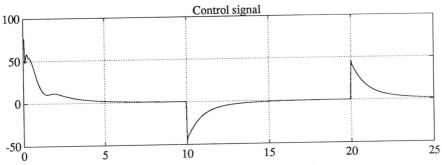

Figure 6.12. Explicit linear-quadratic pole-placement

Description

This example is identical to example 6.2.2, except that the closed-loop poles are chosen to solve equation I-3.4.23:

$$P(s)P(-s) = B(s)B(-s) + \lambda A(s)A(-s)$$

That is, the poles are chosen to correspond to those given by linear-quadratic optimisation theory where λ is the linear-quadratic weighting.

Programme interaction

runex 6 12
Example 6 of chapter 12: Explicit linear-quadratic pole-placement

   ======== *C S T C Version 6.0* ========

Enter all variables (y/n, default n)?

   ======== *Data Source*   ========
   ======== *Filters*   ========
   ======== *Control action* ========
   ======== *Assumed system* ========
A (system denominator)   =   *1.000000   0.000000   0.000000 :=*
B (system numerator)   =   *1.000000   1.000000 :=*
   ======== *Emulator design* ========
Linear-quadratic weight =   *1.000000 :=*
C (emulator denominator) =   *0.500000   1.000000 :=*

    System polynomials

A   1.000000   0.000000   0.000000
B   1.000000   1.000000
D   0.000000   0.000000

    Design polynomials

B+   1.000000
B-   1.000000   1.000000
C   0.500000   1.000000
P   1.000000   1.732051   1.000000
Z+   1.000000
Z-   1.000000   1.000000
Z-+   1.000000

F   1.232051   1.000000
F filter 0.500000   1.000000
G   0.500000   0.633975
G filter 0.500000   1.000000
I
E   0.500000   0.633975
ED   0.000000   0.000000

   ======== *STC type*   ========
Tuning initial conditions = TRUE :=
   ======== *Identification* ========
Initial Variance   = 100000.000000 :=

```
Forget time          =   1000.000000  :=
Cs (emulator denominator) =    1.000000    2.000000    1.000000  :=
======== Controller      ========
======== Simulation      ========
======== Setpoint        ========
======== In Disturbance  ========
======== Out Disturbance ========
======== Actual system   ========
A (system denominator)   =    1.000000    1.000000    0.000000  :=
B (system numerator)     =   -1.000000    1.000000  :=
Number of lags           =       0  :=
Simulation running:
    25% complete
    50% complete
    75% complete
    100% complete
Time now is    25.000000
More time                = FALSE  :=
```

         System polynomials

```
A       1.000000    0.999840    0.000002
B      -1.000117    0.999843
D       0.008655    0.000834
```

         Design polynomials

```
B+       0.999843
B-      -1.000274    1.000000
C        0.500000    1.000000
P        1.000157    2.449737    1.000000
Z+       1.000000
Z-      -1.000274    1.000000
Z-+      1.000000
```

```
F        1.112563    0.999994
F filter 0.500000    1.000000
G        0.500000    2.837449
G filter 0.500000    1.000000
I       -0.010091
E        0.500078    2.837895
ED       0.008656    0.012457
```

Discussion

The upper graph displays three signals: the system output $y(t)$, the setpoint $w(t)$ and the ideal model output $y_m(t)$ where $\overline{y}_m(s) = \dfrac{Z(s)}{P(s)}\overline{w}(s)$.

As in example 3.2.2 note the typical behaviour of a system with right-hand plane zeros: the output initially goes the wrong way in response to a step change.

The desired closed-loop zeros are the same as in example 3.2.2; that is, the system zeros are unchanged; but the poles, and the step rise-time, now depend on $A(s)$, $B(s)$ and λ.

Further investigations

1. Try the effect of varying the linear-quadratic weighting λ. How does this affect the system output and the control signal?

2. Try repeating this example using the same system as example 3.2.1 ($B(s) = 10+s$). How does the closed-loop response when using linear-quadratic control differ from that when using model-reference control?

6.2.13. EXPLICIT LINEAR-QUADRATIC PID

Reference: Section 3.4; page 3-14 and section 3.10; page 3-25.

Description

This example is identical to example 12 except that:

a)   A constant of value -25 is added to the system input.

b)   The assumption that there is a constant offset is built in by setting "Integral action" to "TRUE".

c)   The degree of $C(s)$ is increased by one: $C(s) = (1+0.5s)^2$.

d)   The sample interval is decreased to 0.01 to give a satisfactory approximation.

Programme interaction

runex 6 13
Example 6 of chapter 13: Explicit linear-quadratic PID

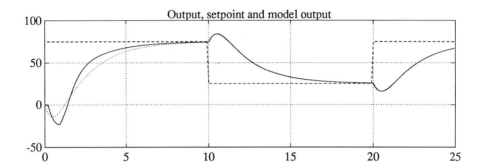

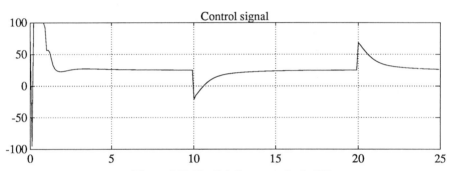

Figure 6.13. Explicit linear-quadratic PID

```
======== C S T C Version 6.0 ========

Enter all variables (y/n, default n)?

======== Data Source    ========
======== Filters        ========
Sample Interval       =    0.010000  :=
======== Control action ========
Integral action       = TRUE  :=
======== Assumed system ========
A (system denominator)  =    1.000000    1.000000    0.000000  :=
B (system numerator)    =   -1.000000    1.000000  :=
======== Emulator design ========
Z has factor B          = TRUE  :=
Linear-quadratic poles  = TRUE  :=
Linear-quadratic weight =    1.000000  :=
C (emulator denominator) =    0.500000    1.000000 *  :=
```

Next factor ...
C (emulator denominator) =   0.500000   1.000000 :=
`-----------------------------------`
     System polynomials
`-----------------------------------`

A	1.000000	1.000000	0.000000	0.000000
B	-1.000000	1.000000	0.000000	
D	0.000000	0.000000	0.000000	

`-----------------------------------`
     Design polynomials
`-----------------------------------`

B+	1.000000	0.000000	
B-	-1.000000	1.000000	
C	0.250000	1.000000	1.000000
P	1.000000	2.449490	1.000000
Z+	1.000000		
Z-	-1.000000	1.000000	
Z-+	1.000000		

`-----------------------------------`

F	3.393304	4.449490	1.000000
F filter	0.250000	1.000000	1.000000
G	0.250000	4.755676	0.000000
G filter	0.250000	1.000000	1.000000
I			
E	0.250000	4.755676	
ED	0.000000	0.000000	

`-----------------------------------`
 `======== ` *STC type* ` ========`
Tuning initial conditions = TRUE :=
 `======== ` *Identification* ` ========`
Initial Variance   = 100000.000000 :=
Forget time   = 1000.000000 :=
*Cs (emulator denominator) =   0.500000   1.000000 * :=*
Next factor ...
*Cs (emulator denominator) =   0.500000   1.000000 * :=*
Next factor ...
Cs (emulator denominator) =   0.500000   1.000000 :=
Normalising Cs so that c0 = 1
Cs   1.000000   6.000000   12.000000   8.000000
 `======== ` *Controller* ` ========`
Maximum control signal   =   100.000000 :=
Minimum control signal   = -100.000000 :=
 `======== ` *Simulation* ` ========`
 `======== ` *Setpoint* ` ========`
 `======== ` *In Disturbance* ` ========`
Step amplitude   =   -25.000000 :=
 `======== ` *Out Disturbance* ` ========`
Step amplitude   =   0.000000 :=
 `======== ` *Actual system* ` ========`

A (system denominator)   =   1.000000   1.000000   0.000000 :=
B (system numerator)   =   -1.000000   1.000000 :=
D (initial conditions)   =   0.000000   0.000000   0.000000 :=
Time delay   =   0.000000 :=
Number of lags   =   0 :=
Simulation running:
    25% complete
    50% complete
    75% complete
    100% complete
Time now is   25.000000
More time   = FALSE :=

     System polynomials

A   1.000000   0.999936   0.000054   0.000000
B   -0.999996   0.999727   0.000000
D   -0.128114   25.128045 -24.994685

     Design polynomials

B+   0.999727   0.000000
B-   -1.000269   1.000000
C   0.250000   1.000000   1.000000
P   1.000273   2.449849   1.000000
Z+   1.000000
Z-   -1.000269   1.000000
Z-+   1.000000

F   3.393938   4.449862   1.000000
F filter 0.250000   1.000000   1.000000
G   0.250000   4.756236   0.000000
G filter 0.250000   1.000000   1.000000
I   -5.769595 -119.037979
E   0.250068   4.757535
ED   -0.128149   0.124881

Discussion

The upper graph displays three signals: the system output $y(t)$, the setpoint $w(t)$ and the ideal model output $y_m(t)$ where $\bar{y}_m(s) = \dfrac{Z(s)}{P(s)} \bar{w}(s)$.

The effect of the disturbance is, in the short term, to spoil the closed-loop response; but, in the long term, the response is not affected. Note that the steady-state control signal has a value of +25 to compensate for the disturbance: the controller has integral action.

Further investigations

1. Try the controller of example 12, but with the disturbance. (Set "Integral action" to FALSE and reduce the orders of $C(s)$ and $C_s(s)$ by one by setting a factor equal to 1). What is the effect of the input disturbance?

2. Repeat step 1, but with an output disturbance in place of an input distubance. Explain what you observe.

6.2.14. IMPLICIT MODEL REFERENCE

Reference: Section 6.4; page 6-11. Section 3.4; page 3-12.

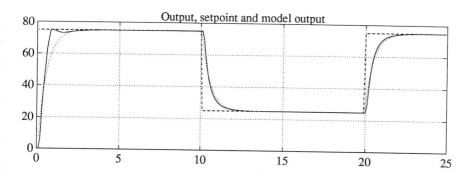

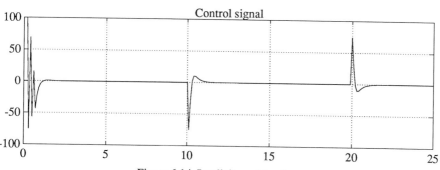

Figure 6.14. Implicit model reference

Description

This is the self-tuning equivalent of example 3.2.1 using the implicit approach with off-line choice of emulator design parameters.

The aim of the controller is to make the system output follow the model:

$$\bar{y}(s) = \frac{Z(s)}{P(s)}\bar{w}(s) \qquad (6.2.14.1)$$

where, in this case, $Z(s)=1$ and $P(s) = 1+Ts$ where the model time-constant $T = 0.5$.

The system parameters are estimated and the corresponding emulator parameters evaluated at each time-step.

As $P(s)/Z(s)$ is improper, a Λ filter is used with

$$\Lambda = \frac{Z(s)}{P(s)} = \frac{1}{0.5s+1} \qquad (6.2.14.2)$$

Programme interaction

runex 6 14
Example 6 of chapter 14: Implicit model reference

======== C S T C Version 6.0 ========

Enter all variables (y/n, default n)?

======== Data Source   ========
======== Filters   ========
======== Control action ========
Integral action   = FALSE :=
======== Assumed system ========
A (system denominator)   =   1.000000   0.000000   0.000000 :=
B (system numerator)   =   1.000000   1.000000 :=
======== Emulator design ========
P (model denominator)   =   0.500000   1.000000 :=
C (emulator denominator) =   0.500000   1.000000 :=

----
*   System polynomials*

A   1.000000   0.000000   0.000000
B   1.000000   1.000000
D   0.000000   0.000000

Design polynomials

```
B+        1.000000    1.000000
B-        1.000000
C         0.500000    1.000000
P         0.500000    1.000000
Z+        1.000000
Z-        1.000000
Z-+       1.000000
```

```
F         1.000000    1.000000
F filter  0.500000    1.000000
G         0.250000    0.250000
G filter  0.500000    1.000000
I
E         0.250000
ED        0.000000
```

```
======== STC type       ========
======== Tuner          ========
Initial Variance    = 100000.000000  :=
Forget time         = 1000.000000  :=
======== Controller     ========
======== Simulation     ========
======== Setpoint       ========
======== In Disturbance ========
======== Out Disturbance ========
======== Actual system  ========
A (system denominator)  =    1.000000    1.000000    0.000000  :=
B (system numerator)    =    1.000000   10.000000  :=
Simulation running:
    25% complete
    50% complete
    75% complete
   100% complete
Time now is    25.000000
```

System polynomials

```
A        1.000000    0.000000    0.000000
B        1.000000    1.000000
D        0.000000    0.000000
```

Design polynomials

```
B+        1.000000    1.000000
B-        1.000000
C         0.500000    1.000000
P         0.500000    1.000000
```

Z+	1.000000	
Z-	1.000000	
Z-+	1.000000	

F	0.746634	1.000119
F filter	0.500000	1.000000
G	0.241125	2.532036
G filter	0.500000	1.000000
I		
E	0.250000	
ED	0.000000	

Discussion

The upper graph displays three signals: the system output $y(t)$, the setpoint $w(t)$ and the ideal model output $y_m(t)$ where $\bar{y}_m(s) = \dfrac{Z(s)}{P(s)}\bar{w}(s)$.

After a short time, the output follows the model output closely despite the initially incorrect parameters.

Further investigations

1. Try the effect of varying the time constant T of the inverse model P. How does this affect the system output and the control signal?

2. The emulator denominator $C(s)$ is also of the form 1+Ts. Try the effect of varying the time constant T of the emulator denominator C. How does this affect the system output and the control signal?

3. Try changing the limits of the control signal so that it is clipped; for example choose 'Maximum control signal' as 10 and 'Minimum control signal' as -10. How does this affect the system output and the control signal?

4. The controller and simulation are implemented as discrete-time systems. Try the effect of vary-

ing the sample interval on closed-loop performance.

6.2.15. IMPLICIT POLE-PLACEMENT CONTROL

Reference: Section 6.4; page 6-11. Section 3.4; page 3-13.

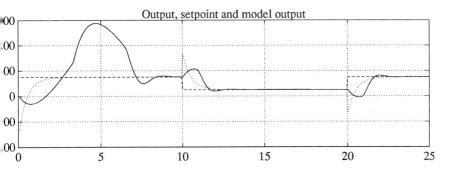

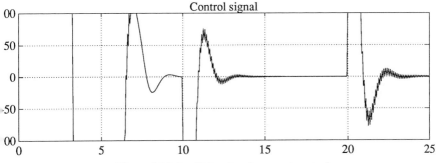

Figure 6.15. Implicit pole-placement control

Description

As discussed in vol.I, the emulator designed in the second example of section I-2.4 may be embedded in a feedback loop to give pole-placement control.

The aim of the controller is to make the system output follow the model:

$$\bar{y}(s) = \frac{Z(s)}{P(s)} \bar{w}(s) \tag{6.2.15.1}$$

where, in this case, $Z(s) = B(s)$ and $P(s) = (1+Ts)^2$ where the model time-constant T = 0.5. Unlik
example 6.2.2, the algorithm is implicit. The design, however, is on-line: the system parameters ar
estimated and $B(s)$ used in the $\Lambda(s)$ filter.

Programme interaction

runex 6 15
Example 6 of chapter 15: Implicit pole-placement control

   ======== C S T C Version 6.0 ========

Enter all variables (y/n, default n)?

```
======== Data Source     ========
======== Filters         ========
======== Control action  ========
======== Assumed system  ========
A (system denominator)   =    1.000000   0.000000   0.000000  :=
B (system numerator)     =    1.000000   1.000000  :=
======== Emulator design ========
Z has factor B           = TRUE  :=
P (model denominator)    =    0.500000   1.000000  :=
C (emulator denominator) =    0.500000   1.000000  :=
-----------------------------------
          System polynomials
-----------------------------------
A        1.000000    0.000000    0.000000
B        1.000000    1.000000
D        0.000000    0.000000
-----------------------------------
          Design polynomials
-----------------------------------
B+       1.000000
B-       1.000000    1.000000
C        0.500000    1.000000
P        0.500000    1.000000
Z+       1.000000
Z-       1.000000    1.000000
Z-+      1.000000
-----------------------------------
F        0.000000    1.000000
F filter 0.500000    1.000000
G        0.250000
G filter 0.500000    1.000000
I
```

```
E          0.250000
CD         0.000000
------------------------------------
======== STC type       ========
Tuning initial conditions = FALSE  :=
======== Identification ========
Initial Variance        = 100000.000000  :=
Forget time             = 1000.000000  :=
Cs (emulator denominator) =    1.000000    2.000000    1.000000  :=
======== Tuner          ========
Initial Variance        = 100000.000000  :=
Forget time             = 1000.000000  :=
======== Controller     ========
======== Simulation     ========
======== Setpoint       ========
======== In Disturbance ========
======== Out Disturbance ========
======== Actual system  ========
A (system denominator)   =    1.000000    1.000000    0.000000  :=
B (system numerator)     =   -1.000000    1.000000  :=
Simulation running:
    25% complete
    50% complete
    75% complete
    100% complete
Time now is    25.000000
------------------------------------
    System polynomials
------------------------------------
A          1.000000    0.999768    0.000013
B         -0.999997    0.999759
D          0.000000    0.000000
------------------------------------
    Design polynomials
------------------------------------
B+         0.999759
B-        -1.000238    1.000000
C          0.500000    1.000000
P          0.500000    1.000000
Z+         1.000000
Z-        -1.000238    1.000000
Z-+        1.000000
------------------------------------
F          0.842645    0.990154
F filter   0.500000    1.000000
G          1.080971
G filter   0.500000    1.000000
J
E          0.250000
```

ED   *0.000000*

Discussion

The upper graph displays three signals: the system output $y(t)$, the setpoint $w(t)$ and the ideal model output $y_m(t)$ where $\bar{y}_m(s) = \dfrac{Z(s)}{P(s)}\bar{w}(s)$.

In this case, note the typical behaviour of a system with right-hand plane zeros: the output initially goes the wrong way in response to a step change. How does the performance compare with that of example 6.2.2?

Further investigations

1. Try the effect of varying the time constant T of the inverse model P. How does this affect the system output and the control signal?

2. Try repeating this example using the same system as the previous example ($B(s) = 10+s$). How does the closed-loop response when using pole-placement differ from that when using model-reference control?

6.2.16. USING A SETPOINT FILTER

Reference: Section 6.4; page 6-11. Section 3.5; page 3-15.

Description

This example is identical to example 6.2.14 except that a setpoint filter is added:

$$w_R(s) = R(s)\bar{w}(s); \ R(s) = \frac{0.5s+1}{s^2 + \sqrt{2}s + 1} \tag{6.2.16.1}$$

The closed loop response is thus:

$$\bar{y}(s) = \frac{Z(s)}{P(s)}R(s)\bar{w}(s) = \frac{1}{0.5s+1}\frac{0.5s+1}{s^2 + \sqrt{2}s + 1}\bar{w}(s) = \frac{1}{s^2 + \sqrt{2}s + 1}\bar{w}(s) \tag{6.2.16.2}$$

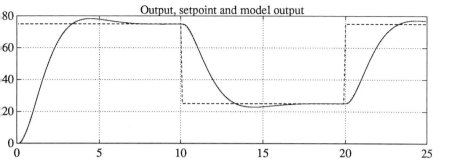

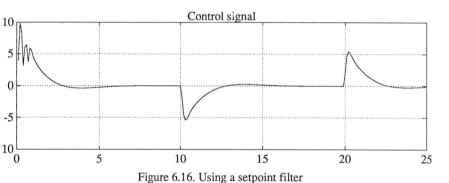

Figure 6.16. Using a setpoint filter

Programme interaction

runex 6 16
Example 6 of chapter 16: Using a setpoint filter

======== C S T C Version 6.0 ========

Enter all variables (y/n, default n)?

======== Data Source   ========
======== Filters   ========
======== Control action ========
Integral action   = FALSE :=
======== Assumed system ========
A (system denominator)   =   1.000000   0.000000   0.000000 :=
B (system numerator)   =   1.000000   1.000000 :=

```
======== Emulator design ========
P (model denominator)     =     0.500000    1.000000   :=
C (emulator denominator)  =     0.500000    1.000000   :=
------------------------------------
        System polynomials
------------------------------------
A          1.000000    0.000000    0.000000
B          1.000000    1.000000
D          0.000000    0.000000
------------------------------------
        Design polynomials
------------------------------------
B+         1.000000    1.000000
B-         1.000000
C          0.500000    1.000000
P          0.500000    1.000000
Z+         1.000000
Z-         1.000000
Z-+        1.000000
------------------------------------
F          1.000000    1.000000
F filter   0.500000    1.000000
G          0.250000    0.250000
G filter   0.500000    1.000000
I
E          0.250000
ED         0.000000
------------------------------------
 ======== STC type       ========
 ======== Tuner          ========
Initial Variance        = 100000.000000  :=
Forget time             = 1000.000000  :=
 ======== Controller     ========
R numerator             =     0.500000    1.000000   :=
R denominator           =     1.000000    1.414000    1.000000   :=
Maximum control signal  =   100.000000  :=
Minimum control signal  =  -100.000000  :=
 ======== Simulation     ========
 ======== Setpoint       ========
 ======== In Disturbance ========
 ======== Out Disturbance ========
 ======== Actual system  ========
A (system denominator)  =     1.000000    1.000000    0.000000   :=
B (system numerator)    =     1.000000   10.000000   :=
Simulation running:
     25% complete
     50% complete
     75% complete
    100% complete
```

Time now is   25.000000

System polynomials

A	1.000000	0.000000	0.000000
B	1.000000	1.000000	
D	0.000000	0.000000	

Design polynomials

B+	1.000000	1.000000
B-	1.000000	
C	0.500000	1.000000
P	0.500000	1.000000
Z+	1.000000	
Z-	1.000000	
Z-+	1.000000	

F	0.748986	1.000014
F filter	0.500000	1.000000
G	0.241512	2.509930
G filter	0.500000	1.000000
I		
E	0.250000	
ED	0.000000	

Discussion

The upper graph displays three signals: the system output $y(t)$, the setpoint $w(t)$ and the ideal model output $y_m(t)$ where $\overline{y}_m(s) = \dfrac{Z(s)}{P(s)}\overline{w}(s)$.

Note that the control signal is considerably reduced.

Further investigations

1.   Try the effect of different choices of $R(s)$ and $P(s)$.

6.2.17. IMPLICIT CONTROL-WEIGHTED MODEL REFERENCE

Reference: Section 6.4; page 6-11. Section 3.6; page 3-16.

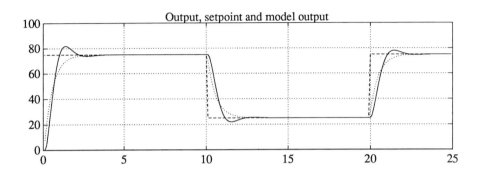

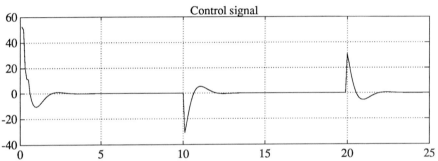

Figure 6.17. Implicit control-weighted model reference

Description

In example 6.2.14, exact model-reference control was achieved by setting $Q(s)=0$. For this example, $Q(s)$ is chosen as

$$Q(s) = \frac{s}{s+1} \qquad (6.2.17.1)$$

this satifies the $Q(s)$ design rule on page 3-17 of vol. 1.

Programme interaction

runex 6 17
Example 6 of chapter 17: Implicit control-weighted model reference

```
======== C S T C Version 6.0 ========

Enter all variables (y/n, default n)?

======== Data Source    ========
======== Filters        ========
======== Control action ========
Integral action         = FALSE  :=
======== Assumed system ========
A (system denominator)  =    1.000000   0.000000   0.000000  :=
B (system numerator)    =    1.000000   1.000000  :=
======== Emulator design ========
P (model denominator)   =    0.500000   1.000000  :=
C (emulator denominator) =   0.500000   1.000000  :=
-----------------------------------
    System polynomials
-----------------------------------
A        1.000000    0.000000    0.000000
B        1.000000    1.000000
D        0.000000    0.000000
-----------------------------------
    Design polynomials
-----------------------------------
B+       1.000000    1.000000
B-       1.000000
C        0.500000    1.000000
P        0.500000    1.000000
Z+       1.000000
Z-       1.000000
Z-+      1.000000
-----------------------------------
F        1.000000    1.000000
F filter 0.500000    1.000000
G        0.250000    0.250000
G filter 0.500000    1.000000
I
E        0.250000
ED       0.000000
-----------------------------------
======== STC type       ========
======== Tuner          ========
Initial Variance        = 100000.000000  :=
Forget time             = 1000.000000  :=
======== Controller     ========
Q numerator             =    1.000000   0.000000  :=
Q denominator           =    1.000000   1.000000  :=
======== Simulation     ========
======== Setpoint       ========
======== In Disturbance ========
```

```
======== Out Disturbance ========
======== Actual system  ========
A (system denominator)  =    1.000000   1.000000   0.000000  :=
B (system numerator)    =    1.000000  10.000000  :=
Simulation running:
    25% complete
    50% complete
    75% complete
   100% complete
Time now is    25.000000
```

       System polynomials

A	1.000000	0.000000	0.000000
B	1.000000	1.000000	
D	0.000000	0.000000	

       Design polynomials

B+	1.000000	1.000000
B-	1.000000	
C	0.500000	1.000000
P	0.500000	1.000000
Z+	1.000000	
Z-	1.000000	
Z-+	1.000000	

F	0.747812	1.000071
F filter	0.500000	1.000000
G	0.241442	2.521147
G filter	0.500000	1.000000
I		
E	0.250000	
ED	0.000000	

Discussion

The upper graph displays three signals: the system output $y(t)$, the setpoint $w(t)$ and the ideal model output $y_m(t)$ where $\bar{y}_m(s) = \dfrac{Z(s)}{P(s)}\bar{w}(s)$.

Notice that the control signal is reduced with respect to that of example 6.2.14. The model following is no longer exact, but the use of the $Q(s)$ design rule ensures that there is no steady-state offset.

Further investigations

1.   Try the effect of varying q in:

$$Q(s) = \frac{qs}{1+s} \tag{6.2.17.2}$$

2.   Try the effect of varying T in:

$$Q(s) = \frac{s}{1+Ts} \tag{6.2.17.3}$$

3.   Replace $Q(s)$ by:

$$Q(s){=}q \tag{6.2.17.4}$$

There is still no offset as, in this case, the system contains an integrator and so the control signal is zero in the steady-state.

4.   Replace $Q(s)$ by:

$$Q(s){=}q \tag{6.2.17.5}$$

and $A(s)$ by:

$$A(s) = s^2 + 2s + 1 \tag{6.2.17.6}$$

Note that there is now an offset dependent on q.

5.   Use the default value of $Q(s)$ but replace $A(s)$ by:

$$A(s) = s^2 + 2s + 1 \tag{6.2.17.7}$$

Note that the offset disappears.

6.2.18.   IMPLICIT CONTROL-WEIGHTED POLE-PLACEMENT

Reference: Section 6.4; page 6-11. Section 3.6; page 3-16.

Description

In example 6.2.15, exact pole-placement control was achieved by setting $Q(s){=}0$. For this example, $Q(s)$ is chosen as

$$Q(s) = \frac{0.1s}{s+1} \tag{6.2.18.1}$$

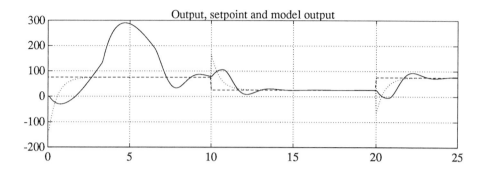

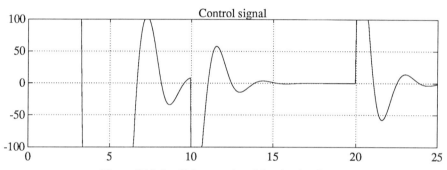

Figure 6.18. Implicit control-weighted pole-placement

this satifies the $Q(s)$ design rule on page 3-17 of vol. 1.

Programme interaction

runex 6 18
Example 6 of chapter 18: Implicit control-weighted pole-placement

======== *C S T C Version 6.0* ========

Enter all variables (y/n, default n)?

======== *Data Source* ========
======== *Filters* ========
======== *Control action* ========
======== *Assumed system* ========

A (system denominator)   =   *1.000000   0.000000   0.000000 :=*
B (system numerator)   =   *1.000000   1.000000 :=*
 ======== *Emulator design* ========
Z has factor B   = *TRUE :=*
P (model denominator)   =   *0.500000   1.000000 :=*
C (emulator denominator) =   *0.500000   1.000000 :=*

      System polynomials

A   *1.000000   0.000000   0.000000*
B   *1.000000   1.000000*
D   *0.000000   0.000000*

      Design polynomials

B+   *1.000000*
B-   *1.000000   1.000000*
C   *0.500000   1.000000*
P   *0.500000   1.000000*
Z+   *1.000000*
Z-   *1.000000   1.000000*
Z-+   *1.000000*

F   *0.000000   1.000000*
F filter *0.500000   1.000000*
G   *0.250000*
G filter *0.500000   1.000000*
I
E   *0.250000*
ED   *0.000000*

 ======== *STC type*   ========
Tuning initial conditions = FALSE :=
 ======== *Identification* ========
Initial Variance   = *100000.000000 :=*
Forget time   = *1000.000000 :=*
Cs (emulator denominator) =   1.000000   2.000000   1.000000 :=
 ======== *Tuner*   ========
Initial Variance   = *100000.000000 :=*
Forget time   = *1000.000000 :=*
 ======== *Controller*   ========
Q numerator   =   *0.100000   0.000000 :=*
Q denominator   =   *1.000000   1.000000 :=*
 ======== *Simulation*   ========
 ======== *Setpoint*   ========
 ======== *In Disturbance* ========
 ======== *Out Disturbance* ========
 ======== *Actual system* ========
A (system denominator)   =   *1.000000   1.000000   0.000000 :=*

B (system numerator)   =   *-1.000000   1.000000 :=*
Simulation running:
    25% complete
    50% complete
    75% complete
    100% complete
Time now is   25.000000

   System polynomials

A	1.000000	0.999768	0.000013
B	-0.999997	0.999758	
D	0.000000	0.000000	

   Design polynomials

B+	0.999758	
B-	-1.000239	1.000000
C	0.500000	1.000000
P	0.500000	1.000000
Z+	1.000000	
Z-	-1.000239	1.000000
Z-+	1.000000	

F	0.844699	0.990051
F filter	0.500000	1.000000
G	1.082946	
G filter	0.500000	1.000000
I		
E	0.250000	
ED	0.000000	

Discussion

The upper graph displays three signals: the system output $y(t)$, the setpoint $w(t)$ and the ideal model output $y_m(t)$ where $\overline{y}_m(s) = \dfrac{Z(s)}{P(s)}\overline{w}(s)$.

Notice that the control signal is reduced with respect to that of example 6.2.15. The model following is no longer exact, but the use of the $Q(s)$ design rule ensures that there is no steady-state offset.

Further investigations

1. Try the effect of varying q in:

$$Q(s) = \frac{qs}{1+s} \tag{6.2.18.2}$$

2. Try the effect of varying T in:

$$Q(s) = \frac{s}{1+Ts} \tag{6.2.18.3}$$

3. Replace $Q(s)$ by:

$$Q(s)=q \tag{6.2.18.4}$$

There is still no offset as, in this case, the system contains an integrator and so the control signal is zero in the steady-state.

4. Replace $Q(s)$ by:

$$Q(s)=q \tag{6.2.18.5}$$

and $A(s)$ by:

$$A(s) = s^2 + 2s + 1 \tag{6.2.18.6}$$

Note that there is now an offset dependent on q.

5. Use the default value of $Q(s)$ but replace $A(s)$ by:

$$A(s) = s^2 + 2s + 1 \tag{6.2.18.7}$$

Note that the offset disappears.

6.2.19. TIME-DELAY SYSTEM (IMPLICIT)

Reference: Section 6.4; page 6-11. Section 3.7; page 3-18.

Description

This example corresponds to example 6.2.14, except that the system now is first order and has a time-delay of one unit.

$$\frac{B(s)}{A(s)} = e^{-t} \frac{1}{s} \tag{6.2.19.1}$$

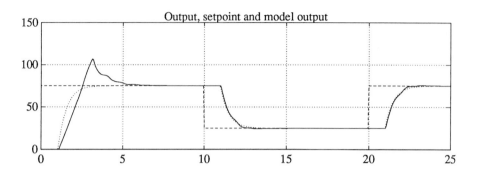

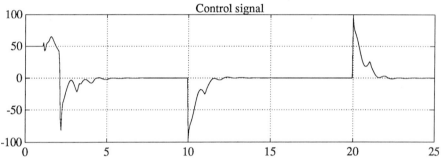

Figure 6.19. Time-delay system (implicit)

The corresponding emulator is based on the Pade approximation approach discussed in section I-2.6. But note that the simulation of the system uses an exact time-delay algorithm.

Programme interaction

runex 6 19
Example 6 of chapter 19: Time-delay system (implicit)

======== C S T C Version 6.0 ========

Enter all variables (y/n, default n)?

======== Data Source   ========
======== Filters   ========

```
======== Control action ========
======== Assumed system ========
A (system denominator)   =    1.000000    2.000000  :=
B (system numerator)     =    3.000000  :=
======== Emulator design ========
P (model denominator)    =    0.500000    1.000000  :=
C (emulator denominator) =    1.000000  :=
Pade approximation order =         3  :=
```

      System polynomials

```
A        1.000000    2.000000
B        3.000000
D        0.000000    0.000000
```

      Design polynomials

```
B+       3.000000
B-       1.000000
C        1.000000
P        0.500000    1.000000
Z+       1.000000
Z-       1.000000
Z-+      1.000000
Pade     0.008333    0.100000    0.500000    1.000000
```

```
F        0.000000
F filter 1.000000
G        0.012500    0.150000    0.750000    1.500000
G filter 0.008333    0.100000    0.500000    1.000000
I
E        0.004167    0.050000    0.250000    0.500000
ED       0.000000    0.000000    0.000000    0.000000
```

```
======== STC type      ========
======== Tuner         ========
Initial Variance      =    10.000000  :=
Forget time           =    1000.000000  :=
======== Controller    ========
======== Simulation    ========
======== Setpoint      ========
======== In Disturbance ========
======== Out Disturbance ========
======== Actual system  ========
A (system denominator)   =    1.000000    0.000000  :=
B (system numerator)     =    1.000000  :=
Time delay            =    1.000000  :=
Simulation running:
    25% complete
```

50% complete
75% complete
100% complete
Time now is   25.000000

       System polynomials

A   *1.000000*   *2.000000*
B   *3.000000*
D   *0.000000*   *0.000000*

       Design polynomials

B+   *3.000000*
B-   *1.000000*
C   *1.000000*
P   *0.500000*   *1.000000*
Z+   *1.000000*
Z-   *1.000000*
Z-+   *1.000000*
Pade   *0.008333*   *0.100000*   *0.500000*   *1.000000*

F   *0.999643*
F filter   *1.000000*
G   *0.003848*   *0.069639*   *0.246801*   *1.503904*
G filter   *0.008333*   *0.100000*   *0.500000*   *1.000000*
I
E   *0.004167*   *0.050000*   *0.250000*   *0.500000*
ED   *0.000000*   *0.000000*   *0.000000*   *0.000000*

Discussion

The upper graph displays three signals: the system output $y(t)$, the setpoint $w(t)$ and the ideal model output $y_m(t)$ where $\bar{y}_m(s) = \dfrac{Z(s)}{P(s)}\bar{w}(s)$.

Despite the approximation involved, the model following is close. Note that the system output is delayed by one time unit.

Further investigations

1.   Try the effect of using a lower order (for example 1) approximation to a time delay in the emula-

tor calculation.

6.2.20. IMPLICIT MODEL REFERENCE - DISTURBANCES

Reference: Section 6.4; page 6-11. Section 3.9; page 3-20.

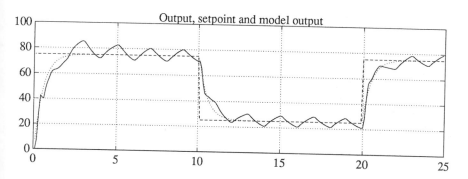

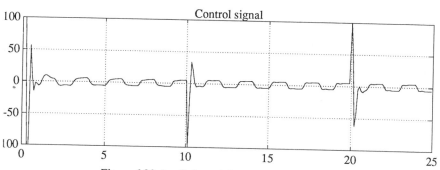

Figure 6.20. Implicit model reference - disturbances

Description

This example is identical to example 6.2.14 except that a square wave disturbance of amplitude 5 units and period two units is added to the system input. The purpose of the example is to illustrate the role of the polynomial $C(s)$ in determining closed-loop disturbance rejection. Initially, $C(s) = 0.5s + 1$.

Programme interaction

runex 6 20
Example 6 of chapter 20: Implicit model reference - disturbances

======== *C S T C Version 6.0* ========

Enter all variables (y/n, default n)?

======== *Data Source*　　========
======== *Filters*　　========
======== *Control action* ========
Integral action　　= *FALSE* :=
======== *Assumed system* ========
A (system denominator)　　=　　*1.000000*　　*0.000000*　　*0.000000* :=
B (system numerator)　　=　　*1.000000*　　*1.000000* :=
======== *Emulator design* ========
P (model denominator)　　=　　*0.500000*　　*1.000000* :=
C (emulator denominator) =　　*0.500000*　　*1.000000* :=

   System polynomials

A	*1.000000*	*0.000000*	*0.000000*
B	*1.000000*	*1.000000*	
D	*0.000000*	*0.000000*	

   Design polynomials

B+	*1.000000*	*1.000000*
B-	*1.000000*	
C	*0.500000*	*1.000000*
P	*0.500000*	*1.000000*
Z+	*1.000000*	
Z-	*1.000000*	
Z-+	*1.000000*	

F	*1.000000*	*1.000000*
F filter	*0.500000*	*1.000000*
G	*0.250000*	*0.250000*
G filter	*0.500000*	*1.000000*
I		
E	*0.250000*	
ED	*0.000000*	

======== *STC type*　　========
======== *Tuner*　　========
Initial Variance　　= *100000.000000* :=

Forget time   = *1000.000000 :=*
======== *Controller*   ========
======== *Simulation*   ========≐
======== *Setpoint*   ========
======== *In Disturbance* ========
Square amplitude   =   *5.000000 :=*
Period   =   *2.000000 :=*
======== *Out Disturbance* ========
======== *Actual system*   ========
A (system denominator) =   *1.000000   1.000000   0.000000 :=*
B (system numerator)   =   *1.000000   10.000000 :=*
Simulation running:
    25% complete
    50% complete
    75% complete
    100% complete
Time now is   25.000000

    System polynomials

A   *1.000000   0.000000   0.000000*
B   *1.000000   1.000000*
D   *0.000000   0.000000*

    Design polynomials

B+   *1.000000   1.000000*
B-   *1.000000*
C   *0.500000   1.000000*
P   *0.500000   1.000000*
Z+   *1.000000*
Z-   *1.000000*
Z-+   *1.000000*

F   *0.883282   0.995968*
F filter   *0.500000   1.000000*
G   *0.067507   1.783383*
G filter   *0.500000   1.000000*
I
E   *0.250000*
ED   *0.000000*

Discussion

The upper graph displays three signals: the system output $y(t)$, the setpoint $w(t)$ and the ideal model output $y_m(t)$ where $\overline{y}_m(s) = \dfrac{Z(s)}{P(s)}\overline{w}(s)$.

The effect of the disturbance is to perturb the system output; the control signal reacts to some extent to counteract this effect. The parameters do not converge to the 'correct' values, yet the control is reasonable.

Further investigations

1.   The emulator denominator $C(s)$ is of the form 1+Ts. Try the effect of varying the time constant T (try, for example, T=0.1) of the emulator denominator C. How does this affect the system output and the control signal?

6.2.21. IMPLICIT MODEL REFERENCE PID

Reference: Section 6.4; page 6-11. Section 3.10; page 3-24.

Description

This example is identical to example 6.2.14 except that:

a)   A constant of value -25 is added to the system input.

b)   The assumption that there is a constant offset is built in by setting "Integral action" to "TRUE".

c)   The degree of C is increased by one: $C = (1+0.5s)^2$.

d)   The degree of $C(s)$ is increased by one: $C(s) = (1+0.5s)^3$.

Programme interaction

runex 6 21
Example 6 of chapter 21: Implicit model reference PID

   ======== C S T C Version 6.0 ========

Enter all variables (y/n, default n)?

   ======== Data Source   ========

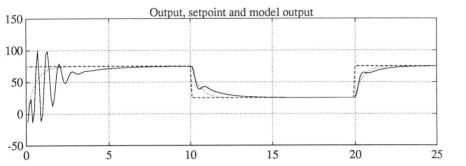

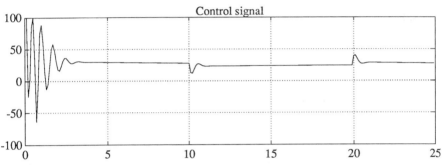

Figure 6.21. Implicit model reference PID

```
======== Filters      ========
======== Control action ========
Integral action       = TRUE  :=
======== Assumed system ========
A (system denominator)   =   1.000000   0.000000   0.000000  :=
B (system numerator)     =   1.000000   1.000000  :=
======== Emulator design ========
P (model denominator)    =   0.500000   1.000000  :=
C (emulator denominator) =   0.500000   1.000000 *  :=
Next factor ...
C (emulator denominator) =   0.500000   1.000000  :=
-----------------------------------
     System polynomials
-----------------------------------
A     1.000000   0.000000   0.000000   0.000000
B     1.000000   1.000000   0.000000
D     0.000000   0.000000   0.000000
```

```
-----------------------------------
    Design polynomials
-----------------------------------
B+       1.000000    1.000000    0.000000
B-       1.000000
C        0.250000    1.000000    1.000000
P        0.500000    1.000000
Z+       1.000000
Z-       1.000000
Z-+      1.000000
-----------------------------------
F        0.750000    1.500000    1.000000
F filter 0.250000    1.000000    1.000000
G        0.125000    0.125000    0.000000
G filter 0.250000    1.000000    1.000000
I
E        0.125000
ED       0.000000
-----------------------------------
======= STC type      =======
Tuning initial conditions = TRUE  :=
======= Tuner         =======
Initial Variance      =   100.000000  :=
Forget time           =  1000.000000  :=
======= Controller    =======
======= Simulation    =======
======= Setpoint      =======
======= In Disturbance =======
Step amplitude        =   -25.000000  :=
======= Out Disturbance =======
======= Actual system  =======
A (system denominator) =    1.000000    1.000000    0.000000  :=
B (system numerator)   =   10.000000    1.000000  :=
Simulation running:
    25% complete
    50% complete
    75% complete
    100% complete
Time now is   25.000000
-----------------------------------
    System polynomials
-----------------------------------
A        1.000000    0.000000    0.000000    0.000000
B        1.000000    1.000000    0.000000
D        0.000000    0.000000    0.000000
-----------------------------------
    Design polynomials
-----------------------------------
B+       1.000000    1.000000    0.000000
```

B-	1.000000		
C	0.250000	1.000000	1.000000
P	0.500000	1.000000	
Z+	1.000000		
Z-	1.000000		
Z-+	1.000000		

F	0.593330	1.599766	1.000000
F filter	0.250000	1.000000	1.000000
G	1.018953	-0.108729	0.000000
G filter	0.250000	1.000000	1.000000
I			
E	0.125000		
ED	0.000000		

Discussion

The upper graph displays three signals: the system output $y(t)$, the setpoint $w(t)$ and the ideal model output $y_m(t)$ where $\overline{y}_m(s) = \dfrac{Z(s)}{P(s)}\overline{w}(s)$.

Note that the response is better than that of the non-adaptive controller (example 3.2.8) because the initial conditions (corresponding to the offset) are estimated.

Further investigations

1. Try the controller of example 6.2.14, but with the disturbance. (Set integral action to FALSE and set $C(s) = 0.5s+1$. What is the effect of the input disturbance?

2. Repeat step 1, but with an output disturbance in place of an input disturbance. Explain what you observe.

3. Try the effect of not estimating an initial condition.

6.2.22. IMPLICIT POLE-PLACEMENT PID

Reference: Section 6.4; page 6-11. Section 3.10; page 3-25.

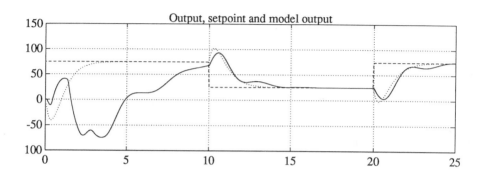

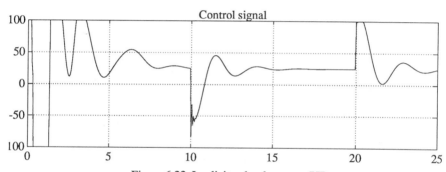

Figure 6.22. Implicit pole-placement PID

Description

   This example is identical to example 6.2.15 except that:

a)   A constant of value -25 is added to the system input

b)   The assumption that there is a constant offset is built in by setting "Integral action" to "TRUE".

c)   The degree of C is increased by one: $C = (1+0.5s)^2$.

d)   The sample interval is decreased to 0.01 to give a satisfactory approximation.

Programme interaction

runex 6 22
Example 6 of chapter 22: Implicit pole-placement PID

```
======== C S T C Version 6.0 ========

Enter all variables (y/n, default n)?

======== Data Source    ========
======== Filters        ========
======== Control action ========
Integral action          = TRUE  :=
======== Assumed system ========
A (system denominator)   =    1.000000    0.000000    0.000000 :=
B (system numerator)     =    1.000000    1.000000 :=
======== Emulator design ========
Z has factor B           = TRUE  :=
P (model denominator)    =    0.500000    1.000000 * :=
Next factor ...
P (model denominator)    =    0.500000    1.000000 :=
C (emulator denominator) =    0.500000    1.000000 * :=
Next factor ...
C (emulator denominator) =    0.500000    1.000000 :=
--------------------------------------
        System polynomials
--------------------------------------
A          1.000000    0.000000    0.000000    0.000000
B          1.000000    1.000000    0.000000
D          0.000000    0.000000    0.000000
--------------------------------------
        Design polynomials
--------------------------------------
B+         1.000000    0.000000
B-         1.000000    1.000000
C          0.250000    1.000000    1.000000
P          0.250000    1.000000    1.000000
Z+         1.000000
Z-         1.000000    1.000000
Z-+        1.000000
--------------------------------------
F          0.500000    1.000000    1.000000
F filter   0.250000    1.000000    1.000000
G          0.062500    0.000000    0.000000
G filter   0.250000    1.000000    1.000000
I
E          0.062500    0.000000
ED         0.000000    0.000000
--------------------------------------
======== STC type       ========
Tuning initial conditions = TRUE  :=
======== Identification ========
Initial Variance         =  100.000000  :=
Forget time              = 1000.000000  :=
```

```
Identifying rational part = TRUE  :=
Identifying delay        = FALSE  :=
======== Tuner           ========
Dead band              =    0.000000  :=
======== Controller      ========
======== Simulation      ========
======== Setpoint        ========
======== In Disturbance  ========
Step amplitude         =  -25.000000  :=
======== Out Disturbance ========
======== Actual system   ========
A (system denominator)  =    1.000000    1.000000    0.000000  :=
B (system numerator)    =   -1.000000    1.000000  :=
Simulation running:
    25% complete
    50% complete
    75% complete
    100% complete
Time now is    25.000000
-----------------------------------
    System polynomials
-----------------------------------
A        1.000000    1.000123    0.001197    0.000000
B       -1.001057    0.995579    0.000000
D       -0.534429   25.114912  -24.766324
-----------------------------------
    Design polynomials
-----------------------------------
B+       0.995579    0.000000
B-      -1.005502    1.000000
C        0.250000    1.000000    1.000000
P        0.250000    1.000000    1.000000
Z+       1.000000
Z-      -1.005502    1.000000
Z-+      1.000000
-----------------------------------
F        2.293963    3.224380    1.000000
F filter 0.250000    1.000000    1.000000
G        0.058552    2.731816    0.000000
G filter 0.250000    1.000000    1.000000
I
E        0.062500    0.000000
ED       0.000000    0.000000
-----------------------------------
```

Discussion

The upper graph displays three signals: the system output $y(t)$, the setpoint $w(t)$ and the ideal model output $y_m(t)$ where $\overline{y}_m(s) = \dfrac{Z(s)}{P(s)}\overline{w}(s)$.

The effect of the disturbance is, in the short term, to spoil the closed-loop response; but, in the long term, the response is not affected. Note that the steady-state control signal has a value of +25 to compensate for the disturbance: the controller has integral action.

Further investigations

1. Try the controller of example 6.2.15, but with the disturbance. (Set "integral action" to "FALSE" and set $C(s) = 0.5s+1$. What is the effect of the input disturbance?

2. Repeat step 1, but with an output disturbance in place of an input disturbance. Explain what you observe.

6.2.23. DETUNED MODEL-REFERENCE

Reference: Section 3.11; page 3-28, section 6.4 p 6-11.

Description

Example 3.2.10 illustrates the use of a reference model with one pole and one zero:

$$\frac{Z(s)}{P(s)} = \frac{0.03s+1}{0.3s+1} \tag{6.2.23.1}$$

together with control weighting:

$$Q(s) = \frac{qs}{0.03s+1} \tag{6.2.23.2}$$

In this example q=0.05 is used initially. An implicit self-tuning version is used in this example.

Programme interaction

runex 6 23
Example 6 of chapter 23: Detuned model-reference

======== C S T C Version 6.0 ========

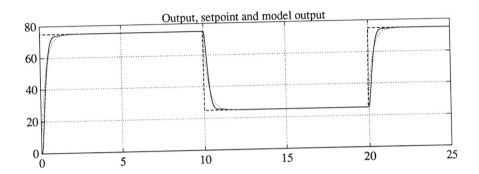

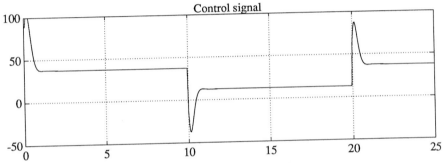

Figure 6.23. Detuned model-reference

Enter all variables (y/n, default n)?

```
======== Data Source    ========
======== Filters        ========
======== Control action ========
Integral action        = TRUE  :=
======== Assumed system ========
A (system denominator)  =    1.000000    0.000000  :=
B (system numerator)    =    1.000000  :=
======== Emulator design ========
Z-+ (Z- not including B) =   0.030000    1.000000  :=
P (model denominator)    =   0.300000    1.000000  :=
C (emulator denominator) =   0.300000    1.000000  :=
-----------------------------------
       System polynomials
-----------------------------------
A          1.000000    0.000000    0.000000
```

```
B          1.000000    0.000000
D          0.000000    0.000000    0.000000
-------------------------------------
    Design polynomials
-------------------------------------
B+          1.000000    0.000000
B-          1.000000
C          0.300000    1.000000
P          0.300000    1.000000
Z+          1.000000
Z-          0.030000    1.000000
Z-+          0.030000    1.000000
-------------------------------------
F          0.570000    1.000000
F filter    0.300000    1.000000
G          0.072900    0.000000
G filter    0.009000    0.330000    1.000000
I
E          0.072900
ED          0.000000
-------------------------------------
 ======== STC type      ========
Tuning initial conditions = FALSE  :=
 ======== Tuner          ========
Initial Variance      = 100000.000000  :=
Forget time          = 1000.000000  :=
 ======== Controller    ========
Q numerator          =    0.050000    0.000000  :=
Q denominator        =    0.030000    1.000000  :=
 ======== Simulation    ========
 ======== Setpoint      ========
 ======== In Disturbance ========
 ======== Out Disturbance ========
 ======== Actual system  ========
A (system denominator)  =    1.000000    1.000000  :=
B (system numerator)    =    2.000000  :=
Simulation running:
    25% complete
    50% complete
    75% complete
    100% complete
Time now is    25.000000
-------------------------------------
    System polynomials
-------------------------------------
A          1.000000    0.000000    0.000000
B          1.000000    0.000000
D          0.000000    0.000000    0.000000
-------------------------------------
```

Design polynomials

```
------------------------------------
B+          1.000000    0.000000
B-          1.000000
C           0.300000    1.000000
P           0.300000    1.000000
Z+          1.000000
Z-          0.030000    1.000000
Z-+         0.030000    1.000000
------------------------------------
F           0.495087    1.000000
F filter    0.300000    1.000000
G           0.150603    0.000000
G filter    0.009000    0.330000    1.000000
I
E           0.072900
ED          0.000000
------------------------------------
```

Discussion

The performance is similar to the non-adaptive case as the parameters rapidly converge to their correct values. This example is taken further in chapter 7, where robustness to neglected dynamics is considered.

Further investigations

1. Examine the effect of varying the parameter q.

2. Examine the effect of varying the initial variance.

6.2.24. IMPLICIT PREDICTIVE CONTROL

Reference: Sections 3.7&8; page 3-18 and section 6.4 page 6-11.

Description

A predictive emulator in a feedback loop was discussed in example 3.2.11. In this example, the emulator is tuned using an implicit algorithm.

The open loop system has a first order rational part with unit time constant together with a unit delay

$$e^{-sT}\ \frac{B(s)}{A(s)} = e^{-s}\ \frac{1}{1+s} \tag{6.2.24.1}$$

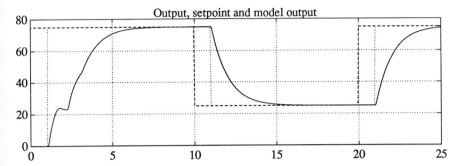

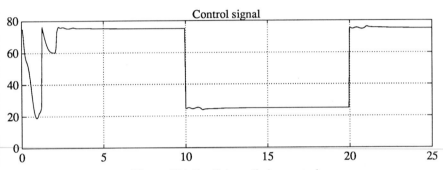

Figure 6.24. Implicit predictive control

$Q(s)$ is chosen to be an inverse PI controller:

$$\frac{1}{Q(s)} = 1 + \frac{1}{s}$$
(6.2.24.2)

Programme interaction

runex 6 24
Example 6 of chapter 24: Implicit predictive control

======== C S T C Version 6.0 ========

Enter all variables (y/n, default n)?

```
======== Data Source    ========
======== Filters        ========
Sample Interval       =    0.050000  :=
======== Control action ========
Integral action       = FALSE  :=
======== Assumed system ========
A (system denominator)  =    1.000000   0.000000  :=
B (system numerator)    =    2.000000  :=
Time delay            =    1.000000  :=
======== Emulator design ========
P (model denominator)   =    1.000000  :=
C (emulator denominator) =    1.000000  :=
------------------------------------
      System polynomials
------------------------------------
A        1.000000    0.000000
B        2.000000
D        0.000000    0.000000
------------------------------------
      Design polynomials
------------------------------------
B+       2.000000
B-       1.000000
C        1.000000
P        1.000000
Z+       1.000000
Z-       1.000000
Z-+      1.000000
Pade     0.000595    0.011905    0.107143    0.500000    1.000000
------------------------------------
F        1.000000
F filter 1.000000
G        0.000000    0.047619    0.000000    2.000000
G filter 0.000595    0.011905    0.107143    0.500000    1.000000
I
E        0.000000    0.023810    0.000000    1.000000
ED       0.000000    0.000000    0.000000    0.000000
------------------------------------
======== STC type       ========
Tuning initial conditions = FALSE  :=
======== Tuner          ========
Initial Variance      = 100000.000000  :=
Forget time           = 1000.000000  :=
======== Controller     ========
Q numerator           =    1.000000   0.000000  :=
Q denominator         =    1.000000   1.000000  :=
======== Simulation     ========
======== Setpoint       ========
======== In Disturbance ========
```

```
======== Out Disturbance ========
Step amplitude         =    0.000000  :=
Cos amplitude          =    0.000000  :=
======== Actual system  ========
A (system denominator) =    1.000000    1.000000  :=
B (system numerator)   =    1.000000  :=
Time delay             =    1.000000  :=
Simulation running:
    25% complete
    50% complete
    75% complete
    100% complete
Time now is    25.000000
```

    System polynomials

A	1.000000	0.000000
B	2.000000	
D	0.000000	0.000000

    Design polynomials

B+	2.000000				
B-	1.000000				
C	1.000000				
P	1.000000				
Z+	1.000000				
Z-	1.000000				
Z-+	1.000000				
Pade	0.000595	0.011905	0.107143	0.500000	1.000000

F	0.366749				
F filter	1.000000				
G	0.000290	0.016045	0.050366	0.633169	
G filter	0.000595	0.011905	0.107143	0.500000	1.000000
I					
E	0.000000	0.023810	0.000000	1.000000	
ED	0.000000	0.000000	0.000000	0.000000	

Discussion

The upper graph displays three signals: the system output $y(t)$, the setpoint $w(t)$ and the ideal model output $y_m(t) = y(t-1)$.

Note that the response is as predicted: a delayed first-order response delayed by one unit.

Further investigations

1. Try the effect of varying the order of the Pade approximation. Note that zero corresponds to having no predictor, and the response is not good. What is the smallest satisfactory order?

2. Try varying the system time delay, keeping the assumed and actual delay the same. For each value of delay, find the minimum satisfactory Pade order. Note that for larger Pade orders, you may need to reduce the sample interval for numerical reasons.

3. Try the effect of choosing an incorrect time-delay, say 0.9 in place of 1.0. Find the maximum and minimum values of the assummed delay (actual delay=1) giving satisfactory performance.

4. Try putting integral action into the predictor (Integral action = TRUE, C = s+1) and use a Pade order of 3. Observe the performance with an output step disturbance, and compare to the integral-free case.

5. Add a sinusoidal disturbance to the system output, how does the performance depend on the amplitude of this signal and the system time-delay?

6.2.25. IMPLICIT LINEAR-QUADRATIC POLE-PLACEMENT

Reference: Section 3.4; page 3-14.

Description

This example is identical to example 6.2.15, except that the closed-loop poles are chosen to solve equation I-3.4.23:

$$P(s)P(-s) = B(s)B(-s) + \lambda A(s)A(-s)$$

That is, the poles are chosen to correspond to those given by linear-quadratic optimisation theory where λ is the linear-quadratic weighting.

Programme interaction

runex 6 25
Example 6 of chapter 25: Implicit linear-quadratic pole-placement

======== C S T C Version 6.0 ========

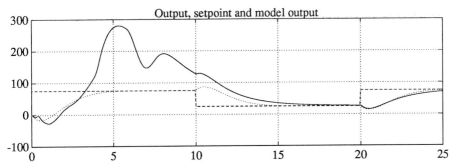

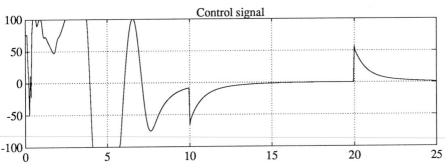

Figure 6.25. Implicit linear-quadratic pole-placement

Enter all variables (y/n, default n)?

```
======== Data Source    ========
======== Filters        ========
======== Control action ========
======== Assumed system ========
A (system denominator)  =   1.000000   0.000000   0.000000  :=
B (system numerator)    =   1.000000   1.000000  :=
======== Emulator design ========
Linear-quadratic weight =   1.000000  :=
C (emulator denominator) =   0.500000   1.000000  :=
```

      System polynomials

```
A      1.000000   0.000000   0.000000
B      1.000000   1.000000
D      0.000000   0.000000
```

Design polynomials

B+	1.000000		
B-	1.000000	1.000000	
C	0.500000	1.000000	
P	1.000000	1.732051	1.000000
Z+	1.000000		
Z-	1.000000	1.000000	
Z-+	1.000000		

F	1.232051	1.000000
F filter	0.500000	1.000000
G	0.500000	0.633975
G filter	0.500000	1.000000
I		
E	0.500000	0.633975
ED	0.000000	0.000000

======== STC type   ========
Tuning initial conditions = FALSE :=
======== Identification ========
Initial Variance   = 100000.000000 :=
Forget time   = 1000.000000 :=
Cs (emulator denominator) =   1.000000   2.000000   1.000000 :=
======== Tuner   ========
Initial Variance   = 100000.000000 :=
Forget time   = 1000.000000 :=
======== Controller   ========
======== Simulation   ========
======== Setpoint   ========
======== In Disturbance ========
======== Out Disturbance ========
======== Actual system ========
A (system denominator)   =   1.000000   1.000000   0.000000 :=
B (system numerator)   =   -1.000000   1.000000 :=
Simulation running:
    25% complete
    50% complete
    75% complete
    100% complete
Time now is   25.000000

System polynomials

A	1.000000	0.999750	0.000011
B	-0.999998	0.999742	
D	0.000000	0.000000	

Design polynomials

B+	0.999742		
B-	-1.000256	1.000000	
C	0.500000	1.000000	
P	1.000258	2.449587	1.000000
Z+	1.000000		
Z-	-1.000256	1.000000	
Z-+	1.000000		

F	1.090896	0.976832
F filter	0.500000	1.000000
G	0.402335	2.656042
G filter	0.500000	1.000000
I		
E	0.500000	0.633975
ED	0.000000	0.000000

Discussion

The upper graph displays three signals: the system output $y(t)$, the setpoint $w(t)$ and the ideal model output $y_m(t)$ where $\bar{y}_m(s) = \dfrac{Z(s)}{P(s)}\bar{w}(s)$.

As in example 3.2.2 note the typical behaviour of a system with right-hand plane zeros: the output initially goes the wrong way in response to a step change.

Further investigations

1. Try the effect of varying the linear-quadratic weighting λ. How does this affect the system output and the control signal?

2. Try repeating this example using the same system as example 3.2.1 ($B(s) = 10+s$). How does the closed-loop response when using linear-quadratic control differ from that when using model-reference control?

6.2.26. IMPLICIT LINEAR-QUADRATIC PID

Reference: Section 3.4; page 3-14 and section 3.10; page 3-25.

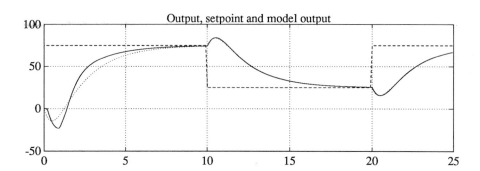

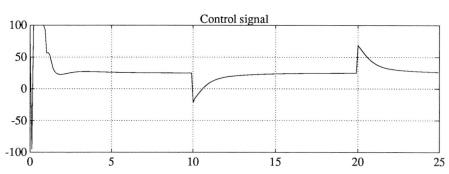

Figure 6.26. Implicit linear-quadratic PID

Description

This example is identical to example 25 except that:

a)   A constant of value -25 is added to the system input.

b)   The assumption that there is a constant offset is built in by setting "Integral action" to "TRUE".

c)   The degree of $C(s)$ is increased by one: $C(s) = (1+0.5s)^2$.

d)   The sample interval is decreased to 0.01 to give a satisfactory approximation.

Programme interaction

runex 6 26
Example 6 of chapter 26: Implicit linear-quadratic PID

```
======== C S T C Version 6.0 ========

Enter all variables (y/n, default n)?

======== Data Source    ========
======== Filters        ========
Sample Interval      =    0.010000  :=
======== Control action ========
Integral action      = TRUE  :=
======== Assumed system ========
A (system denominator)  =    1.000000    1.000000    0.000000  :=
B (system numerator)    =   -1.000000    1.000000  :=
======== Emulator design ========
Z has factor B         = TRUE  :=
Linear-quadratic poles = TRUE  :=
Linear-quadratic weight =    1.000000  :=
C (emulator denominator) =    0.500000    1.000000 *  :=
Next factor ...
C (emulator denominator) =    0.500000    1.000000  :=
```

System polynomials

A	1.000000	1.000000	0.000000	0.000000
B	-1.000000	1.000000	0.000000	
D	0.000000	0.000000	0.000000	

Design polynomials

B+	1.000000	0.000000	
B-	-1.000000	1.000000	
C	0.250000	1.000000	1.000000
P	1.000000	2.449490	1.000000
Z+	1.000000		
Z-	-1.000000	1.000000	
Z-+	1.000000		

F	3.393304	4.449490	1.000000
F filter	0.250000	1.000000	1.000000
G	0.250000	4.755676	0.000000
G filter	0.250000	1.000000	1.000000
I			
E	0.250000	4.755676	
ED	0.000000	0.000000	

```
======== STC type       ========
Tuning initial conditions = TRUE  :=
======== Identification ========
Initial Variance     = 100000.000000  :=
Forget time          = 1000.000000  :=
```

*Cs (emulator denominator) =　0.500000　1.000000 * :=*
Next factor ...
*Cs (emulator denominator) =　0.500000　1.000000 * :=*
Next factor ...
Cs (emulator denominator) =　0.500000　1.000000 :=
Normalising Cs so that c0 = 1
Cs　1.000000　6.000000　12.000000　8.000000
======== Controller　========
Maximum control signal　=　100.000000 :=
Minimum control signal　= -100.000000 :=
======== Simulation　========
======== Setpoint　========
======== In Disturbance ========
Step amplitude　=　-25.000000 :=
======== Out Disturbance ========
Step amplitude　=　0.000000 :=
======== Actual system　========
Simulation running:
*　25% complete*
*　50% complete*
*　75% complete*
*　100% complete*
Time now is　25.000000
----
*　　System polynomials*

A	*1.000000*	*0.999936*	*0.000054*	*0.000000*
B	*-0.999996*	*0.999727*	*0.000000*	
D	*-0.128114*	*25.128045*	*-24.994685*	

----
*　　Design polynomials*

B+	*0.999727*	*0.000000*	
B-	*-1.000269*	*1.000000*	
C	*0.250000*	*1.000000*	*1.000000*
P	*1.000273*	*2.449849*	*1.000000*
Z+	*1.000000*		
Z-	*-1.000269*	*1.000000*	
Z-+	*1.000000*		

F	*3.393938*	*4.449862*	*1.000000*
F filter	*0.250000*	*1.000000*	*1.000000*
G	*0.250000*	*4.756236*	*0.000000*
G filter	*0.250000*	*1.000000*	*1.000000*
I	*-5.769595*	*-119.037979*	
E	*0.250068*	*4.757535*	
ED	*-0.128149*	*0.124881*	

Discussion

The upper graph displays three signals: the system output $y(t)$, the setpoint $w(t)$ and the ideal model output $y_m(t)$ where $\bar{y}_m(s) = \dfrac{Z(s)}{P(s)}\bar{w}(s)$.

The effect of the disturbance is, in the short term, to spoil the closed-loop response; but, in the long term, the response is not affected. Note that the steady-state control signal has a value of +25 to compensate for the disturbance: the controller has integral action.

Further investigations

1. Try the controller of example 6.2.25, but with the disturbance. (Set "integral action" to "FALSE" and set $C(s) = 0.5s+1$ by setting the second factor =1). What is the effect of the input disturbance?

2. Repeat step 1, but with an output disturbance in place of an input disturbance. Explain what you observe.

6.2.27. DISCRETE-TIME IMPLICIT CONTROL

Reference: Section 6.4; page 6-11. Section 3.4; page 3-13.

Description

CSTC may be used for discrete-time simulation as well as continuous-time simulation. The system considered in this example is

$$\frac{z+0.9}{z^2 - 1.8z + 0.81} = \frac{z+0.9}{(z-0.9)^2} \qquad (6.2.27.1)$$

This system is controlled by a self-tuning model-reference controller with desired closed-loop system

$$\frac{1}{z-0.5} \qquad (6.2.27.2)$$

Programme interaction

runex 6 27
Example 6 of chapter 27: Discrete-time implicit control

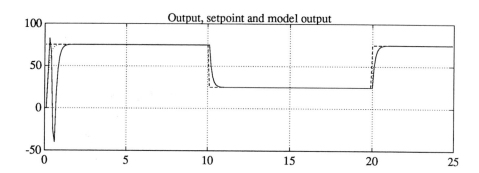

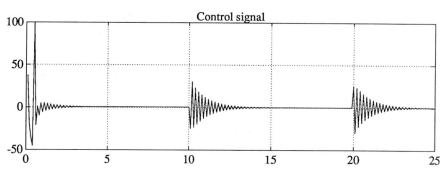

Figure 6.27. Discrete-time implicit control

======== C S T C Version 6.0 ========

Enter all variables (y/n, default n)?

======== Data Source   ========
======== Filters   ========
Continuous-time?   = FALSE :=
======== Control action ========
======== Assumed system ========
A (system denominator) =   1.000000   -2.000000   1.000000   :=
B (system numerator)   =   1.000000   0.000000   :=
======== Emulator design ========
Z has factor B   = FALSE :=
Z+ (nice model numerator) =   0.500000   :=
P (model denominator)   =   1.000000   -0.500000   :=
C (emulator denominator) =   1.000000   -0.500000   :=

System polynomials

A	1.000000	-2.000000	1.000000
B	1.000000	0.000000	
D	0.000000	0.000000	

Design polynomials

B+	1.000000	0.000000
B-	1.000000	
C	1.000000	-0.500000
P	1.000000	-0.500000
Z+	0.500000	
Z-	1.000000	
Z-+	1.000000	

F	1.000000	-0.750000
F filter	0.500000	-0.250000
G	2.000000	0.000000
G filter	1.000000	-0.500000
I		
E	2.000000	
ED	0.000000	

```
======== STC type        ========
Using lambda filter     = TRUE   :=
Tuning initial conditions = FALSE   :=
======== Tuner           ========
Initial Variance        = 100000.000000   :=
Forget time             = 1000.000000   :=
======== Controller      ========
======== Simulation      ========
======== Setpoint        ========
======== In Disturbance  ========
======== Out Disturbance ========
======== Actual system   ========
```

| A (system denominator) | = | 1.000000 | -1.800000 | 0.810000 | := |
| B (system numerator) | = | 1.000000 | 0.900000 | := | |

Simulation running:
     25% complete
     50% complete
     75% complete
     100% complete
Time now is 25.000000

System polynomials

A	1.000000	-2.000000	1.000000
B	1.000000	0.000000	

D	0.000000	0.000000

Design polynomials

B+	1.000000	0.000000
B-	1.000000	
C	1.000000	-0.500000
P	1.000000	-0.500000
Z+	0.500000	
Z-	1.000000	
Z-+	1.000000	

F	0.800000	-0.560000
F filter	0.500000	-0.250000
G	2.000000	1.800000
G filter	1.000000	-0.500000
I		
E	2.000000	
ED	0.000000	

Discussion

The upper graph displays three signals: the system output y_i, the setpoint w_i and the ideal model output y_m

After an initial tuning period, the self-tuning controller adjusts its parameters to give exact model-following control. Note, however, the rather oscillatory control signal due to the cancellation of the system zero at $z=-0.9$. Such zeros are typical of discrete-time models of continuous-time systems.

Further investigations

1. In discrete-time, it is possible to set the roots of both $P(s)$ and $C(s)$ to be at the z-plane origin. Try this by setting $P(s) = C(s) = z + 0$ and $Z + = 1$ to give unit steady-state gain.

6.2.28. DISCRETE-TIME EXPLICIT CONTROL

Reference: Section 6.4; page 6-11. Section 3.4; page 3-13.

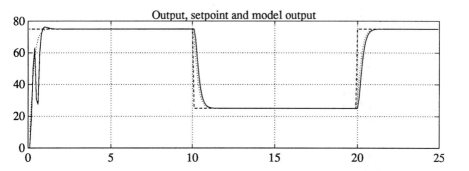

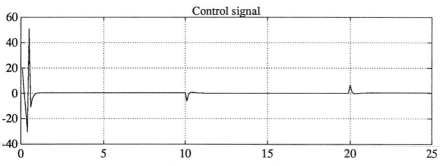

Figure 6.28. Discrete-time explicit control

Description

This is another discrete-time example based on the previous example. The difference here is that an explicit pole-placement algorithm is used in place of the implicit model-reference algorithm. The two closed-loop poles are placed at $z=0.5$, using

$$\frac{Z(z)}{P(z)} = \frac{0.25B(z)}{(z-0.5)^2}$$ (6.2.28.1)

Programme interaction

runex 6 28
Example 6 of chapter 28: Discrete-time explicit control

```
======== C S T C Version 6.0 ========

Enter all variables (y/n, default n)?

======== Data Source    ========
======== Filters        ========
Continuous-time?        = FALSE  :=
======== Control action ========
======== Assumed system ========
A (system denominator)  =    1.000000  -2.000000   1.000000  :=
B (system numerator)    =    1.000000   0.000000  :=
======== Emulator design ========
Z has factor B          = TRUE  :=
Z+ (nice model numerator) =   0.250000  :=
P (model denominator)   =    1.000000  -0.500000 *  :=
Next factor ...
P (model denominator)   =    1.000000  -0.500000  :=
C (emulator denominator) =   1.000000  -0.500000  :=
-----------------------------------
        System polynomials
-----------------------------------
A        1.000000   -2.000000    1.000000
B        1.000000    0.000000
D        0.000000    0.000000
-----------------------------------
        Design polynomials
-----------------------------------
B+       1.000000
B-       1.000000    0.000000
C        1.000000   -0.500000
P        1.000000   -1.000000    0.250000
Z+       0.250000
Z-       1.000000    0.000000
Z-+      1.000000
-----------------------------------
F        0.625000   -0.500000
F filter 0.250000   -0.125000
G        4.000000   -0.500000
G filter 1.000000   -0.500000
I
E        4.000000   -0.500000
ED       0.000000    0.000000
-----------------------------------
======== STC type       ========
Explicit self-tuning    = TRUE  :=
Identifying system      = TRUE  :=
Tuning initial conditions = FALSE  :=
======== Identification ========
Initial Variance        = 100000.000000  :=
```

Forget time   =   *1000.000000 :=*
Cs (emulator denominator) =   1.000000   2.000000   1.000000 :=
======= Controller   ========
======= Simulation   ========
======= Setpoint   =======
======= In Disturbance ========
======= Out Disturbance ========
======= Actual system   =======
A (system denominator)   =   1.000000   -1.800000   0.810000 :=
B (system numerator)   =   1.000000   0.900000 :=
Simulation running:
      25% complete
      50% complete
      75% complete
      100% complete
Time now is   25.000000

      System polynomials

A	*1.000000*	*-1.800000*	*0.810000*
B	*1.000000*	*0.900000*	
D	*0.000000*	*0.000000*	

      Design polynomials

B+	*1.900000*		
B-	*0.526316*	*0.473684*	
C	*1.000000*	*-0.500000*	
P	*1.000000*	*-1.000000*	*0.250000*
Z+	*0.250000*		
Z-	*0.526316*	*0.473684*	
Z-+	*1.000000*		

F	*0.469136*	*-0.354667*
F filter	*0.250000*	*-0.125000*
G	*7.600000*	*0.403457*
G filter	*1.000000*	*-0.500000*
I		
E	*4.000000*	*0.212346*
ED	*0.000000*	*0.000000*

Discussion

The displyed results are similar to those of the previous example exept taht the control is now much smoother as the system zero at z=-0.9 is no longer cancelled.

Further investigations

1. In discrete-time, it is possible to set the roots of both P and C to be at the Z plane origin. Try this by setting $P = (z + 0)*(z + 0)$ and $C = z + 0$ and $Z + = 1$ to give unit steady-state gain.

CHAPTER 7
Robustness of Self-Tuning Controllers

Aims. To investigate the effect of unmodelled system dynamics on the performance of self-tuning controllers. To investigate the role of control weighting on the robustness of self-tuning controllers with respect to unmodelled system dynamics.

7.1. IMPLEMENTATION DETAILS

The implementation is identical to that described in chapter 6, except that two additional methods of describinng the actual system are used. As in chapter 4, the neglected dynamics can be introduced into the simulated system by including additional factors in the system polynomials. This approach is not very satisfactory from the numerical point of view and high precision floating point arithmetic is required. Additionally, dynamics of two additional types can be included in the actual system:

$$G(s) = \frac{1}{(1+s\frac{T}{N})^N}$$

(7.1.1)

and

$$G(s) = be^{-\sqrt{s}T}$$

(7.1.2)

The former can be regarded as N (non-interacting) lags with time-constant $\frac{T}{N}$ in series; the latter can be regarded as the limiting case of N *interacting* lags with time constant $\frac{T}{\sqrt{N}}$ in series.

Both systems are implemented in procedure **MultiLag**. The former is implemented if the Boolean variable **Interactive** is FALSE; the latter is implemented if the Boolean variable **Interactive** is TRUE. N is contained in the variable **Lags**; if N=0, these additional dynamics are not implemented.

7.2. EXAMPLES

7.2.1. RHORS EXAMPLE: MODEL REFERENCE

Reference: Section 7.6&7, pages 7-20 - 7-30.

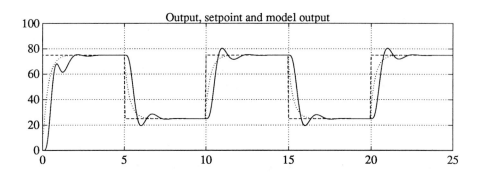

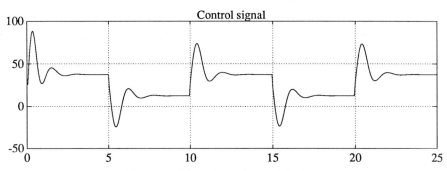

Figure 7.1. Rhors example: model reference

Description

In section I-7.7, a number of simulations are presented relating to an example of Rohrs. This example corresponds to the first simulation in that section; simulations 2 to 4 can be performed by changing parameters as described under "further investigations".

Programme interaction

runex 7 1
Example 7 of chapter 1: Rhors example: model reference

======== *C S T C Version 6.0* ========

Enter all variables (y/n, default n)?

======== *Data Source*   ========
======== *Filters*   ========
======== *Control action* ========
Integral action   = TRUE :=
======== *Assumed system* ========
A (system denominator)   =   1.000000   3.000000 :=
B (system numerator)   =   0.000000 :=
======== *Emulator design* ========
Z has factor B   = FALSE :=
Z-+ (Z- not including B) =   0.030000   1.000000 :=
P (model denominator)   =   0.300000   1.000000 :=
C (emulator denominator) =   0.300000   1.000000 :=

        System polynomials

A   *1.000000   3.000000   0.000000*
B   *0.000000   0.000000*
D   *0.000000   0.000000*

        Design polynomials

B+   *0.000000   0.000000*
B-   *1.000000*
C   *0.300000   1.000000*
P   *0.300000   1.000000*
Z+   *1.000000*
Z-   *0.030000   1.000000*
Z-+   *0.030000   1.000000*

F   *0.329670   1.000000*

```
F filter    0.300000    1.000000
G           0.000000    0.000000
G filter    0.009000    0.330000    1.000000
I
E           0.080110
ED
```

```
------------------------------------
======== STC type        ========
Using lambda filter    = FALSE  :=
======== Tuner           ========
Initial Variance         =   100.000000  :=
Forget time              =   100.000000  :=
======== Controller      ========
Q numerator              =     0.200000    0.000000  :=
Q denominator            =     0.030000    1.000000  :=
======== Simulation      ========
======== Setpoint        ========
======== In Disturbance  ========
Square amplitude         =     0.000000  :=
Period                   =    25.000000  :=
======== Out Disturbance ========
Cos amplitude            =     0.000000  :=
Period                   =     0.123400  :=
======== Actual system   ========
A (system denominator)   =     1.000000    1.000000 *  :=
Next factor ...
A (system denominator)   =     1.000000    8.000000  100.000000  :=
B (system numerator)     =     2.000000 *  :=
Next factor ...
B (system numerator)     =   100.000000  :=
Simulation running:
      25% complete
      50% complete
      75% complete
      100% complete
Time now is    25.000000
```

```
------------------------------------
        System polynomials
------------------------------------

A        1.000000    3.000000    0.000000
B        0.000000    0.000000
D        0.000000    0.000000
```

```
------------------------------------
        Design polynomials
------------------------------------

B+        0.000000    0.000000
B-        1.000000
C         0.300000    1.000000
P         0.300000    1.000000
```

Z+	1.000000		
Z-	0.030000	1.000000	
Z-+	0.030000	1.000000	

F	0.598435	1.000000	
F filter	0.300000	1.000000	
G	0.186110	0.000000	
G filter	0.009000	0.330000	1.000000
I			
E	0.080110		
ED			

Discussion

The upper graph displays three signals: the system output $y(t)$, the setpoint $w(t)$ and the ideal model output $y_m(t)$ where $\bar{y}_m(s) = \dfrac{Z(s)}{P(s)} \bar{w}(s)$.

The system output does not follow the model due to the neglected dynamics, but the self-tuning control system is stable.

Further investigations

1. Perform simulation 2 of section I-7.7 by setting

$$Q_n(s) = 0.05s + 0.0 \qquad\qquad (7.2.1.1)$$

   (Q numerator := 0.05 0).

2. Perform simulation 3 of section I-7.7 by setting

$$Z^+(s) = 1; \; Q_d(s) = 1 \qquad\qquad (7.2.1.2)$$

   and setting "Using lambda filter" to TRUE.

3. Perform simulation 4 of section I-7.7 by setting

$$Z^+(s) = 1; \; Q_d(s) = 1 \qquad\qquad (7.2.1.3)$$

   setting "Using lambda filter" to TRUE and

$$Q_n(s) = 0.05s + 0.0 \qquad\qquad (7.2.1.4)$$

4.   Try the effect of the other example of Rohrs where:

$$N(s) = \frac{229}{s^2 + 30s + 229}$$

(7.2.1.5)

5.   Try the effect of a sinusoidal output disturbance on simulations 1 and 3 .

6.   Try the effect of an input square-wave disturbance on simulations 1 and 3.

7.2.2. RHORS EXAMPLE: POLE PLACEMENT

Reference: Section 7.6&7, pages 7-20 - 7-30.

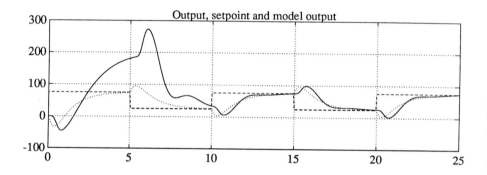

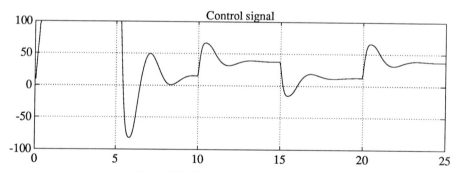

Figure 7.2. Rhors example: pole placement

Description

In section I-7.7, a number of simulations are presented relating to an example of Rohrs. This example corresponds to the 5th simulation; simulation 6 can be performed by changing parameters as described under "further investigations".

The control signal has been limited to a maximum value of 100.

Programme interaction

runex 7 2
Example 7 of chapter 2: Rhors example: pole placement

======== C S T C Version 6.0 ========

Enter all variables (y/n, default n)?

======== Data Source   ========
======== Filters   ========
======== Control action ========
======== Assumed system ========
A (system denominator) =   1.000000   0.000000   0.000000 :=
B (system numerator)   =   1.000000   1.000000 :=
======== Emulator design ========
Z has factor B   = TRUE :=
*P (model denominator)   =   0.300000   1.000000 * :=*
Next factor ...
P (model denominator)   =   1.000000   1.000000 :=
C (emulator denominator) =   0.300000   1.000000 :=

System polynomials

A	*1.000000*	*0.000000*	*0.000000*
B	*1.000000*	*1.000000*	
D	*0.000000*	*0.000000*	

Design polynomials

B+	*1.000000*		
B-	*1.000000*	*1.000000*	
C	*0.300000*	*1.000000*	
P	*0.300000*	*1.300000*	*1.000000*
Z+	*1.000000*		
Z-	*1.000000*	*1.000000*	
Z-+	*1.000000*		

```
F           0.600000    1.000000
F filter    0.300000    1.000000
G           0.090000    0.090000
G filter    0.300000    1.000000
I
E           0.090000    0.090000
ED          0.000000    0.000000
```

```
======== STC type       ========
Tuning initial conditions = FALSE  :=
======== Identification ========
Initial Variance      =   100.000000  :=
Forget time           =   100.000000  :=
Cs (emulator denominator) =   1.000000    2.000000    1.000000  :=
======== Controller     ========
Q numerator           =   0.200000    0.000000  :=
Q denominator         =   1.000000  :=
======== Simulation     ========
======== Setpoint       ========
======== In Disturbance ========
======== Out Disturbance ========
======== Actual system  ========
A (system denominator)  =   1.000000    2.000000    1.000000 *  :=
Next factor ...
A (system denominator)  =   1.000000    8.000000  100.000000  :=
B (system numerator)    =  -2.000000    2.000000 *  :=
Next factor ...
B (system numerator)    =   100.000000  :=
Simulation running:
    25% complete
    50% complete
    75% complete
   100% complete
Time now is    25.000000
```

```
        System polynomials
```

```
A           1.000000    1.787453    0.891984
B          -1.893522    1.770595
D           0.000000    0.000000
```

```
        Design polynomials
```

```
B+          1.770595
B-         -1.069427    1.000000
C           0.300000    1.000000
P           0.300000    1.300000    1.000000
Z+          1.000000
Z-         -1.069427    1.000000
```

Z-+	1.000000	
F	0.289599	0.251774
F filter	0.300000	1.000000
G	0.159354	1.485235
G filter	0.300000	1.000000
I		
E	0.090000	0.838834
ED	0.000000	0.000000

Discussion

The upper graph displays three signals: the system output $y(t)$, the setpoint $w(t)$ and the ideal model output $y_m(t)$ where $\bar{y}_m(s) = \dfrac{Z(s)}{P(s)} \bar{w}(s)$.

The system output does not follow the model due to the neglected dynamics, but the self-tuning control system is stable.

Further investigations

1. Perform simulation 6 of section 7.7 by setting

$$Q_n(s) = 0.05s + 0.0 \tag{7.2.2.1}$$

(Q numerator := 0.05 0).

2. Try the effect of the other example of Rohrs where:

$$N(s) = \frac{229}{s^2 + 30s + 229} \tag{7.2.2.2}$$

3. Try the effect of a sinusoidal output disturbance on simulations 1 and 3.

4. Try the effect of an input square-wave disturbance on simulation 5.

7.2.3. CONTROL OF TRANSMISSION LINE

Reference: Section 7.6&7, pages 7-20 - 7-30.

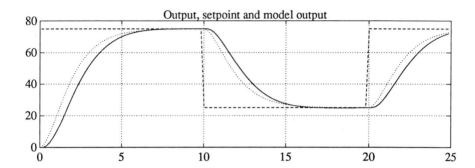

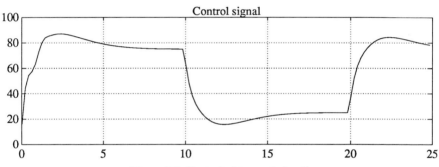

Figure 7.3. Control of transmission line

Description

A number of industrial processes, for example extruder barrel temperature, can be modelled as a large number of interacting first-order lags in series. An electrical analogy is an R-C ladder network. Such systems can be approximated by the transfer function:

$$G(s) = be^{-\sqrt{sT}} \qquad\qquad (7.2.3.1)$$

where

$$T = \frac{RC}{N^2} ; \, b=1 \qquad\qquad (7.2.3.2)$$

This simulation examines such a system with 5 interacting lags with time constant T=5 and b=1. The STC assumes a system with two poles and no zeros and an integrator in the disturbance. As discussed in chapter 6, the corresponding controller structure is PID.

These assumptions lead to neglected dynamics, and the purpose of this example is to investigate this.

Programme interaction

runex 7 3
Example 7 of chapter 3: Control of transmission line

======== *C S T C Version 6.0* ========

Enter all variables (y/n, default n)?
Chapter   =   7 :=

======== *Data Source   ========*
======== *Filters   ========*
======== *Control action ========*
Integral action   = TRUE :=
======== *Assumed system ========*
A (system denominator)   =   1.000000   2.000000   1.000000 :=
B (system numerator)   =   1.000000 :=
======== *Emulator design ========*
Z-+ (Z- not including B) =   1.000000 :=
*P (model denominator)   =   1.000000   1.000000 * :=*
Next factor ...
P (model denominator)   =   1.000000   1.000000 :=
*C (emulator denominator) =   0.500000   1.000000 * :=*
Next factor ...
C (emulator denominator) =   0.500000   1.000000 :=

     System polynomials

A   1.000000   2.000000   1.000000   0.000000
B   1.000000   0.000000
D   0.000000   0.000000

     Design polynomials

B+   1.000000   0.000000
B-   1.000000
C   0.250000   1.000000   1.000000
P   1.000000   2.000000   1.000000
Z+   1.000000
Z-   1.000000
Z-+   1.000000

```
-------------------------------------
F          1.000000   2.000000   1.000000
F filter   0.250000   1.000000   1.000000
G          0.250000   1.000000   0.000000
G filter   0.250000   1.000000   1.000000
I
E          0.250000   1.000000
ED         0.000000
-------------------------------------
```

======== STC type   ========
Using lambda filter   = TRUE :=
======== Tuner   ========
======== Controller   ========
Q numerator   =   0.400000   0.000000 :=
Q denominator   =   0.100000   1.000000 :=
======== Simulation   ========
======== Setpoint   ========
======== In Disturbance ========
Cos amplitude   =   0.000000 :=
======== Out Disturbance ========
======== Actual system   ========
A (system denominator) =   1.000000 :=
B (system numerator)   =   1.000000 :=
D (initial conditions) =   0.000000 :=
Number of lags   =   5 :=
Lag time constant   =   5.000000 :=
Interactive lags   = TRUE :=
Simulation running:
    25% complete
    50% complete
    75% complete
    100% complete
Time now is   25.020000

```
-------------------------------------
        System polynomials
-------------------------------------
A     1.000000   2.000000   1.000000   0.000000
B     1.000000   0.000000
D     0.000000   0.000000
-------------------------------------
        Design polynomials
-------------------------------------
B+        1.000000   0.000000
B-        1.000000
C         0.250000   1.000000   1.000000
P         1.000000   2.000000   1.000000
Z+        1.000000
Z-        1.000000
Z-+       1.000000
```

```
-----------------------------------
F          -0.128252   1.790089   1.000000
F filter    0.250000   1.000000   1.000000
G           0.100435   1.212803   0.000000
G filter    0.250000   1.000000   1.000000
I
E           0.250000   1.000000
ED          0.000000
-----------------------------------
```

Discussion

The upper graph displays three signals: the system output $y(t)$, the setpoint $w(t)$ and the ideal model output $y_m(t)$ where $\bar{y}_m(s) = \dfrac{Z(s)}{P(s)}\bar{w}(s)$.

The system output does not exactly follow the model due to the neglected dynamics and to control weighting, but the self-tuning control system is stable.

Further investigations

1. Try varying P and Q to investigate the region of stability.

7.2.4. LQ CONTROL OF TRANSMISSION LINE

Reference: Section 7.6&7, pages 7-20 - 7-30.

Description

This example uses the identical system to the previous example, but the controller is of the explicit LQ variety.

Programme interaction

runex 7 4
Example 7 of chapter 4: LQ control of transmission line

======== C S T C Version 6.0 ========

Enter all variables (y/n, default n)?

======== Data Source ========

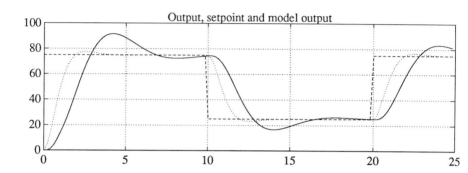

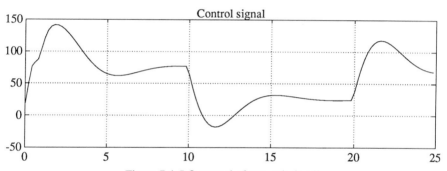

Figure 7.4. LQ control of transmission line

```
======== Filters        ========
======== Control action ========
Integral action        = TRUE  :=
======== Assumed system ========
A (system denominator)   =    1.000000    2.000000    1.000000  :=
B (system numerator)     =    1.000000  :=
======== Emulator design ========
Z-+ (Z- not including B) =    1.000000  :=
C (emulator denominator) =    0.500000    1.000000 *  :=
Next factor ...
C (emulator denominator) =    0.500000    1.000000  :=
-----------------------------------
       System polynomials
-----------------------------------
A        1.000000    2.000000    1.000000    0.000000
B        1.000000    0.000000
D        0.000000    0.000000
```

```
-----------------------------------
    Design polynomials
-----------------------------------
B+        1.000000    0.000000
B-        1.000000
C         0.250000    1.000000    1.000000
P         0.301511    0.799616    1.000000
Z+        1.000000
Z-        1.000000
Z-+       1.000000
-----------------------------------
F         0.574430    1.448957    1.000000
F filter  0.250000    1.000000    1.000000
G         0.075378    0.350660    0.000000
G filter  0.250000    1.000000    1.000000
I
E         0.075378    0.350660
ED        0.000000
-----------------------------------
======== STC type      ========
Explicit self-tuning    = TRUE  :=
Identifying system      = TRUE  :=
Tuning initial conditions = FALSE  :=
======== Identification ========
======== Controller    ========
Q numerator        =    0.400000    0.000000 :=
Q denominator      =    0.100000    1.000000 :=
======== Simulation    ========
======== Setpoint      ========
======== In Disturbance ========
======== Out Disturbance ========
Cos amplitude      =    0.000000 :=
======== Actual system  ========
A (system denominator) =    1.000000 :=
B (system numerator)   =    1.000000 :=
D (initial conditions) =    0.000000 :=
Number of lags     =       5 :=
Lag time constant  =    5.000000 :=
Interactive lags   = TRUE  :=
Simulation running:
    25% complete
    50% complete
    75% complete
    100% complete
Time now is    25.020000
-----------------------------------
    System polynomials
-----------------------------------
A         1.000000    2.501832    0.959328    0.000000
```

B	0.955590	0.000000	
D	0.000000	0.000000	

Design polynomials

$B+$	0.955590	0.000000	
$B-$	1.000000		
C	0.250000	1.000000	1.000000
P	0.315411	0.904572	1.000000
$Z+$	1.000000		
$Z-$	1.000000		
$Z-+$	1.000000		

F	0.533013	1.574297	1.000000
F filter	0.250000	1.000000	1.000000
G	0.075351	0.328989	0.000000
G filter	0.250000	1.000000	1.000000
I			
E	0.078853	0.344278	
ED	0.000000		

Discussion

The upper graph displays three signals: the system output $y(t)$, the setpoint $w(t)$ and the ideal model output $y_m(t)$ where $\bar{y}_m(s) = \dfrac{Z(s)}{P(s)}\bar{w}(s)$. In this case, the value of $P(s)$ used to generate $\bar{y}_m(s)$ is the initial value based on initial parameter estimates. The desired closed-loop denominator $P(s)$ is now chosen automatically by the LQ algorithm.

Further investigations

1. Try varying the control weighting λ to investigate the region of stability.

2. Try varying T, and note how both $A(s)$ and $P(s)$ change in sympathy.

CHAPTER 8

Non-Adaptive and Adaptive Robustness

Aims. To compare and contrast the non-adaptive and adaptive control of uncertain systems.

8.1. IMPLEMENTATION DETAILS

In addition to the self-tuning control algorithms described in chapter 6, the high-gain control given in equation I-8.3.3 (page I-8-9) is implemented. If the Boolean variable **UsingHighGainControl** is TRUE, then procedure **HighGainControl** is invoved in place of the self-tuning controller implemented in procedure

SelfTuningControl. To enable ready comparison between the two approaches, CSTC is organised so that the same parameters are read in for each case: the only difference between the **inlog.dat** files is the value of the Boolean variable **UsingHighGainControl**.

8.2. EXAMPLES

8.2.1. AN EXAMPLE OF HOROWITZ (IMPLICIT)

Reference: Section 8.2; page 8-4.

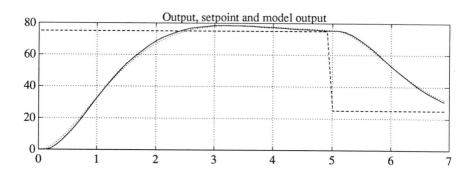

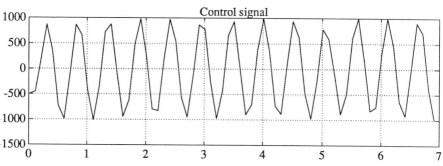

Figure 8.1. An example of Horowitz (Implicit)

Description

In section I-8.2, an example due to Horowitz is used to illustrate the theme of chapter 8, namely that self-tuning can be used in conjunction with Quantitative Feedback Theory to give a design which achieves robust control of uncertain but constant plants without undesirable sensor noise amplification.

This simulation uses this example with the time scales normalised by a factor of 10. The assumed plant has a gain K=1 and poles at :   0 , -0.1000 + 0.1732j and -0.1000 - 0.1732j.

The actual plant has a gain K=4 and poles at: 0, 0 + 0.2000j 0 - 0.2000j. The non-adaptive two-degree of freedom QFT controller is used in the simulation.

An implicit algorithm without the $\Lambda(s)$ filter is used. $Z(s)$ is chosen as:

$$Z(s) = Z^{+}(s) = P(0.1s) = 0.005970s^2 + 0.107460s + 1 \qquad (8.2.1.1)$$

Consequently, assuming no setpoint prefilter in the QFT design, $R(s)$ is chosen as:

$$R(s) = \frac{1}{Z(s)} = \frac{1}{0.005970s^2 + 0.107460s + 1} \tag{8.2.1.2}$$

The sensor noise properties are illustrated by adding a sinusoidal signal of amplitude 0.1 (0.2% of the average setpoint) to the plant output.

The emulator-based and the self-tuning versions are illustrated as further examples.

Programme interaction

```
runex 8 1
Example 8 of chapter 1:  An example of Horowitz (Implicit)

======== C S T C Version 6.0 ========

Enter all variables (y/n, default n)?
Chapter            =        8  :=

======== Data Source    ========
======== Filters        ========
Sample Interval     =    0.010000  :=
======== Control action ========
Integral action     = FALSE  :=
======== Assumed system ========
A (system denominator)  = 1000.000000 200.000000   40.000000    0.000000  :=
B (system numerator)    = 1250.000000 *  :=
Next factor ...
B (system numerator)    =    1.000000  :=
Normalising A and B so that a0 = 1
A    1.000000    0.200000    0.040000    0.000000
B    1.250000
======== Emulator design ========
Z-+ (Z- not including B)  =    0.005970    0.107460    1.000000  :=
P (model denominator)     =    0.597000    1.074600    1.000000  :=
C (emulator denominator)  =    0.250000    1.000000    1.000000  :=
-------------------------------------
    System polynomials
-------------------------------------
A    1.000000    0.200000    0.040000    0.000000
B    1.250000
D    0.000000    0.000000
-------------------------------------
    Design polynomials
-------------------------------------
```

```
B+        1.250000
B-        1.000000
C         0.250000    1.000000    1.000000
P         0.597000    1.074600    1.000000
Z+        1.000000
Z-        0.005970    0.107460    1.000000
Z-+       0.005970    0.107460    1.000000
-----------------------------------
F         1.569997    1.940845    1.000000
F filter  0.250000    1.000000    1.000000
G         0.174846    0.821720
G filter  0.001493    0.032835    0.363430    1.107460    1.000000
I
E         0.139877    0.657376
ED
-----------------------------------
======== STC type      ========
Using lambda filter   = FALSE   :=
======== Tuner         ========
Estimator on          = FALSE   :=
======== Controller    ========
Q numerator           =    0.116700 *  :=
Next factor ...
Q numerator           =    0.000287    0.029880    1.000000  :=
Q denominator         =    0.005970    0.107460    1.000000  :=
R numerator           =    1.000000  :=
R denominator         =    0.005970    0.107460    1.000000  :=
======== Simulation    ========
======== Setpoint      ========
======== In Disturbance ========
======== Out Disturbance ========
Cos amplitude         =    0.100000  :=
======== Actual system  ========
A (system denominator) = 1000.000000    0.000000    40.000000    0.000000  :=
B (system numerator)   = 1250.000000 *  :=
Next factor ...
B (system numerator)   =    2.000000  :=
Simulation running:
    25% complete
    50% complete
    75% complete
    100% complete
Time now is    7.010000
```

Discussion

The upper graph displays three signals: the system output $y(t)$, the setpoint $w(t)$ and the ideal model output $y_m(t)$ where $\bar{y}_m(s) = \dfrac{Z(s)}{P(s)}\bar{w}(s)$.

The system output is held close to the model output by the high gain control. The small ripple is due to the additive sinusoidal sensor noise. The control signal is, however, unsatisfactory due to the large sinusoidal component caused by the sensor noise.

Further investigations

1. Repeat the example but with the high-gain control replaced by the emulator version. This is achieved by setting "Chapter" to 7, and "Estimator on" to FALSE. Notice that the control signal fluctuations (due to the sinusoidal disturbances) are reduced. However, the reponse is now unsatifactory due to the sensitivity of this design method coupled with the error in the assumed system.

2. Repeat the example but with the high-gain control replaced by the self-tuning version. This is achieved by setting "Chapter" to 7, and "Estimator on" to TRUE. As in the previous case, the control signal fluctuations (due to the sinousoidal disturbances) are reduced. However, in contrast, the output response is now satisfactory.

3. If the $\Lambda(s)$ filter is used, then the use of $Z^{-+}(s)$ is not necessary. Try this by setting "Using lambda filter" to TRUE and resetting the terms corresponding to $Z^{-+}(s)$ in $Z^{-+}(s)$, $Q(s)$ and $R(s)$. Why is the result better?

8.2.2. AN EXAMPLE OF HOROWITZ (EXPLICIT)

Reference: Section 8.2; page 8-4.

Description

This is identical to example 8.2.1 except that an explicit self-tuning emulator is used in place of the implicit version. The theory does not cover this case - but it seems to work rather better than the implicit version.

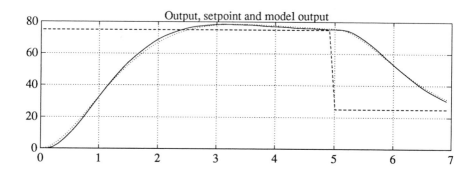

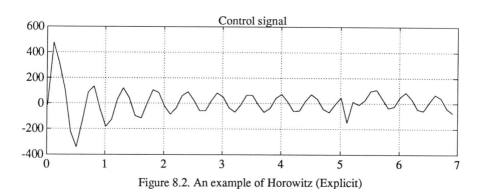

Figure 8.2. An example of Horowitz (Explicit)

The self-tuning version is implemented in the example; other versions are examined under 'further investigations'.

Programme interaction

runex 8 2
Example 8 of chapter 2: An example of Horowitz (Explicit)

======== C S T C Version 6.0 ========

Enter all variables (y/n, default n)?
Chapter   =   7 :=

======== Data Source   ========

```
======== Filters      ========
Sample Interval     =    0.010000  :=
======== Control action ========
Integral action     = FALSE  :=
======== Assumed system ========
A (system denominator)  = 1000.000000 200.000000   40.000000    0.000000  :=
B (system numerator)    = 1250.000000 *  :=
Next factor ...
B (system numerator)    =    1.000000  :=
Normalising A and B so that a0 = 1
A    1.000000   0.200000   0.040000   0.000000
B    1.250000
======== Emulator design ========
Z-+ (Z- not including B)  =    0.005970   0.107460   1.000000  :=
P (model denominator)     =    0.597000   1.074600   1.000000  :=
C (emulator denominator)  =    0.250000   1.000000   1.000000  :=
Small positive number     =    0.000001  :=
```

System polynomials

```
A      1.000000   0.200000   0.040000   0.000000
B      1.250000
D      0.000000   0.000000
```

Design polynomials

```
B+      1.250000
B-      1.000000
C       0.250000   1.000000   1.000000
P       0.597000   1.074600   1.000000
Z+      1.000000
Z-      0.005970   0.107460   1.000000
Z-+     0.005970   0.107460   1.000000
```

```
F        1.569997   1.940845   1.000000
F filter 0.250000   1.000000   1.000000
G        0.174846   0.821720
G filter 0.001493   0.032835   0.363430   1.107460   1.000000
I
E        0.139877   0.657376
ED
```

```
======== STC type      ========
======== Identification ========
Estimator on        = TRUE  :=
======== Controller   ========
Q numerator        =    0.116700 *  :=
Next factor ...
Q numerator        =    0.000287   0.029880   1.000000  :=
```

```
Q denominator          =     0.005970    0.107460    1.000000   :=
R numerator            =     1.000000   :=
R denominator          =     0.005970    0.107460    1.000000   :=
======== Simulation      ========
======== Setpoint        ========
======== In Disturbance  ========
======== Out Disturbance ========
Cos amplitude          =     0.100000   :=
======== Actual system   ========
A (system denominator)  =    1000.000000   0.000000   40.000000   0.000000   :=
B (system numerator)    =    1250.000000 *   :=
Next factor ...
B (system numerator)    =       2.000000   :=
Simulation running:
    25% complete
    50% complete
    75% complete
    100% complete
Time now is     7.010000
```

System polynomials

```
A        1.000000    -0.000049    0.040018    -0.000003
B        2.499750
D        0.000000     0.000000
```

Design polynomials

```
B+       2.499750
B-       1.000000
C        0.250000     1.000000    1.000000
P        0.597000     1.074600    1.000000
Z+       1.000000
Z-       0.005970     0.107460    1.000000
Z-+      0.005970     0.107460    1.000000
```

```
F        1.701595     1.940279    1.000002
F filter 0.250000     1.000000    1.000000
G        0.347694     1.677883
G filter 0.001493     0.032835    0.363430    1.107460    1.000000
I
E        0.139091     0.671220
ED
```

Discussion

The upper graph displays three signals: the system output $y(t)$, the setpoint $w(t)$ and the ideal model output $y_m(t)$ where $\bar{y}_m(s) = \dfrac{Z(s)}{P(s)}\bar{w}(s)$.

The system output is held close to the model output; not by the high gain control, but by the tuning of the emulator. The small ripple is due to the additive sinusoidal sensor noise. The control signal is does not have a large sensor noise component.

Further investigations

1. Repeat the example but with the tuning switched off. This is achieved by setting"Estimator on" to FALSE. T. As in the previous case, the control signal fluctuations (due to the sinusoidal disturbances) are small, but the response is now poor.

2. In this explicit version, it is not necessary to use a realisable ϕ. Try the effect of deleting the $0.005970s^2 + 0.107460s + 1$ from $Z^{-+}(s)$, $R(s)$ and $Q(s)$.

8.2.3. AN EXAMPLE OF ASTROM (IMPLICIT)

Reference: Section 8.2; page 8-4.

Description

Another example of applying QFT design to self-tuning controllers appears in a recent paper [1]. This example corresponds to that presented in the paper; the QFT design is to found in a paper by Astrom et al [2].

The plant is described by

$$\frac{B(s)}{A(s)} = \frac{k}{(1+Ts)^2}; \ 1<k<4, \ 0.5<T<2. \tag{8.2.3.1}$$

As discussed in the paper [1] a possible set of self-tuning controller design parameters is:

1 Gawthrop, P.J.: "Quantitative feedback theory and self-tuning control", Proceedings of IEE conference "Control 88", Oxford, 1988.

2 Astrom, K.J., Neumann, L. and Gutman, P.O: (1986) "A comparison between robust and adaptive control of uncertain systems", Proceedings of the 2nd IFAC workshop on "Adaptive systems in Control and Signal Processing" Lund, Sweden.

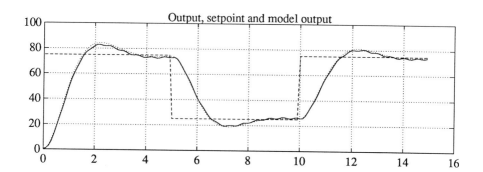

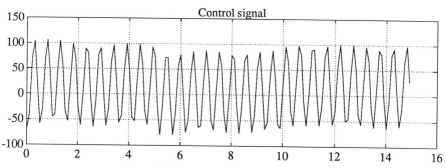

Figure 8.3. An example of Astrom (Implicit)

$$P(s) = (1+4s)(1+0.6666s);$$
$$(8.2.3.2)$$

$$Z(s) = P(0.1s) = (1+0.4s)(1+0.06666s)$$
$$(8.2.3.3)$$

$$Q(s)$$
$$(8.2.3.4)$$

$$= \frac{s(1+0.03333s)(1+0.0020s+0.0000040s^2)}{2Z(s)}$$

$$= \frac{s(1+0.03333s)(1+0.0020s+0.0000040s^2)}{2(1+0.4s)(1+0.06666s)}$$

and

$$R(s) = \frac{(1+4s)(1+0.6666s)}{(1+0.4s)(1+0.06666s)(1+0.6471s+0.3460s^2)}$$
$$(8.2.3.5)$$

In addition, the effect of the low-pass neglected dynamics:

$$N(s) = \frac{1}{1+0.05s} \tag{8.2.3.6}$$

will be illustrated.

This example is set up to use the QFT controller; the corresponding emulator and self-tuning versions are discussed as further examples.

Programme interaction

runex 8 3
Example 8 of chapter 3: An example of Astrom (Implicit)

======== C S T C Version 6.0 ========

Enter all variables (y/n, default n)?
Chapter   =   8 :=

======== Data Source   ========
======== Filters   ========
Sample Interval   =   0.010000 :=
======== Control action ========
======== Assumed system ========
*A (system denominator) =   1.000000   1.000000 * :=*
Next factor ...
A (system denominator) =   1.000000   1.000000 :=
B (system numerator)   =   2.000000 :=
======== Emulator design ========
*Z-+ (Z- not including B) =   0.400000   1.000000 * :=*
Next factor ...
Z-+ (Z- not including B) =   0.066660   1.000000 :=
*P (model denominator)   =   4.000000   1.000000 * :=*
Next factor ...
P (model denominator)   =   0.666600   1.000000 :=
C (emulator denominator) =   1.000000   1.000000   1.000000 :=
----
*   System polynomials*

A   1.000000   2.000000   1.000000   0.000000
B   2.000000   0.000000
D   0.000000   0.000000   0.000000
----
*   Design polynomials*

$B+$	2.000000	0.000000			
$B-$	1.000000				
C	1.000000	1.000000	1.000000		
P	2.666400	4.666600	1.000000		
$Z+$	1.000000				
$Z-$	0.026664	0.466660	1.000000		
$Z-+$	0.026664	0.466660	1.000000		

F	0.871367	3.657425	1.000000		
F filter	1.000000	1.000000	1.000000		
G	5.286332	3.085029	0.000000		
G filter	0.026664	0.493324	1.493324	1.466660	1.000000
I					
E	2.643166	1.542515			
ED					

```
======== STC type      ========
======== Tuner         ========
Initial Variance    =   100.000000  :=
Forget time         =  1000.000000  :=
Estimator on        = TRUE  :=
======== Controller    ========
Q numerator         =     1.000000    0.000000 *  :=
Next factor ...
Q numerator         =     0.033300    1.000000   :=
Q denominator       =     2.000000 *  :=
Next factor ...
Q denominator       =     0.400000    1.000000 *  :=
Next factor ...
Q denominator       =     0.066660    1.000000   :=
R numerator         =     4.000000    1.000000 *  :=
Next factor ...
R numerator         =     0.666600    1.000000   :=
R denominator       =     0.346000    0.647000    1.000000 *  :=
Next factor ...
R denominator       =     0.400000    1.000000 *  :=
Next factor ...
R denominator       =     0.066660    1.000000   :=
======== Simulation    ========
======== Setpoint      ========
======== In Disturbance  ========
======== Out Disturbance ========
Cos amplitude       =     0.500000   :=
======== Actual system ========
A (system denominator)  =     0.500000    1.000000 *  :=
Next factor ...
A (system denominator)  =     0.500000    1.000000   :=
B (system numerator)    =     4.000000   :=
Simulation running:
```

25% complete
50% complete
75% complete
100% complete
Time now is 15.010000

Discussion

The upper graph displays three signals: the system output $y(t)$, the setpoint $w(t)$ and the ideal model output $y_m(t)$ where $\bar{y}_m(s) = \dfrac{Z(s)}{P(s)} \bar{w}(s)$.

The system output is held close to the model output; not by the high gain control, but by the tuning of the emulator. The small ripple is due to the additive sinusoidal sensor noise. The control signal is does not have a large sensor noise component.

Further investigations

1. Repeat the example but with the high-gain control replaced by the emulated version. This is achieved by setting "Chapter" to 7, and "Estimator on" to FALSE. To speed things up, it is possible to reduce the sample interval from 0.002 to 0.1 and still retain stability. Notice that the control signal fluctuations (due to the sinusoidal disturbances) are reduced. However, the reponse is now unsatifactory due to the sensitivity of this design method coupled with the error in the assumed system.

2. Repeat the example but with the high-gain control replaced by the emulated version. This is achieved by setting "Chapter" to 7, and "Estimator on" to TRUE. To speed things up, it is possible to reduce the sample interval from 0.002 to 0.1 and still retain stability. As in the previous case, the control signal fluctuations (due to the sinusoidal disturbances) are reduced. However, in contrast, the output response is now satisfactory.

8.2.4. AN EXAMPLE OF ASTROM (EXPLICIT)

Reference: Section 8.2; page 8-4.

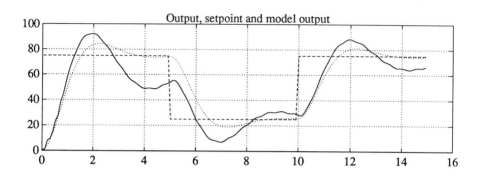

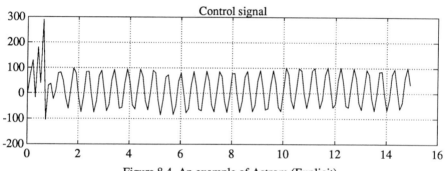

Figure 8.4. An example of Astrom (Explicit)

Description

This is identical to example 8.2.3 except that an explicit self-tuning emulator is used in place of the implicit version. The theory does not cover this case - but it seems to work.

The self-tuning version is used initially.

Programme interaction

runex 8 4
Example 8 of chapter 4: An example of Astrom (Explicit)

======== C S T C Version 6.0 ========

Enter all variables (y/n, default n)?

Chapter   =   *7* :=

======== *Data Source*   ========
======== *Filters*   ========
Sample Interval   =   *0.010000* :=
======== *Control action* ========
======== *Assumed system* ========
A (system denominator)   =   *1.000000   1.000000* * :=
Next factor ...
A (system denominator)   =   *1.000000   1.000000* :=
B (system numerator)   =   *2.000000* :=
======== *Emulator design* ========
Z-+ (Z- not including B)   =   *0.400000   1.000000* * :=
Next factor ...
Z-+ (Z- not including B)   =   *0.066660   1.000000* :=
P (model denominator)   =   *4.000000   1.000000* * :=
Next factor ...
P (model denominator)   =   *0.666600   1.000000* :=
C (emulator denominator)   =   *1.000000   1.000000   1.000000* :=

     System polynomials

A   *1.000000   2.000000   1.000000   0.000000*
B   *2.000000   0.000000*
D   *0.000000   0.000000   0.000000*

     Design polynomials

B+   *2.000000   0.000000*
B-   *1.000000*
C   *1.000000   1.000000   1.000000*
P   *2.666400   4.666600   1.000000*
Z+   *1.000000*
Z-   *0.026664   0.466660   1.000000*
Z-+   *0.026664   0.466660   1.000000*

F   *0.871367   3.657425   1.000000*
F filter   *1.000000   1.000000   1.000000*
G   *5.286332   3.085029   0.000000*
G filter   *0.026664   0.493324   1.493324   1.466660   1.000000*
I
E   *2.643166   1.542515*
ED

======== *STC type*   ========
======== *Identification* ========
Initial Variance   =   *100.000000* :=
Forget time   =   *1000.000000* :=
Estimator on   = *TRUE* :=

Cs (emulator denominator) =   *1.000000   3.000000   3.000000   1.000000 :=*
======== *Controller*   ========
Q numerator   =   *1.000000   0.000000 * :=*
Next factor ...
Q numerator   =   *0.033300   1.000000 :=*
Q denominator   =   *2.000000 * :=*
Next factor ...
Q denominator   =   *0.400000   1.000000 * :=*
Next factor ...
Q denominator   =   *0.066660   1.000000 :=*
R numerator   =   *4.000000   1.000000 * :=*
Next factor ...
R numerator   =   *0.666600   1.000000 :=*
R denominator   =   *0.346000   0.647000   1.000000 * :=*
Next factor ...
R denominator   =   *0.400000   1.000000 * :=*
Next factor ...
R denominator   =   *0.066660   1.000000 :=*
======== *Simulation*   ========
======== *Setpoint*   ========
======== *In Disturbance* ========
======== *Out Disturbance* ========
Cos amplitude   =   *0.500000 :=*
======== *Actual system*   ========
A (system denominator)   =   *0.500000   1.000000 * :=*
Next factor ...
A (system denominator)   =   *0.500000   1.000000 :=*
B (system numerator)   =   *4.000000 :=*
Simulation running:
    25% complete
    50% complete
    75% complete
    100% complete
Time now is   15.010000

    System polynomials

A	*1.000000*	*4.000064*	*4.000088*	*0.000000*
B	*16.000220*	*0.000000*		
D	*0.000000*	*0.000000*	*0.000000*	

    Design polynomials

B+	*16.000220*	*0.000000*	
B-	*1.000000*		
C	*1.000000*	*1.000000*	*1.000000*
P	*2.666400*	*4.666600*	*1.000000*
Z+	*1.000000*		
Z-	*0.026664*	*0.466660*	*1.000000*

Z-+	0.026664	0.466660	1.000000		
F	104.214448	188.734479	1.000000		
F filter	1.000000	1.000000	1.000000		
G	-1.798009	-734.132125	0.000000		
G filter	0.026664	0.493324	1.493324	1.466660	1.000000
I					
E	-0.112374	-45.882627			
ED					

Discussion

The upper graph displays three signals: the system output $y(t)$, the setpoint $w(t)$ and the ideal model output $y_m(t)$ where $\overline{y}_m(s) = \dfrac{Z(s)}{P(s)}\overline{w}(s)$.

The system output is held close to the model output; not by the high gain control, but by the tuning of the emulator. The small ripple is due to the additive sinusoidal sensor noise. The control signal is does not have a large sensor noise component. The performance is not as good as that of the implicit algorithm.

Further investigations

1. Repeat the example but with the tuning switched off. This is achieved by setting"Estimator on" to FALSE. T. As in the previous case, the control signal fluctuations (due to the sinusoidal disturbances) are small, but the response is now poor.

CHAPTER 9
Cascade Control

Aims. To investigate the effect of a neglected inner loop adaptive controller on outer-loop performance when two self-tuning controllers are operated in cascade.

9.1. IMPLEMENTATION DETAILS

The implementation of the self-tuning controllers, and the corresponding simulation, is identical to that described in chapter 6 except that CSTC is configured in a multi-loop form. This is accomplished by storing all variables pertaining to a given loop in the a record data structure called **Loop-VAR** of type **TypeLoopVAR**. In cascade mode, the output of one system forms the input to the next; this is implemented (when the Boolean variable **Cascade** is set to TRUE) in procedure **Simulate** by the statement:

uD := LoopVAR[ThisLoop - 1].y;

Similarly, in cascade mode, the setpoint of one controller is the control signal from the next controller; this is implemented in procedure **Simulate** by the statement:

w := LoopVAR[ThisLoop + 1].u;

The Boolean variable **Cascade** is set to TRUE when **Chapter** is set to 9.

9.2. EXAMPLES

9.2.1. IMPLICIT CASCADE CONTROL

Reference: Section 9.2, page 9-2.

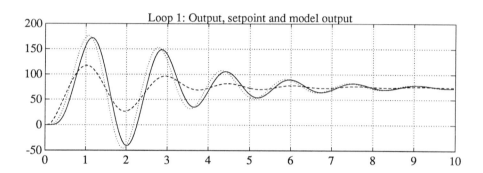

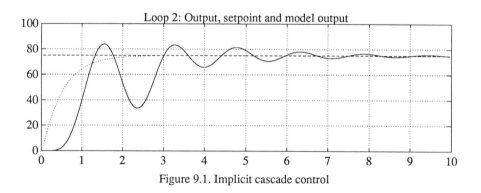

Figure 9.1. Implicit cascade control

Description

Chapter 9 of volume I considers various possible ways of implementing self-tuning cascade control. This example looks at the naive approach of ignoring the inner loop when designing the outer loop.

The example is based on a paper* which also discusses the theoretical properties of this method.

---

* Gawthrop, P.J. and Kharbouch, M. (1988): "Two-loop self-tuning cascade control", Proc. IEE pt D, Vol. 135, No. 4, pp. 232-238.

The inner loop system, and corresponding design parameters ,are given by:

$$\frac{B_1(s)}{A_1(s)} = \frac{1}{s+1}$$ (9.2.1.1)

$$P_1(s) = C_1(s) = 0.1s+1; \; Z_1(s) = 1; \; Q_1(s) = 0.05s$$ (9.2.1.2)

The corresponding outer-loop parameters are:

$$\frac{B_2(s)}{A_2(s)} = \frac{1}{s+1}$$ (9.2.1.3)

$$P_2(s) = C_2(s) = 0.5s+1; \; Z_2(s) = 1; \; Q_2(s) = 0.4s$$ (9.2.1.4)

Notice that the inner loop is chosen to be faster than the outer loop.

Programme interaction

runex 9 1
Example 9 of chapter 1: Implicit cascade control

======== C S T C Version 6.0 ========

Enter all variables (y/n, default n)?
Chapter   =   9 Example 1 of chapter 9   :=

======== Data Source   ========
======== Filters   ========

======== LOOP 1   ========
======== Control action ========
Integral action   = TRUE :=
======== Assumed system ========
A (system denominator) =   1.000000   0.000000 Denominator: s+1 :=
B (system numerator)   =   1.000000 Numerator: 1 :=
======== Emulator design ========
Z-+ (Z- not including B) =   1.000000 :=
P (model denominator)   =   0.100000   1.000000 (0.1s+1) :=
C (emulator denominator) =   0.100000   1.000000 (0.1s+1) :=

     System polynomials

```
------------------------------------
A        1.000000    0.000000    0.000000
B        1.000000    0.000000
D        0.000000    0.000000
------------------------------------
        Design polynomials
------------------------------------
B+       1.000000    0.000000
B-       1.000000
C        0.100000    1.000000
P        0.100000    1.000000
Z+       1.000000
Z-       1.000000
Z-+      1.000000
------------------------------------
F        0.200000    1.000000
F filter 0.100000    1.000000
G        0.010000    0.000000
G filter 0.100000    1.000000
I
E        0.010000
ED       0.000000
------------------------------------
```

======== STC type　　========
Using lambda filter　　= TRUE　:=
======== Tuner　　========
Initial Variance　　= 100000.000000　:=
Forget time　　= 1000.000000　:=
Estimator on　　= TRUE　:=
======== Controller　　========
Q numerator　　=　0.050000　0.000000　:=
Q denominator　　=　1.000000　:=
======== Simulation　　========
======== In Disturbance　========
======== Out Disturbance ========
======== Actual system　========
A (system denominator)　=　1.000000　1.000000　:=
B (system numerator)　　=　1.000000　:=

======== LOOP 2　　========
======== Control action ========
Integral action　　= TRUE　:=
======== Assumed system ========
A (system denominator)　=　1.000000　1.000000 Denominator: s+1 :=
B (system numerator)　　=　1.000000 Numerator: 1 :=
======== Emulator design ========
Z-+ (Z- not including B) =　1.000000　:=
P (model denominator)　　=　0.500000　1.000000 (0.5s+1) :=
C (emulator denominator) =　0.500000　1.000000 (0.5s+1)　:=

```
-----------------------------------
    System polynomials
-----------------------------------
A        1.000000    1.000000    0.000000
B        1.000000    0.000000
D        0.000000    0.000000
-----------------------------------
    Design polynomials
-----------------------------------
B+        1.000000    0.000000
B-        1.000000
C         0.500000    1.000000
P         0.500000    1.000000
Z+        1.000000
Z-        1.000000
Z-+       1.000000
-----------------------------------
F         0.750000    1.000000
F filter  0.500000    1.000000
G         0.250000    0.000000
G filter  0.500000    1.000000
I
E         0.250000
ED        0.000000
-----------------------------------
======== STC type      ========
======== Tuner         ========
Estimator on          = TRUE  :=
======== Controller    ========
Q numerator       =    0.400000    0.000000  :=
Q denominator     =    1.000000  :=
======== Simulation    ========
======== Setpoint      ========
Step amplitude    =    50.000000  :=
Square amplitude  =    25.000000  :=
Period            =    20.000000  :=
======== In Disturbance ========
======== Out Disturbance ========
======== Actual system  ========
A (system denominator)   =    1.000000    1.000000  :=
B (system numerator)     =    1.000000  :=
Simulation running:
     25% complete
     50% complete
     75% complete
     100% complete
Time now is   10.000000

======== LOOP 1        ========
```

```
------------------------------------
     System polynomials
------------------------------------
A        1.000000    0.000000    0.000000
B        1.000000    0.000000
D        0.000000    0.000000
------------------------------------
     Design polynomials
------------------------------------
B+         1.000000    0.000000
B-         1.000000
C          0.100000    1.000000
P          0.100000    1.000000
Z+         1.000000
Z-         1.000000
Z-+        1.000000
------------------------------------
F          0.190241    1.000000
F filter   0.100000    1.000000
G          0.010006    0.000000
G filter   0.100000    1.000000
I
E          0.010000
ED         0.000000
------------------------------------


======== LOOP 2      ========
------------------------------------
     System polynomials
------------------------------------
A        1.000000    1.000000    0.000000
B        1.000000    0.000000
D        0.000000    0.000000
------------------------------------
     Design polynomials
------------------------------------
B+         1.000000    0.000000
B-         1.000000
C          0.500000    1.000000
P          0.500000    1.000000
Z+         1.000000
Z-         1.000000
Z-+        1.000000
------------------------------------
F          0.849471    1.000000
F filter   0.500000    1.000000
G          0.314538    0.000000
G filter   0.500000    1.000000
I
```

E   *0.250000*
ED   *0.000000*

Discussion

The upper graph shows the system output, setpoint, and model output for the inner loop; the lower graph shows the corresponding signals for the outer loop. The setpoint for the inner loop is the control signal generated by the outer loop.

As designed, the inner loop gives close tracking of the setpoint. The outer-loop response displays overshoot due to the neglected inner-loop dynamics; it is, however, stable. The algorithm treated in the cited paper does not use the $\Lambda(s)$ filter, so the theory is not strictly applicable, but nevertheless, does give the correct prediction in this case.

Further investigations

1. Following the cited paper, try $Q_2(s) = 0.15s$ (set Q numerator to 0.15 in loop 2). This is not predicted to give stability.

2. Try the algorithm given in the paper by setting:

$$Z^{-+}(s) = Q_d(s) = 0.01s + 1 \qquad\qquad (9.2.1.5)$$

in loop 1 and

$$Z^{-+}(s) = Q_d(s) = 0.05s + 1 \qquad\qquad (9.2.1.6)$$

in loop 2. For each loop set "Using lambda filter" to FALSE, and you will need to set the sample interval to 0.02. How does the performance compare?

9.2.2. EXPLICIT CASCADE CONTROL

Reference: Section 9.2, page 9-2.

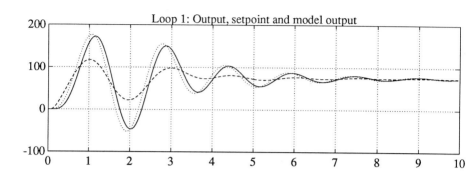

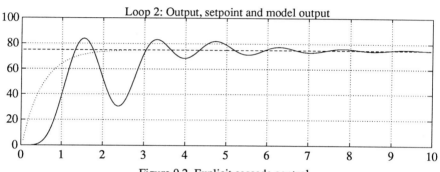

Figure 9.2. Explicit cascade control

Description

This example is identical to the previous one except that an explicit algorithm is used.

Programme interaction

runex 9 2
Example 9 of chapter 2: Explicit cascade control

======== C S T C Version 6.0 ========

Enter all variables (y/n, default n)?
Chapter = 9 *Example 1 of chapter 9* :=

```
======== Data Source    ========
======== Filters        ========

======== LOOP 1         ========
======== Control action ========
Integral action       = TRUE  :=
======== Assumed system ========
A (system denominator)  =    1.000000    0.000000 Denominator: s+1 :=
B (system numerator)    =    1.000000 Numerator: 1 :=
======== Emulator design ========
Z-+ (Z- not including B) =   1.000000  :=
P (model denominator)    =   0.100000    1.000000 (0.1s+1) :=
C (emulator denominator) =   0.100000    1.000000 (0.1s+1) :=
```

```
------------------------------------
    System polynomials
------------------------------------
A       1.000000    0.000000    0.000000
B       1.000000    0.000000
D       0.000000    0.000000
------------------------------------
    Design polynomials
------------------------------------
B+      1.000000    0.000000
B-      1.000000
C       0.100000    1.000000
P       0.100000    1.000000
Z+      1.000000
Z-      1.000000
Z-+     1.000000
------------------------------------
F       0.200000    1.000000
F filter 0.100000   1.000000
G       0.010000    0.000000
G filter 0.100000   1.000000
I
E       0.010000
ED      0.000000
------------------------------------
```

```
======== STC type       ========
Explicit self-tuning  = TRUE  :=
======== Identification ========
Initial Variance      = 100000.000000  :=
Forget time           = 1000.000000  :=
Estimator on          = TRUE  :=
======== Controller     ========
Q numerator           =    0.050000    0.000000  :=
Q denominator         =    1.000000  :=
======== Simulation     ========
======== In Disturbance ========
```

```
======== Out Disturbance ========
======== Actual system  ========
A (system denominator)   =    1.000000    1.000000  :=
B (system numerator)     =    1.000000  :=


======== LOOP 2          ========
======== Control action ========
Integral action        = TRUE  :=
======== Assumed system ========
A (system denominator)   =    1.000000    1.000000 Denominator: s+1 :=
B (system numerator)     =    1.000000 Numerator: 1 :=
======== Emulator design ========
Z-+ (Z- not including B)  =    1.000000  :=
P (model denominator)     =    0.500000    1.000000 (0.5s+1) :=
C (emulator denominator)  =    0.500000    1.000000 (0.5s+1)  :=

-----------------------------------
      System polynomials
-----------------------------------

A        1.000000    1.000000    0.000000
B        1.000000    0.000000
D        0.000000    0.000000

-----------------------------------
      Design polynomials
-----------------------------------

B+        1.000000    0.000000
B-        1.000000
C         0.500000    1.000000
P         0.500000    1.000000
Z+        1.000000
Z-        1.000000
Z-+       1.000000

-----------------------------------
F         0.750000    1.000000
F filter  0.500000    1.000000
G         0.250000    0.000000
G filter  0.500000    1.000000
I
E         0.250000
ED        0.000000

-----------------------------------
======== STC type       ========
Explicit self-tuning   = TRUE  :=
======== Identification ========
Initial Variance       = 100000.000000  :=
Forget time            = 1000.000000  :=
Estimator on           = TRUE  :=
======== Controller     ========
Q numerator            =    0.400000    0.000000  :=
Q denominator          =    1.000000  :=
```

```
======== Simulation     ========
======== Setpoint       ========
tep amplitude        =    50.000000  :=
quare amplitude      =    25.000000  :=
eriod                =    20.000000  :=
======== In Disturbance ========
======== Out Disturbance ========
======== Actual system  ========
A (system denominator)  =     1.000000   1.000000  :=
B (system numerator)    =     1.000000  :=
imulation running:
    25% complete
    50% complete
    75% complete
    100% complete
Time now is    10.000000
```

```
======== LOOP 1        ========
-------------------------------------
      System polynomials
-------------------------------------
A       1.000000    0.998652    0.000000
B       0.999791    0.000000
D       0.000000    0.000000
-------------------------------------
      Design polynomials
-------------------------------------
B+      0.999791    0.000000
B-      1.000000
C       0.100000    1.000000
P       0.100000    1.000000
Z+      1.000000
Z-      1.000000
Z-+     1.000000
-------------------------------------
F       0.190013    1.000000
F filter 0.100000   1.000000
G       0.009998    0.000000
G filter 0.100000   1.000000
J
E       0.010000
ED      0.000000
-------------------------------------
```

```
======== LOOP 2        ========
-------------------------------------
      System polynomials
-------------------------------------
A       1.000000    0.922202    0.000000
```

B	1.088899	0.000000
D	0.000000	0.000000

Design polynomials

B+	1.088899	0.000000
B-	1.000000	
C	0.500000	1.000000
P	0.500000	1.000000
Z+	1.000000	
Z-	1.000000	
Z-+	1.000000	

F	0.769449	1.000000
F filter	0.500000	1.000000
G	0.272225	0.000000
G filter	0.500000	1.000000
I		
E	0.250000	
ED	0.000000	

Discussion

The upper graph shows the system output, setpoint, and model output for the inner loop; the lower graph shows the corresponding signals for the outer loop. The setpoint for the inner loop is the control signal generated by the outer loop.

As designed, the inner loop gives close tracking of the setpoint. The outer-loop response displays overshoot due to the neglected inner-loop dynamics; it is, however, stable. The algorithm treated in the cited paper does not use explicit estimation, so the theory is not strictly applicable, but nevertheless, does give the correct prediction in this case.

Note that the inner loop estimated parameters are correct, but that the outer-loop estimated parameters are not. Why is this?

Further investigations

1. Following the cited paper, try $Q_2(s) = 0.15s$ (set Q numerator to 0.15 in loop 2). This is not predicted to give stability. What do you observe?

CHAPTER 10

Two-Input Two-Output Systems

Aims. To investigate the behaviour of self-tuning controllers operating in a multi-loop environment. To compare the performance when coupling is ignored and included in the algorithm.

10.1. IMPLEMENTATION DETAILS

As with the implementation discussed in Chapter 9 (section 9.1), this chapter requires a multi-loop simulation. Once again, this is handled using the record data structure **LoopVAR** of type **TypeLoopVAR**.

The difference between the impementation of Chapter 9 and this chapter is that the Boolean variable **Cascade** is set to FALSE. In this case, the interaction signals are set equal the systems output if the Boolean variable **OutputCoupled** is TRUE; otherwise they are set equal to the system inputs. This occurs within procedure **Run** using the statements

FOR Loop := 1 TO Loops DO
    IF OutputCoupled THEN
        LoopInteraction[Loop] := LoopVAR[Loop].y
    ELSE
        LoopInteraction[Loop] := LoopVAR[Loop].u;

The self-tuning algorithms are extended to incorporate these additional interaction signals. In particular, procedures: **Emulator, SetData** and **TuneEmulator** all include loops involving the variable

NumberInteractions.

10.2. EXAMPLES

10.2.1. OUTPUT-COUPLED TANKS (IMPLICIT)

Reference: Section 10.2; page 10-7.

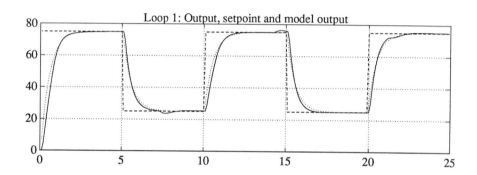

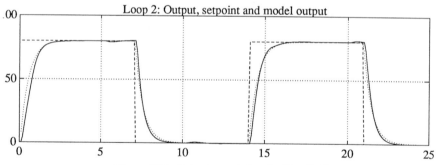

Figure 10.1. Output-coupled tanks (Implicit)

Description

　　Example 1 of chapter I-10 considers a simple model comprising two connected tanks of liquid ; the effective interaction is thus from output to input. This example is a special case where the outflow constants (k_1 and k_2) are both 0.5, giving two identical sets of transfer functions:

$$R_{11}(s) = R_{22}(s) = \frac{1}{s+1} \qquad\qquad (10.2.1.1)$$

$$R_{12}(s) = R_{21}(s) = 0.5 \qquad\qquad (10.2.1.2)$$

That is:

$$A_1(s) = A_2(s) = s+1 \qquad\qquad (10.2.1.3)$$

$$B_1(s) = B_2(s) = 1 \qquad\qquad (10.2.1.4)$$

$$B_{12}(s) = B_{21}(s) = 0.5 \qquad\qquad (10.2.1.5)$$

In this example, the initial parameters for $A_1(s)$, $A_2(s)$, $B_1(s)$, $B_2(s)$ are correct, but $B_{12}(s)$ and $B_{21}(s)$ are set to zero. An implicit self-tuning algorithm with $\Lambda = 1/P(s)$ is used.

Programme interaction

runex 10 1
Example 10 of chapter 1: Output-coupled tanks (Implicit)

======== C S T C Version 6.0 ========

Enter all variables (y/n, default n)?

======== Data Source   ========
======== Filters   ========
Sample Interval   =   0.100000 :=

======== LOOP 1   ========
======== Control action ========
Integral action   = TRUE :=
======== Assumed system ========
A (system denominator)   =   1.000000   0.000000 Denominator: s :=
B (system numerator)   =   1.000000 Numerator: 1 :=
Number of interactions   =   1 Account for the other loop   :=
Interaction polynomial   =   0.000000 :=
======== Emulator design ========
P (model denominator)   =   0.500000   1.000000 (0.5s+1) :=
C (emulator denominator) =   1.000000   1.000000 :=
----
*   System polynomials*

A   1.000000   0.000000   0.000000
B   1.000000   0.000000
B[1]   0.000000   0.000000

```
D          0.000000    0.000000
-------------------------------------
      Design polynomials
-------------------------------------
B+         1.000000    0.000000
B-         1.000000
C          1.000000    1.000000
P          0.500000    1.000000
Z+         1.000000
Z-         1.000000
Z-+        1.000000
-------------------------------------
F          1.500000    1.000000
F filter   1.000000    1.000000
G          0.500000    0.000000
G filter   1.000000    1.000000
G[1]       0.000000    0.000000
I
E          0.500000
ED         0.000000
-------------------------------------
  ======== STC type       ========
  ======== Tuner          ========
Estimator on            = TRUE  :=
  ======== Controller     ========
  ======== Simulation     ========
  ======== Setpoint       ========
Step amplitude          =    50.000000  :=
Square amplitude        =    25.000000  :=
Period                  =    10.000000  :=
  ======== In Disturbance ========
  ======== Out Disturbance ========
  ======== Actual system  ========
A (system denominator)  =    1.000000    1.000000  :=
B (system numerator)    =    1.000000  :=
Number of interactions  =          1 Account for the other loop        :=
Interaction polynomial  =    0.500000 k=0.5 :=

  ======== LOOP 2         ========
  ======== Control action ========
Integral action         = TRUE  :=
  ======== Assumed system ========
A (system denominator)  =    1.000000    0.000000 Denominator: s :=
B (system numerator)    =    1.000000 Numerator: 1 :=
Interaction polynomial  =    0.000000  :=
  ======== Emulator design ========
P (model denominator)   =    0.500000    1.000000 (0.5s+1) :=
C (emulator denominator) =   1.000000    1.000000  :=
-------------------------------------
```

System polynomials

A	1.000000	0.000000	0.000000
B	1.000000	0.000000	
B[1]	0.000000	0.000000	
D	0.000000	0.000000	

Design polynomials

B+	1.000000	0.000000
B-	1.000000	
C	1.000000	1.000000
P	0.500000	1.000000
Z+	1.000000	
Z-	1.000000	
Z-+	1.000000	

F	1.500000	1.000000
F filter	1.000000	1.000000
G	0.500000	0.000000
G filter	1.000000	1.000000
G[1]	0.000000	0.000000
I		
E	0.500000	
ED	0.000000	

======== STC type   ========
======== Tuner   ========
Estimator on   = TRUE :=
======== Controller   ========
======== Simulation   ========
======== Setpoint   ========
Step amplitude   =   40.000000 :=
Square amplitude   =   40.000000 :=
Period   =   14.000000 :=
======== In Disturbance ========
======== Out Disturbance ========
======== Actual system   ========
A (system denominator)   =   1.000000   1.000000 :=
B (system numerator)   =   1.000000 :=
Number of interactions   =   1 Account for the other loop   :=
Interaction polynomial   =   0.500000 :=
Simulation running:
    25% complete
    50% complete
    75% complete
    100% complete
Time now is   25.000000

======== LOOP 1 ========

    System polynomials

A	1.000000	0.000000	0.000000
B	1.000000	0.000000	
B[1]	0.000000	0.000000	
D	0.000000	0.000000	

    Design polynomials

B+	1.000000	0.000000
B-	1.000000	
C	1.000000	1.000000
P	0.500000	1.000000
Z+	1.000000	
Z-	1.000000	
Z-+	1.000000	

F	1.000787	1.000000
F filter	1.000000	1.000000
G	0.499590	0.000000
G filter	1.000000	1.000000
G[1]	0.249854	0.000000
I		
E	0.500000	
ED	0.000000	

======== LOOP 2 ========

    System polynomials

A	1.000000	0.000000	0.000000
B	1.000000	0.000000	
B[1]	0.000000	0.000000	
D	0.000000	0.000000	

    Design polynomials

B+	1.000000	0.000000
B-	1.000000	
C	1.000000	1.000000
P	0.500000	1.000000
Z+	1.000000	
Z-	1.000000	
Z-+	1.000000	

F	1.000788	1.000000

F filter	1.000000	1.000000
G	0.499571	0.000000
G filter	1.000000	1.000000
G[1]	0.249878	0.000000
I		
E	0.500000	
ED	0.000000	

Discussion

The upper graph displays three signals associated with the first loop: the system output $y(t)$, the setpoint $w(t)$ and the ideal model output $y_m(t)$; the lower graph displays the corresponding signals for the second loop.

The interaction is essentially eliminated by the self-tuning decoupling terms. Note that the G[1] parameter is correctly estimated to be 0.25 in each loop.

Further investigations

1. Observe the effect of the tuning by setting "Estimation on" to FALSE in each loop. Note that the $A(s)$ and $B(s)$ parameters are correct, but that the interaction terms are (incorrectly) set to zero.

2. Repeat for different values of a and k; observe that the interaction is always eliminated when tuning is enabled.

10.2.2. OUTPUT-COUPLED TANKS IGNORING INTERACTION

Reference: Section 10.2; page 10-7.

Description

This example is identical to example 10.2.1, except that the interaction terms are ignored in the emulators for each loop.

Programme interaction

runex 10 2
Example 10 of chapter 2: Output-coupled tanks ignoring interaction

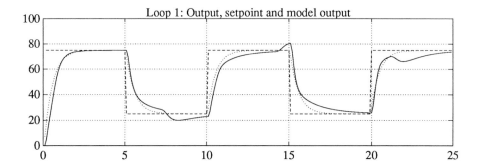

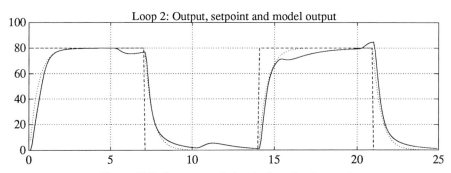

Figure 10.2. Output-coupled tanks ignoring interaction

======== *C S T C Version 6.0* ========

Enter all variables (y/n, default n)?

======== *Data Source*   ========
======== *Filters*   ========
Sample Interval   =   *0.100000* :=

======== *LOOP 1*   ========
======== *Control action* ========
Integral action   = *TRUE* :=
======== *Assumed system* ========
A (system denominator)   =   *1.000000   0.000000 Denominator: s :=*
B (system numerator)   =   *1.000000 Numerator: 1 :=*
Number of interactions   =   *0 Ignore the other loop*   :=
======== *Emulator design* ========
P (model denominator)   =   *0.500000   1.000000 (0.5s+1) :=*

C (emulator denominator) =   *1.000000   1.000000 :=*

     System polynomials

A   *1.000000   0.000000   0.000000*
B   *1.000000   0.000000*
D   *0.000000   0.000000*

     Design polynomials

B+   *1.000000   0.000000*
B-   *1.000000*
C   *1.000000   1.000000*
P   *0.500000   1.000000*
Z+   *1.000000*
Z-   *1.000000*
Z-+   *1.000000*

F   *1.500000   1.000000*
F filter   *1.000000   1.000000*
G   *0.500000   0.000000*
G filter   *1.000000   1.000000*
I
E   *0.500000*
ED   *0.000000*

  ======== *STC type*   ========
  ======== *Tuner*   ========
Estimator on   = *TRUE :=*
  ======== *Controller*   ========
  ======== *Simulation*   ========
  ======== *Setpoint*   ========
Step amplitude   =   *50.000000 :=*
Square amplitude   =   *25.000000 :=*
Period   =   *10.000000 :=*
  ======== *In Disturbance* ========
  ======== *Out Disturbance* ========
  ======== *Actual system* ========
A (system denominator)   =   *1.000000   1.000000 :=*
B (system numerator)   =   *1.000000 :=*
Number of interactions   =   *1 Account for the other loop*   *:=*
Interaction polynomial   =   *0.500000 k=0.5 :=*

  ======== *LOOP 2*   ========
  ======== *Control action* ========
Integral action   = *TRUE :=*
  ======== *Assumed system* ========
A (system denominator)   =   *1.000000   0.000000 Denominator: s :=*
B (system numerator)   =   *1.000000 Numerator: 1 :=*

Number of interactions   =   0 Ignore the other loop   :=
======== Emulator design ========
P (model denominator)   =   0.500000   1.000000 (0.5s+1) :=
C (emulator denominator) =   1.000000   1.000000 :=

        System polynomials

A   1.000000   0.000000   0.000000
B   1.000000   0.000000
D   0.000000   0.000000

        Design polynomials

B+   1.000000   0.000000
B-   1.000000
C   1.000000   1.000000
P   0.500000   1.000000
Z+   1.000000
Z-   1.000000
Z-+   1.000000

F   1.500000   1.000000
F filter   1.000000   1.000000
G   0.500000   0.000000
G filter   1.000000   1.000000
I
E   0.500000
ED   0.000000

======== STC type   ========
======== Tuner   ========
Estimator on   = TRUE :=
======== Controller   ========
======== Simulation   ========
======== Setpoint   ========
Step amplitude   =   40.000000 :=
Square amplitude   =   40.000000 :=
Period   =   14.000000 :=
======== In Disturbance ========
======== Out Disturbance ========
======== Actual system ========
A (system denominator)   =   1.000000   1.000000 :=
B (system numerator)   =   1.000000 :=
Number of interactions   =   1 Account for the other loop   :=
Interaction polynomial   =   0.500000 :=
Simulation running:
      25% complete
      50% complete
      75% complete

100% complete
Time now is   25.000000

======== *LOOP 1*   ========

System polynomials

A   *1.000000   0.000000   0.000000*
B   *1.000000   0.000000*
D   *0.000000   0.000000*

Design polynomials

B+   *1.000000   0.000000*
B-   *1.000000*
C   *1.000000   1.000000*
P   *0.500000   1.000000*
Z+   *1.000000*
Z-   *1.000000*
Z-+   *1.000000*

F   *1.195862   1.000000*
F filter *1.000000   1.000000*
G   *0.343553   0.000000*
G filter *1.000000   1.000000*
I
E   *0.500000*
ED   *0.000000*

======== *LOOP 2*   ========

System polynomials

A   *1.000000   0.000000   0.000000*
B   *1.000000   0.000000*
D   *0.000000   0.000000*

Design polynomials

B+   *1.000000   0.000000*
B-   *1.000000*
C   *1.000000   1.000000*
P   *0.500000   1.000000*
Z+   *1.000000*
Z-   *1.000000*
Z-+   *1.000000*

F   *1.096956   1.000000*

F filter	1.000000	1.000000
G	0.437673	0.000000
G filter	1.000000	1.000000
I		
E	0.500000	
ED	0.000000	

Discussion

The upper graph displays three signals associated with the first loop: the system output $y(t)$, the setpoint $w(t)$ and the ideal model output $y_m(t)$; the lower graph displays the corresponding signals for the second loop.

The interaction cannot any longer be eliminated by the self-tuning controllers as the corresponding terms do not appear in the emulators. Note that the estimated parameters are incorrect due to the neglected interaction.

Further investigations

1. Repeat for different values of a and k; determine the maximum value of k for which the response remains satisfactory.

10.2.3. OUTPUT-COUPLED TANKS (EXPLICIT&IMPLICIT)

Reference: Section 10.2; page 10-7.

Description

This example is identical to example 10.2.1 except that an *explicit* self-tuning algorithm is used in loop 1 and an *implicit* algorithm in loop 2.

Programme interaction

runex 10 3
Example 10 of chapter 3: Output-coupled tanks (Explicit&implicit)

======== C S T C Version 6.0 ========

Enter all variables (y/n, default n)?

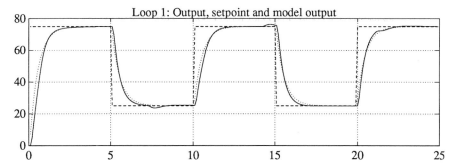

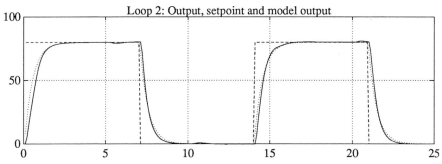

Figure 10.3. Output-coupled tanks (Explicit&implicit)

```
======== Data Source    ========
======== Filters        ========
Sample Interval      =    0.100000  :=

======== LOOP 1         ========
======== Control action ========
Integral action      = TRUE  :=
======== Assumed system ========
A (system denominator)   =    1.000000   0.000000 Denominator: 1 :=
B (system numerator)     =    1.000000 Numerator: 1 :=
Number of interactions   =           1 Account for the other loop        :=
Interaction polynomial   =    0.000000  :=
======== Emulator design ========
P (model denominator)    =    0.500000   1.000000 (0.5s+1) :=
C (emulator denominator) =    1.000000   1.000000  :=
------------------------------------
    System polynomials
```

```
------------------------------------
A           1.000000    0.000000    0.000000
B           1.000000    0.000000
B[1]        0.000000    0.000000
D           0.000000    0.000000
------------------------------------
        Design polynomials
------------------------------------
B+          1.000000    0.000000
B-          1.000000
C           1.000000    1.000000
P           0.500000    1.000000
Z+          1.000000
Z-          1.000000
Z-+         1.000000
------------------------------------
F           1.500000    1.000000
F filter    1.000000    1.000000
G           0.500000    0.000000
G filter    1.000000    1.000000
G[1]        0.000000    0.000000
I
E           0.500000
ED          0.000000
------------------------------------
```

======== STC type   ========
======== Identification ========
Estimator on   = TRUE :=
Cs (emulator denominator) =   1.000000   0.000000   0.000000 :=
Identifying rational part = TRUE :=
Identifying delay   = FALSE :=
======== Controller   ========
======== Simulation   ========
======== Setpoint   ========
Step amplitude   =   50.000000 :=
Square amplitude   =   25.000000 :=
Period   =   10.000000 :=
======== In Disturbance ========
======== Out Disturbance ========
======== Actual system ========
A (system denominator) =   1.000000   1.000000 :=
B (system numerator)   =   1.000000 :=
Number of interactions =   1 Account for the other loop   :=
Interaction polynomial =   0.500000 k=0.5 :=

======== LOOP 2   ========
======== Control action ========
Integral action   = TRUE :=
======== Assumed system ========

A (system denominator)   =   1.000000   0.000000 Denominator: 1 :=
B (system numerator)   =   1.000000 Numerator: 1 :=
Interaction polynomial   =   0.000000   :=
======== Emulator design ========
P (model denominator)   =   0.500000   1.000000 (0.5s+1) :=
C (emulator denominator) =   1.000000   1.000000   :=

    System polynomials

A	1.000000	0.000000	0.000000
B	1.000000	0.000000	
B[1]	0.000000	0.000000	
D	0.000000	0.000000	

    Design polynomials

B+	1.000000	0.000000
B-	1.000000	
C	1.000000	1.000000
P	0.500000	1.000000
Z+	1.000000	
Z-	1.000000	
Z-+	1.000000	

F	1.500000	1.000000
F filter	1.000000	1.000000
G	0.500000	0.000000
G filter	1.000000	1.000000
G[1]	0.000000	0.000000
I		
E	0.500000	
ED	0.000000	

======== STC type   ========
======== Tuner   ========
Estimator on   = TRUE :=
======== Controller ========
======== Simulation ========
======== Setpoint   ========
Step amplitude   =   40.000000 :=
Square amplitude   =   40.000000 :=
Period   =   14.000000 :=
======== In Disturbance ========
======== Out Disturbance ========
======== Actual system ========
A (system denominator)   =   1.000000   1.000000 :=
B (system numerator)   =   1.000000 :=
Number of interactions   =   1 Account for the other loop   :=
Interaction polynomial   =   0.500000 :=

Simulation running:
  25% complete
  50% complete
  75% complete
  100% complete
Time now is   25.000000

======== *LOOP 1*   ========

System polynomials

A	1.000000	1.000105	0.000000
B	1.000048	0.000000	
B[1]	0.500084	0.000000	
D	0.000000	0.000000	

Design polynomials

B+	1.000048	0.000000
B-	1.000000	
C	1.000000	1.000000
P	0.500000	1.000000
Z+	1.000000	
Z-	1.000000	
Z-+	1.000000	

F	0.999948	1.000000
F filter	1.000000	1.000000
G	0.500024	0.000000
G filter	1.000000	1.000000
G[1]	0.250042	0.000000
I		
E	0.500000	
ED	0.000000	

======== *LOOP 2*   ========

System polynomials

A	1.000000	0.000000	0.000000
B	1.000000	0.000000	
B[1]	0.000000	0.000000	
D	0.000000	0.000000	

Design polynomials

B+	1.000000	0.000000
B-	1.000000	

C	1.000000	1.000000
P	0.500000	1.000000
Z+	1.000000	
Z-	1.000000	
Z-+	1.000000	
---	---	---
F	1.000788	1.000000
F filter	1.000000	1.000000
G	0.499571	0.000000
G filter	1.000000	1.000000
G[1]	0.249878	0.000000
I		
E	0.500000	
ED	0.000000	

Discussion

The upper graph displays three signals associated with the first loop: the system output $y(t)$, the setpoint $w(t)$ and the ideal model output $y_m(t)$; the lower graph displays the corresponding signals for the second loop.

The interaction is essentially eliminated by the self-tuning decoupling terms.

Further investigations

1. Observe the effect of the tuning by setting "Estimation on" to FALSE in each loop. Note that the $A(s)$ and $B(s)$ parameters are correct, but that the interaction terms are (incorrectly) set to zero.

2. Repeat for different values of a and k; observe that the interaction is always eliminated when tuning is enabled.

10.2.4. INPUT-COUPLED TANKS (IMPLICIT)

Reference: Section 10.2; page 10-7.

Description

Example 2 of chapter I-10 (page I-10-8) considers a simple model comprising two tanks of liquid which share a common inflow; the effective interaction is thus from input to input. Unlike the example in the book, however, the input, not the output, is used as a feedforward signal so it is possible to decouple the system exactly. In practice, discrepancies arise due to the non-zero sample

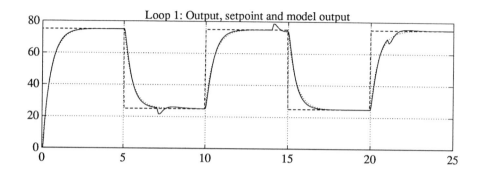

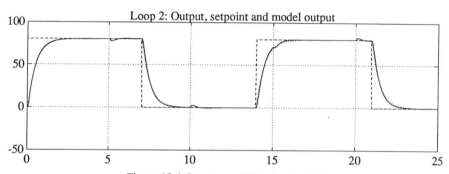

Figure 10.4. Input-coupled tanks (Implicit)

interval.

Programme interaction

runex 10 4
Example 10 of chapter 4: Input-coupled tanks (Implicit)

======== C S T C Version 6.0 ========

Enter all variables (y/n, default n)?

======== Data Source ========
======== Filters ========
Sample Interval   =   0.050000 :=

```
======== LOOP 1        ========
======== Control action ========
Integral action      = TRUE  :=
======== Assumed system ========
A (system denominator)  =    1.000000    0.000000 Denominator: s :=
B (system numerator)    =    1.000000 Numerator: 1 :=
Number of interactions  =          1 Account for the other loop          :=
Interaction polynomial  =    0.000000 :=
======== Emulator design ========
P (model denominator)   =    0.500000    1.000000 (0.5s+1) :=
C (emulator denominator) =   1.000000    1.000000 :=
```

         System polynomials

A	1.000000	0.000000	0.000000
B	1.000000	0.000000	
B[1]	0.000000	0.000000	
D	0.000000	0.000000	

         Design polynomials

B+	1.000000	0.000000
B-	1.000000	
C	1.000000	1.000000
P	0.500000	1.000000
Z+	1.000000	
Z-	1.000000	
Z-+	1.000000	

F	1.500000	1.000000
F filter	1.000000	1.000000
G	0.500000	0.000000
G filter	1.000000	1.000000
G[1]	0.000000	0.000000
I		
E	0.500000	
ED	0.000000	

```
======== STC type      ========
======== Tuner         ========
Estimator on         = TRUE  :=
======== Controller    ========
======== Simulation    ========
======== Setpoint      ========
Step amplitude       =    50.000000 :=
Square amplitude     =    25.000000 :=
Period               =    10.000000 :=
======== In Disturbance ========
======== Out Disturbance ========
```

```
======== Actual system   ========
A (system denominator)   =    1.000000   1.000000  :=
B (system numerator)     =    1.000000  :=
Number of interactions   =         1 Account for the other loop           :=
Interaction polynomial   =    0.500000 k=0.5 :=


======== LOOP 2          ========
======== Control action  ========
Integral action         = TRUE  :=
======== Assumed system  ========
A (system denominator)   =    1.000000   0.000000 Denominator: s :=
B (system numerator)     =    1.000000 Numerator: 1 :=
Interaction polynomial   =    0.000000  :=
======== Emulator design ========
P (model denominator)    =    0.500000   1.000000 (0.5s+1) :=
C (emulator denominator) =    1.000000   1.000000  :=
-------------------------------------
        System polynomials
-------------------------------------

A        1.000000    0.000000    0.000000
B        1.000000    0.000000
B[1]     0.000000    0.000000
D        0.000000    0.000000
-------------------------------------
        Design polynomials
-------------------------------------

B+       1.000000    0.000000
B-       1.000000
C        1.000000    1.000000
P        0.500000    1.000000
Z+       1.000000
Z-       1.000000
Z-+      1.000000
-------------------------------------
F        1.500000    1.000000
F filter 1.000000    1.000000
G        0.500000    0.000000
G filter 1.000000    1.000000
G[1]     0.000000    0.000000
I
E        0.500000
ED       0.000000
-------------------------------------
======== STC type        ========
======== Tuner           ========
Estimator on            = TRUE  :=
======== Controller      ========
======== Simulation      ========
======== Setpoint        ========
```

Step amplitude   =   *40.000000 :=*
Square amplitude   =   *40.000000 :=*
Period   =   *14.000000 :=*
======== In Disturbance ========
======== Out Disturbance ========
======== Actual system   ========
A (system denominator)   =   *1.000000   1.000000 :=*
B (system numerator)   =   *1.000000 :=*
Number of interactions   =   *1 Account for the other loop   :=*
Interaction polynomial   =   *0.500000 :=*
Simulation running:
     25% complete
     50% complete
     75% complete
     100% complete
Time now is   25.000000

======== LOOP 1   ========

     System polynomials

A   *1.000000   0.000000   0.000000*
B   *1.000000   0.000000*
B[1]   *0.000000   0.000000*
D   *0.000000   0.000000*

     Design polynomials

B+   *1.000000   0.000000*
B-   *1.000000*
C   *1.000000   1.000000*
P   *0.500000   1.000000*
Z+   *1.000000*
Z-   *1.000000*
Z-+   *1.000000*

F   *1.000198   1.000000*
F filter *1.000000   1.000000*
G   *0.499897   0.000000*
G filter *1.000000   1.000000*
G[1]   *0.249952   0.000000*
I
E   *0.500000*
ED   *0.000000*

======== LOOP 2   ========

     System polynomials

```
---------------------------------
A          1.000000    0.000000    0.000000
B          1.000000    0.000000
B[1]       0.000000    0.000000
D          0.000000    0.000000
---------------------------------
           Design polynomials
---------------------------------
B+         1.000000    0.000000
B-         1.000000
C          1.000000    1.000000
P          0.500000    1.000000
Z+         1.000000
Z-         1.000000
Z-+        1.000000
---------------------------------
F          1.000200    1.000000
F filter   1.000000    1.000000
G          0.499899    0.000000
G filter   1.000000    1.000000
G[1]       0.249961    0.000000
I
E          0.500000
ED         0.000000
---------------------------------
```

Discussion

The upper graph displays three signals associated with the first loop: the system output $y(t)$, the setpoint $w(t)$ and the ideal model output $y_m(t)$; the lower graph displays the corresponding signals for the second loop.

The interaction is essentially eliminated by the self-tuning decoupling terms; and the estimated parameters are correct.

Further investigations

1. Observe the effect of the tuning by setting "Estimation on" to FALSE in each loop. Note that the $A(s)$ and $B(s)$ parameters are correct, but that the interaction terms are (incorrectly) set to zero.

2. Repeat for different values of a and k; observe that the interaction is always eliminated when

tuning is enabled.

10.2.5. INPUT-COUPLED TANKS IGNORING INTERACTION

Reference: Section 10.2; page 10-7.

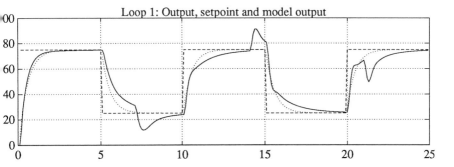

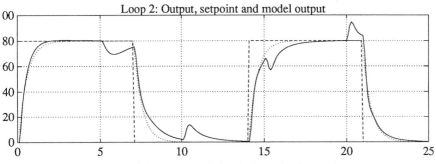

Figure 10.5. Input-coupled tanks ignoring interaction

Description

This example is identical to example 10.2.4, except that the interaction terms are ignored in the emulators for each loop.

Programme interaction

runex 10 5
Example 10 of chapter 5: Input-coupled tanks ignoring interaction

    ======== C S T C Version 6.0 ========

Enter all variables (y/n, default n)?

        ======== Data Source   ========
        ======== Filters   ========
    Sample Interval   =   0.100000   :=

        ======== LOOP 1   ========
        ======== Control action ========
    Integral action   = TRUE   :=
        ======== Assumed system ========
    A (system denominator)   =   1.000000   0.000000 Denominator: s :=
    B (system numerator)   =   1.000000 Numerator: 1 :=
    Number of interactions   =   0 Ignore the other loop   :=
        ======== Emulator design ========
    P (model denominator)   =   0.500000   1.000000 (0.5s+1) :=
    C (emulator denominator) =   1.000000   1.000000   :=

        System polynomials

    A   1.000000   0.000000   0.000000
    B   1.000000   0.000000
    D   0.000000   0.000000

        Design polynomials

    B+   1.000000   0.000000
    B-   1.000000
    C   1.000000   1.000000
    P   0.500000   1.000000
    Z+   1.000000
    Z-   1.000000
    Z-+   1.000000

    F   1.500000   1.000000
    F filter 1.000000   1.000000
    G   0.500000   0.000000
    G filter 1.000000   1.000000
    I
    E   0.500000
    ED   0.000000

```
--------------------------------------
======== STC type        ========
======== Tuner           ========
Estimator on             = TRUE  :=
======== Controller      ========
======== Simulation      ========
======== Setpoint        ========
Step amplitude           =    50.000000  :=
Square amplitude         =    25.000000  :=
Period                   =    10.000000  :=
======== In Disturbance ========
======== Out Disturbance ========
======== Actual system  ========
A (system denominator)   =    1.000000    1.000000  :=
B (system numerator)     =    1.000000  :=
Number of interactions   =         1 Account for the other loop          :=
Interaction polynomial   =    0.500000 k=0.5 :=

======== LOOP 2          ========
======== Control action ========
Integral action          = TRUE  :=
======== Assumed system ========
A (system denominator)   =    1.000000    0.000000 Denominator: s :=
B (system numerator)     =    1.000000 Numerator: 1 :=
Number of interactions   =         0 Ignore the other loop               :=
======== Emulator design ========
P (model denominator)    =    0.500000    1.000000 (0.5s+1) :=
C (emulator denominator) =    1.000000    1.000000  :=
--------------------------------------
        System polynomials
--------------------------------------
A          1.000000    0.000000    0.000000
B          1.000000    0.000000
D          0.000000    0.000000
--------------------------------------
        Design polynomials
--------------------------------------
B+         1.000000    0.000000
B-         1.000000
C          1.000000    1.000000
P          0.500000    1.000000
Z+         1.000000
Z-         1.000000
Z-+        1.000000
--------------------------------------
F          1.500000    1.000000
F filter   1.000000    1.000000
G          0.500000    0.000000
G filter   1.000000    1.000000
```

```
I
E          0.500000
ED         0.000000
------------------------------------
======== STC type        ========
======== Tuner           ========
Estimator on             = TRUE  :=
======== Controller      ========
======== Simulation      ========
======== Setpoint        ========
Step amplitude        =    40.000000  :=
Square amplitude      =     40.000000  :=
Period                =     14.000000  :=
======== In Disturbance  ========
======== Out Disturbance ========
======== Actual system   ========
A (system denominator)   =    1.000000   1.000000  :=
B (system numerator)     =    1.000000  :=
Number of interactions   =           1 Account for the other loop       :=
Interaction polynomial   =    0.500000  :=
Simulation running:
     25% complete
     50% complete
     75% complete
    100% complete
Time now is    25.000000


======== LOOP 1          ========
------------------------------------
     System polynomials
------------------------------------
A        1.000000   0.000000    0.000000
B        1.000000   0.000000
D        0.000000   0.000000
------------------------------------
     Design polynomials
------------------------------------
B+         1.000000   0.000000
B-         1.000000
C          1.000000   1.000000
P          0.500000   1.000000
Z+         1.000000
Z-         1.000000
Z-+        1.000000
------------------------------------
F          1.245325   1.000000
F filter   1.000000   1.000000
G          0.240999   0.000000
G filter   1.000000   1.000000
```

```
I
E          0.500000
ED         0.000000
-------------------------------------

========= LOOP 2        ========
-------------------------------------
   System polynomials
-------------------------------------
A          1.000000   0.000000   0.000000
B          1.000000   0.000000
D          0.000000   0.000000
-------------------------------------
   Design polynomials
-------------------------------------
B+         1.000000   0.000000
B-         1.000000
C          1.000000   1.000000
P          0.500000   1.000000
Z+         1.000000
Z-         1.000000
Z-+        1.000000
-------------------------------------
F          1.034773   1.000000
F filter   1.000000   1.000000
G          0.354875   0.000000
G filter   1.000000   1.000000
I
E          0.500000
ED         0.000000
-------------------------------------
```

Discussion

The upper graph displays three signals: the system output $y(t)$ the setpoint $w(t)$ and the ideal model output $y_m(t)$ where $\overline{y}_m(s) = \dfrac{Z(s)}{P(s)}\overline{w}(s)$.

Note that the interaction cannot any longer be eliminated by the self-tuning controllers as the corresponding terms do not appear in the emulators.

Further investigations

1.   Repeat for different values of a and k; determine the maximum value of k for which the response remains satisfactory.

CHAPTER 11

CSTC: The Programme

Aims. To explicitly describe the continuous-time self tuning algorithm as Pascal code. There are three sections: a summary of the programme in terms of procedure headings, procedure cross-references and the line-numbered code.

11.1. THE PROGRAMME SUMMARY

```
  4  PROGRAM CSTC(Input, Output, InLog, OutLog, InData, OutData,
  5  OutSysPar, OutEmPar);
```

```
{-------------------------------------------------}
{--   Polynomial output procedures        --}
{-------------------------------------------------}
```

```
304      PROCEDURE PolWrite(VAR ListFile: TEXT;
305              Pol: Polynomial);
323      PROCEDURE PolLineWrite(VAR ListFile: TEXT;
324              Pol: Polynomial);
```

```
{-------------------------------------------------}
{--   Polynomial manipulation procedures    --}
{-------------------------------------------------}
```

```
339      FUNCTION PolNorm(Pol: Polynomial): REAL;
359      PROCEDURE PolRemove(VAR A: Polynomial;
360              N: INTEGER);
382      PROCEDURE PolTruncate(VAR A: Polynomial);
403      PROCEDURE PolZero(VAR Result: Polynomial;
404              Deg: Degree);
417      PROCEDURE PolUnity(VAR Result: Polynomial;
418              Deg: Degree);
434      PROCEDURE PolEquate(VAR Result: Polynomial;
435              Pol: Polynomial);
450      PROCEDURE PolOfMinusS(VAR Result: Polynomial;
```

```
451                    Pol: Polynomial);
469        PROCEDURE PolAdd(VAR Result: Polynomial;
470                    A, B: Polynomial);
504        PROCEDURE PolMinus(VAR Result: Polynomial;
505                    A, B: Polynomial);
539        PROCEDURE PolWeightedAdd(VAR Result: Polynomial;
540                    u: REAL;
541                    A: Polynomial;
542                    v: REAL;
543                    B: Polynomial);
577        PROCEDURE PolScalarMultiply(VAR Result: Polynomial;
578                    A: REAL;
579                    B: Polynomial);
594        PROCEDURE PolsMultiply(VAR sA: Polynomial;
595                    A: Polynomial);
610        PROCEDURE PolsDivide(VAR A: Polynomial;
611                    sA: Polynomial);
628        PROCEDURE PolMultiply(VAR Result: Polynomial;
629                    A, B: Polynomial);
647        PROCEDURE PolSquare(VAR S: Polynomial;
648                    A: Polynomial);
658         FUNCTION Even(i: INTEGER): BOOLEAN;
685        PROCEDURE PolSqrt(VAR A: Polynomial;
686                    S: Polynomial);
718        PROCEDURE PolNormalise(VAR A, B: Polynomial;
719                    i: INTEGER);
743         FUNCTION PolGain(VAR A: Polynomial;
744                    ContinuousTime: BOOLEAN): REAL;
766        PROCEDURE PolUnitGain(VAR A: Polynomial;
767                    ContinuousTime: BOOLEAN);
782        PROCEDURE PolMarkovRecursion(VAR MarkovParameter: REAL;
783                    VAR E, F: Polynomial;
784                    A: Polynomial);
813        PROCEDURE PolDerivativeEmulator
814                   (VAR E, F: Polynomial;
815                    P, C, A: Polynomial);
848        PROCEDURE PolDivide(VAR E, F: Polynomial;
849                    B, A: Polynomial);
865        PROCEDURE PolEuclid(VAR GCD, E, F: Polynomial;
866                    A, B: Polynomial);
882          PROCEDURE FindGCD(AlphaIminus1 {A} ,
883                    AlphaI {B} : Polynomial);
919          PROCEDURE DeduceEandF(VAR Beta {F} ,
920                    Gamma {E} : Polynomial);
956          PROCEDURE NormaliseGCD;
981        PROCEDURE PolDioRecursion(VAR E, F: Polynomial;
982                    A, B: Polynomial);
1022       PROCEDURE PolDiophantine(VAR E, F: Polynomial;
1023                    VAR GCD: Polynomial;
1024                    A, B, PC: Polynomial);
1068       PROCEDURE PolZeroCancellingEmulator
1069                   (VAR E, F: Polynomial;
1070                    P, C, A: Polynomial;
1071                    ZMinus, ZPlus: Polynomial;
1072                    VAR GCDAZ: Polynomial {GCD of A and Z-} );
1089       PROCEDURE PolPade(VAR Pade: Polynomial;
1090                    Deg: INTEGER;
1091                    Delay: REAL);
```

```
{-------------------------------------------------}
{--   Emulator design for self-tuning      --}
{-------------------------------------------------}
```

```
1118      PROCEDURE SetDesignKnobs(VAR DesignKnobs: TypeDesignKnobs;
1119                    A, B: Polynomial;
1120                    ZeroAtOrigin, ZHasFactorB,
1121                    ContinuousTime: BOOLEAN);
1126         PROCEDURE DesignP(A, B: Polynomial);
1185      PROCEDURE PolInitialConditions
1186         (VAR InitialCondition, ED: Polynomial;
1187         A, D, E: Polynomial;
1188         DesignKnobs: TypeDesignKnobs);
1226      PROCEDURE PolEmulator(VAR F, G, InitialCondition,
1227         {Emulator numerators}
1228                    FFilter, GFilter  {Emulator
1229                          denominators}
1230                    : Polynomial;
1231                    VAR E, ED: {error} Polynomial;
1232                    VAR GCDAZ: Polynomial {GCD of A and
1233                          Z-} ;
1234                    A: Polynomial {System denominator} ;
1235                    D: Polynomial {Initial condition} ;
1236                    DesignKnobs: TypeDesignKnobs);
1247         PROCEDURE FindEandF;
1291      PROCEDURE PolDelayEmulator(VAR F, G, InitialCondition,
1292                    FFilter, GFilter: Polynomial;
1293                    VAR E, ED: Polynomial;
1294                    VAR GCDAZ, PadeDenominator,
1295                    PadeNumerator: Polynomial;
1296                    A, D: Polynomial;
1297                    DesignKnobs: TypeDesignKnobs;
1298                    Delay: REAL;
1299                    PadeOrder: INTEGER);
1336      PROCEDURE DesignEmulator(VAR STCKnobs: TypeSTCKnobs;
1337                    VAR STCState: TypeSTCState);
```

```
{-------------------------------------------------}
{-- Input output  procedures           --}
{-------------------------------------------------}
```

```
1368      PROCEDURE WriteTitle(Title: TypeTitle);
1376      PROCEDURE WriteLoopTitle(Loop, Loops: INTEGER);
1397      PROCEDURE Skip(VAR F: TEXT);
1406      PROCEDURE GetSymbol(VAR F: TEXT;
1407               VAR ChangeChar: CHAR);
1416      FUNCTION NameMatched(i: INTEGER;
1417               VAR Name: TypeName): BOOLEAN;
1441      FUNCTION NewValue(All: BOOLEAN;
1442               VAR ChangeChar: CHAR): BOOLEAN;
1461      PROCEDURE GetComment(VAR F: TEXT;
1462               VAR Comment: TypeComment);
1477      PROCEDURE PutComment(VAR F: TEXT;
1478               Comment: TypeComment);
1492      PROCEDURE EnterReal(VAR x: REAL;
1493               Default: REAL;
1494               Name: TypeName;
1495               All: BOOLEAN);
```

```
1540   PROCEDURE EnterInteger(VAR x: INTEGER;
1541              Default: INTEGER;
1542              Name: TypeName;
1543              All: BOOLEAN);
1587   PROCEDURE EnterBoolean(VAR x: BOOLEAN;
1588              Default: BOOLEAN;
1589              Name: TypeName;
1590              All: BOOLEAN);
1598     PROCEDURE ReadBoolean(VAR F: TEXT);
1646   PROCEDURE EnterPolynomial(VAR x: Polynomial;
1647              Default: Polynomial;
1648              Name: TypeName;
1649              All: BOOLEAN);
1659     PROCEDURE GetPolynomial(VAR F: TEXT;
1660              VAR x: Polynomial;
1661              VAR AnotherFactor: BOOLEAN);
1741   PROCEDURE WriteParameters(VAR LoopVAR: TypeLoopVAR);
1768   PROCEDURE WriteDesign(VAR LoopVAR: TypeLoopVAR);
```

```
{-------------------------------------------------}
{-- Data filtering procedures              --}
{-------------------------------------------------}
```

```
1845   PROCEDURE StateVariableFilter
1846       (u {Signal to be filtered} : REAL;
1847       A: Polynomial;
1848       FilterKnobs: TypeFilterKnobs;
1849       VAR FilterState: TypeFilterState);
1851   PROCEDURE cStateVariableFilter
1852       (u {Signal to be filtered} : REAL;
1853       A: Polynomial;
1854       FilterKnobs: TypeFilterKnobs;
1855       VAR FilterState: TypeFilterState);
1931   PROCEDURE dStateVariableFilter
1932       (u {Signal to be filtered} : REAL;
1933       A: Polynomial; {Now a discrete-time polynomial}
1934       FilterKnobs: TypeFilterKnobs;
1935       VAR FilterState: TypeFilterState);
1974   PROCEDURE FilterInitialise(VAR FilterState:
1975              TypeFilterState;
1976              ContinuousTime: BOOLEAN;
1977              InitialValue: REAL);
1992   FUNCTION StateOutput(FilterState: TypeFilterState;
1993              Numerator,
1994       Denominator: Polynomial): REAL;
2014   FUNCTION Filter(u {Input to filter} : REAL;
2015       Numerator, Denominator: Polynomial;
2016       FilterKnobs: TypeFilterKnobs;
2017       VAR FilterState: TypeFilterState): REAL;
2030   FUNCTION Delayed(u: REAL;
2031       Delay: INTEGER;
2032       VAR State: TypeDelayState): REAL;
2047   FUNCTION DelayFilter(u {Input to filter} : REAL;
2048       Numerator, Denominator: Polynomial;
2049       Delay: REAL;
2050       FilterKnobs: TypeFilterKnobs;
2051       VAR FilterState: TypeFilterState;
2052       VAR DelFilterState: TypeDelayState):
```

```
2053    REAL;
2080    PROCEDURE TimeDelayInitialise
2081        (VAR State: TypeDelayState;
2082        InitialValue: REAL);
2096    FUNCTION TimeFor(Interval: INTEGER;
2097        VAR Counter: INTEGER): BOOLEAN;
    END {TimeFor} ;
```

```
{-------------------------------------------------}
{--    CSTC initialisation procedures      --}
{-------------------------------------------------}
```

```
2108    PROCEDURE SigGenInitialise(VAR SigGenKnobs:
2109                        TypeSigGenKnobs);
2125    PROCEDURE tSystemInitialise(STCKnobs: TypeSTCKnobs;
2126                        STCState: TypeSTCState;
2127                        VAR tSystemKnobs:
2128                        TypeSystemKnobs;
2129                        VAR tSystemState:
2130                        TypeSystemState;
2131                        ContinuousTime: BOOLEAN;
2132                        RunKnobs: TypeRunKnobs);
2211    PROCEDURE ModelKnobsInitialise
2212        (STCKnobs: TypeSTCKnobs;
2213        tSystemKnobs: TypeSystemKnobs;
2214        VAR ModelKnobs: TypeSystemKnobs;
2215        ContinuousTime: BOOLEAN);
2232    PROCEDURE ModelInitialise(STCKnobs: TypeSTCKnobs;
2233                        STCState: TypeSTCState;
2234                        tSystemKnobs: TypeSystemKnobs;
2235                        VAR ModelKnobs: TypeSystemKnobs;
2236                        VAR ModelState: TypeSystemState;
2237                        ContinuousTime: BOOLEAN);
2255    PROCEDURE SystemInitialise(VAR STCKnobs: TypeSTCKnobs;
2256                        VAR STCState: TypeSTCState;
2257                        RunKnobs: TypeRunKnobs);
2318    PROCEDURE DesignInitialise(VAR STCKnobs: TypeSTCKnobs;
2319                        VAR STCState: TypeSTCState;
2320                        ContinuousTime: BOOLEAN);
2384    PROCEDURE InitFilterKnobs(VAR FilterKnobs: TypeFilterKnobs
2385                        );
2400    PROCEDURE STCInitialise(VAR LoopVAR: TypeLoopVAR;
2401                        FilterKnobs: TypeFilterKnobs;
2402                        RunKnobs: TypeRunKnobs);
2407        PROCEDURE KnobsInitialise(FilterKnobs: TypeFilterKnobs;
2408                        RunKnobs: TypeRunKnobs;
2409                        VAR PutDataKnobs:
2410                        TypePutDataKnobs;
2411                        VAR STCKnobs: TypeSTCKnobs;
2412                        VAR STCState: TypeSTCState);
2414        PROCEDURE TunerInitialise
2415            (SampleInterval: REAL;
2416            VAR Knobs: TypeTunerKnobs;
2417            VAR State: TypeTunerState);
2459        PROCEDURE TuneEmInitialise
2460            (SampleInterval: REAL;
2461            VAR TunerKnobs: TypeTunerKnobs;
2462            VAR TunerState: TypeTunerState);
```

```
2469          PROCEDURE IdentifyInitialise
2470               (SampleInterval: REAL;
2471               VAR STCKnobs: TypeSTCKnobs;
2472               VAR STCState: TypeSTCState);
2522          PROCEDURE ControlInitialise
2523               (VAR ControlKnobs: TypeControlKnobs);
2545          PROCEDURE PutDatInitialise
2546               (VAR PutDataKnobs: TypePutDataKnobs);
2622          PROCEDURE StateInitialise(STCKnobs: TypeSTCKnobs;
2623               VAR STCState: TypeSTCState;
2624               ContinuousTime: BOOLEAN);
2629          PROCEDURE InitEmulator(EmKnobs: TypeEmKnobs;
2630               VAR EmState: TypeEmState;
2631               ContinuousTime: BOOLEAN);
```

```
{------------------------------------------------}
{--    System simulation procedures        --}
{------------------------------------------------}
```

```
2719          FUNCTION SigGen(SigGenKnobs: TypeSigGenKnobs;
2720               Time: REAL): REAL;
2744          FUNCTION System(u: REAL;
2745               Knobs: TypeSystemKnobs;
2746               FilterKnobs: TypeFilterKnobs;
2747               VAR State: TypeSystemState): REAL;
2766          FUNCTION MultiLag(u: REAL;
2767               Lags: INTEGER;
2768               TimeConstant: REAL;
2769               Interactive: BOOLEAN;
2770               FilterKnobs: TypeFilterKnobs;
2771               VAR State: TypeLagState): REAL;
```

```
{------------------------------------------------}
{--    Self-tuner input/output procedures    --}
{------------------------------------------------}
```

```
2799          PROCEDURE GetData(VAR ThisLoopVAR: TypeLoopVAR;
2800               VAR LoopVAR: LoopVARs;
2801               VAR InData: TEXT;
2802               VAR Time: REAL;
2803               RunKnobs: TypeRunKnobs;
2804               FilterKnobs: TypeFilterKnobs);
2806          PROCEDURE GetDataFromFile(VAR InData: TEXT);
2827          PROCEDURE Simulate;
2876          PROCEDURE PutData(VAR u: REAL;
2877               PutDataKnobs: TypePutDataKnobs);
```

```
{------------------------------------------------}
{--    High-gain (emulator-free) control    --}
{------------------------------------------------}
```

```
2895          PROCEDURE HighGainControl(VAR u: REAL;
2896               w, y: REAL;
2897               FilterKnobs: TypeFilterKnobs;
2898               VAR STCKnobs: TypeSTCKnobs;
2899               VAR STCState: TypeSTCState);
```

```
{------------------------------------------------}
```

```
{--      Self-tuning  control                    --}
{------------------------------------------------}

2917        PROCEDURE SelfTuningControl(VAR u: REAL
2918           { The control signal } ;
2919                            w, y: REAL
2920                            { The setpoint and system output }
2921                            ;
2922                            Interaction: TypeInteraction
2923                            {Interaction terms} ;
2924                            FilterKnobs: TypeFilterKnobs
2925                            { The digital filter parameters }
2926                            ;
2927                            ExternalData: BOOLEAN;
2928                            VAR PutDataKnobs:
2929                            TypePutDataKnobs
2930                            { The control signal limits etc.  }
2931                            ;
2932                            VAR STCKnobs: TypeSTCKnobs
2933                            { The user defined STC variables }
2934                            ;
2935                            VAR STCState: TypeSTCState
2936                            { The internal state of the STC }
2937                            );
      {------------------------------------------------}
      {--     Emulator-based control procedures     --}
      {------------------------------------------------}

2949        FUNCTION Emulator(y, u: REAL;
2950                            Interaction: TypeInteraction;
2951                            NumberInteractions: INTEGER;
2952                            F, FFilter, G, GFilter,
2953                            InitialCondition: Polynomial;
2954                            GInteraction: InterPolynomial;
2955                            InputDelay: REAL;
2956                            FilterKnobs: TypeFilterKnobs;
2957                            VAR EmState: TypeEmState): REAL;
2998        FUNCTION Control(y, w: REAL;
2999                            Interaction: TypeInteraction;
3000                            STCKnobs: TypeSTCKnobs;
3001                            VAR STCState: TypeSTCState;
3002                            FilterKnobs: TypeFilterKnobs): REAL;
3004           FUNCTION ImplicitSolution
3005              (y, w: REAL;
3006              Interaction: TypeInteraction;
3007              Em0State, Em1State: TypeEmState;
3008              Q0State, Q1State: TypeFilterState;
3009              STCKnobs: TypeSTCKnobs;
3010              VAR STCState: TypeSTCState;
3011              FilterKnobs: TypeFilterKnobs): REAL;

      {------------------------------------------------}
      {--     Emulator tuning procedures        --}
      {------------------------------------------------}

3068        PROCEDURE SetData(VAR DataVector: TypeDataVector;
3069                            State: TypeEmState;
3070                            Knobs: TypeEmKnobs;
```

```
3071                    TuningInitialConditions,
3072                    IntegralAction: BOOLEAN;
3073                    NumberInteractions: INTEGER);
3126    PROCEDURE TuneEmulator(VAR Knobs: TypeEmKnobs;
3127                    State: TypeTunerState;
3128                    TuningInitialConditions,
3129                    IntegralAction: BOOLEAN;
3130                    NumberInteractions: INTEGER);
3182    PROCEDURE UpdateLeastSquaresGain
3183            (VAR TunerState: TypeTunerState;
3184            TunerKnobs: TypeTunerKnobs;
3185            DataVector: TypeDataVector);
3193    FUNCTION UTX(j: INTEGER): REAL; { computes jth element
3275    PROCEDURE IdentifySystem(y, u: REAL;
3276                    Interaction: TypeInteraction;
3277                    FilterKnobs: TypeFilterKnobs;
3278                    VAR STCKnobs: TypeSTCKnobs;
3279                    VAR STCState: TypeSTCState);
3286    PROCEDURE TuneDelay(VAR Delay: REAL;
3287                    State: TypeTunerState;
3288                    NumberOfParameters: INTEGER);
3299    PROCEDURE SetDelayData(VAR DataVector: TypeDataVector;
3300                    State: TypeEmState;
3301                    Knobs: TypeEmKnobs);
3378    PROCEDURE TunePhiEmulator(y: REAL;
3379                    FilterKnobs: TypeFilterKnobs;
3380                    VAR STCKnobs: TypeSTCKnobs;
3381                    VAR STCState: TypeSTCState);
3415    PROCEDURE TuneLambdaEmulator
3416            (y, u: REAL;
3417            Interaction: TypeInteraction;
3418            FilterKnobs: TypeFilterKnobs;
3419            LambdaNumerator, LambdaDenominator: Polynomial;
3420            ZLambda, PLambda: Polynomial;
3421            VAR STCKnobs: TypeSTCKnobs;
3422            VAR STCState: TypeSTCState);

        {-------------------------------------------------}
        {--   Self-tuning  control: procedure body   --}
        {-------------------------------------------------}

3494    BEGIN {SelfTuningControl}

3572    PROCEDURE RunInitialise;
3611    PROCEDURE SimulationInitialise
3612            (VAR ThisLoopVAR: TypeLoopVAR;
3613            FilterKnobs: TypeFilterKnobs;
3614            RunKnobs: TypeRunKnobs);
3648    PROCEDURE Run;
3655            PROCEDURE WriteData(VAR ThisLoopVAR: TypeLoopVAR);
3706            PROCEDURE WriteLnData;
3714            PROCEDURE OneTimeStep(VAR ThisLoopVAR: TypeLoopVAR);
3749            PROCEDURE Splice(VAR ThisLoopVAR: TypeLoopVAR);
3777            FUNCTION NoMore: BOOLEAN;
3783                PROCEDURE PreventBump;
3937    FUNCTION Chapter(VAR All: BOOLEAN): INTEGER;

        {-------------------------------------------------}
```

```
{--     Body of CSTC                      --}
{----------------------------------------------}
3967   BEGIN {CSTC}
```

11.2. THE PROGRAMME PROCEDURAL INDEX

Chapter   Head: 3937   Body: 3943
Calls   EnterInteger
Called by   CSTC
Control   Head: 2998   Body: 3049
Calls   ImplicitSolution Filter
Called by   SelfTuningContro
ControlInitialis Head: 2522   Body: 2525
Calls   WriteTitle   EnterPolynomial
Called by   KnobsInitialise
cStateVariableFi Head: 1851   Body: 1876
Called by   StateVariableFil
CSTC   Head: 4   Body: 3967
Calls   PolZero   PolUnity   Chapter
RunInitialise   InitFilterKnobs STCInitialise
SimulationInitia EnterBoolean   Run
SystemInitialise DesignInitialise DesignEmulator
WriteDesign   WriteParameters EnterInteger
WriteLoopTitle
DeduceEandF   Head: 919   Body: 926
Calls   PolScalarMultipl PolZero   PolUnity
PolEquate   PolMultiply   PolAdd
Called by   PolEuclid
Delayed   Head: 2030   Body: 2036
Called by   DelayFilter   System
DelayFilter   Head: 2047   Body: 2064
Calls   Delayed   StateVariableFil StateOutput
Called by   Emulator   TuneLambdaEmulat
DesignEmulator   Head: 1336   Body: 1346
Calls   PolDelayEmulator PolMultiply   PolZero
Called by   KnobsInitialise SelfTuningContro CSTC
DesignInitialise Head: 2318   Body: 2325
Calls   PolZero   PolUnity   WriteTitle
EnterBoolean   EnterPolynomial EnterReal
SetDesignKnobs   EnterInteger
Called by   KnobsInitialise CSTC
DesignP   Head: 1126   Body: 1131
Calls   PolsDivide   PolSquare   PolWeightedAdd
PolSqrt   PolScalarMultipl
Called by   SetDesignKnobs
dStateVariableFi Head: 1931   Body: 1944
Called by   StateVariableFil
Emulator   Head: 2949   Body: 2966
Calls   DelayFilter   Filter
Called by   ImplicitSolution IdentifySystem   TuneLambdaEmulat
SelfTuningContro
EnterBoolean   Head: 1587   Body: 1608
Calls   GetSymbol   NameMatched   ReadBoolean
GetComment   PutComment   NewValue
Called by   tSystemInitialis DesignInitialise InitFilterKnobs
TunerInitialise   IdentifyInitiali PutDatInitialise
KnobsInitialise   STCInitialise   RunInitialise
NoMore   CSTC
EnterInteger   Head: 1540   Body: 1550
Calls   GetSymbol   NameMatched   GetComment
PutComment   NewValue
Called by   tSystemInitialis SystemInitialise DesignInitialise

InitFilterKnobs TunerInitialise   RunInitialise
     Chapter   CSTC
EnterPolynomial   Head: 1646 Body: 1685
    Calls   PolEquate   GetSymbol   NameMatched
     GetPolynomial   GetComment   PutComment
     NewValue   EnterPolynomial   PolMultiply
    Called by EnterPolynomial tSystemInitialis SystemInitialise
     DesignInitialise IdentifyInitiali ControlInitialis
     NoMore
EnterReal   Head: 1492 Body: 1502
    Calls   GetSymbol   NameMatched   GetComment
     PutComment   NewValue
    Called by SigGenInitialise tSystemInitialis SystemInitialise
     DesignInitialise InitFilterKnobs   TunerInitialise
     PutDatInitialise RunInitialise   NoMore
Even   Head: 658 Body: 660
    Called by PolSquare
Filter   Head: 2014 Body: 2020
    Calls   StateVariableFil StateOutput
    Called by System   Simulate   HighGainControl
     Emulator   ImplicitSolution Control
     TunePhiEmulator   TuneLambdaEmulat OneTimeStep
FilterInitialise Head: 1974 Body: 1983
    Called by tSystemInitialis ModelInitialise   InitEmulator
     StateInitialise Splice
FindEandF   Head: 1247 Body: 1249
    Calls   PolMultiply   PolDerivativeEmu PolZeroCancellin
    Called by PolEmulator
FindGCD   Head: 882 Body: 897
    Calls   PolDivide   PolNorm   PolEquate
    Called by PolEuclid
GetComment   Head: 1461 Body: 1464
    Calls   Skip
    Called by EnterReal   EnterInteger   EnterBoolean
     EnterPolynomial
GetData   Head: 2799 Body: 2871
    Calls   GetDataFromFile Simulate
    Called by OneTimeStep
GetDataFromFile Head: 2806 Body: 2811
    Called by GetData
GetPolynomial   Head: 1659 Body: 1666
    Calls   Skip
    Called by EnterPolynomial
GetSymbol   Head: 1406 Body: 1409
    Called by EnterReal   EnterInteger   EnterBoolean
     EnterPolynomial
HighGainControl Head: 2895 Body: 2901
    Calls   Filter
    Called by OneTimeStep
IdentifyInitiali Head: 2469 Body: 2478
    Calls   WriteTitle   TunerInitialise   EnterPolynomial
     PolScalarMultipl PolLineWrite   EnterBoolean
     PolEquate   PolMinus   PolRemove
    Called by KnobsInitialise
IdentifySystem   Head: 3275 Body: 3317
    Calls   Emulator   TimeFor   SetData
     SetDelayData   UpdateLeastSquar TuneEmulator
     TuneDelay   PolMinus   PolEquate

PolTruncate
Called by   SelfTuningContro
ImplicitSolution Head: 3004 Body: 3016
    Calls   Emulator   Filter
    Called by Control
InitEmulator   Head: 2629 Body: 2636
    Calls   FilterInitialise
    Called by StateInitialise
InitFilterKnobs Head: 2384 Body: 2387
    Calls   WriteTitle   EnterReal   EnterInteger
        EnterBoolean
    Called by CSTC
KnobsInitialise Head: 2407 Body: 2560
    Calls   SystemInitialise DesignInitialise DesignEmulator
        WriteDesign   WriteTitle   EnterBoolean
        IdentifyInitiali TuneEmInitialise ControlInitialis
        PutDatInitialise PolEquate
    Called by STCInitialise
ModelInitialise Head: 2232 Body: 2239
    Calls   ModelKnobsInitia PolEquate   FilterInitialise
        TimeDelayInitial
    Called by SimulationInitia
ModelKnobsInitia Head: 2211 Body: 2217
    Calls   PolUnitGain   PolMultiply   PolEquate
    Called by ModelInitialise
MultiLag   Head: 2766 Body: 2776
    Called by Simulate
NameMatched   Head: 1416 Body: 1422
    Calls   NameMatched
    Called by NameMatched   EnterReal   EnterInteger
        EnterBoolean   EnterPolynomial
NewValue   Head: 1441 Body: 1447
    Called by EnterReal   EnterInteger   EnterBoolean
        EnterPolynomial
NoMore   Head: 3777 Body: 3803
    Calls   EnterBoolean   EnterReal   WriteLoopTitle
        WriteTitle   EnterPolynomial PreventBump
    Called by Run
NormaliseGCD   Head: 956 Body: 961
    Calls   PolScalarMultipl
    Called by PolEuclid
OneTimeStep   Head: 3714 Body: 3716
    Calls   GetData   Filter   System
        HighGainControl PutData   SelfTuningContro
        WriteData
    Called by Run
PolAdd   Head: 469 Body: 477
    Called by DeduceEandF
PolDelayEmulator Head: 1291 Body: 1314
    Calls   PolPade   PolOfMinusS   PolMultiply
        PolEmulator
    Called by DesignEmulator
PolDerivativeEmu Head: 813 Body: 822
    Calls   PolZero   PolMultiply   PolEquate
        PolScalarMultipl PolMarkovRecursi PolWeightedAdd
    Called by PolDivide   PolInitialCondit FindEandF
PolDiophantine   Head: 1022 Body: 1045
    Calls   PolEuclid   PolEquate   PolScalarMultipl

              PolDioRecursion PolWeightedAdd
    Called by   PolZeroCancellin
PolDioRecursion Head: 981 Body: 997
    Calls   PolsMultiply   PolWeightedAdd   PolTruncate
    Called by   PolDiophantine
PolDivide   Head: 848 Body: 860
    Calls   PolUnity   PolDerivativeEmu
    Called by   FindGCD   PolInitialCondit PolEmulator
PolEmulator   Head: 1226 Body: 1263
    Calls   FindEandF   PolMultiply   PolDivide
              PolInitialCondit
    Called by   PolDelayEmulator
PolEquate   Head: 434 Body: 442
    Called by   PolDerivativeEmu FindGCD   DeduceEandF
              PolDiophantine SetDesignKnobs   EnterPolynomial
              tSystemInitialis ModelKnobsInitia ModelInitialise
              IdentifyInitiali KnobsInitialise IdentifySystem
PolEuclid   Head: 865 Body: 968
    Calls   FindGCD   DeduceEandF   PolTruncate
              NormaliseGCD
    Called by   PolDiophantine
PolGain   Head: 743 Body: 755
    Called by   PolUnitGain   SetDesignKnobs
PolInitialCondit Head: 1185 Body: 1201
    Calls   PolMultiply   PolDerivativeEmu PolZeroCancellin
              PolWeightedAdd PolDivide   PolTruncate
    Called by   PolEmulator
PolLineWrite   Head: 323 Body: 330
    Calls   PolWrite
    Called by   WriteParameters WriteDesign   SystemInitialise
              IdentifyInitiali
PolMarkovRecursi Head: 782 Body: 792
    Calls   PolsMultiply   PolWeightedAdd   PolRemove
    Called by   PolDerivativeEmu
PolMinus   Head: 504 Body: 512
    Called by   IdentifyInitiali IdentifySystem
PolMultiply   Head: 628 Body: 636
    Calls   PolZero
    Called by   PolDerivativeEmu DeduceEandF   PolZeroCancellin
              SetDesignKnobs PolInitialCondit FindEandF
              PolEmulator   PolDelayEmulator DesignEmulator
              EnterPolynomial ModelKnobsInitia
PolNorm   Head: 339 Body: 349
    Called by   FindGCD
PolNormalise   Head: 718 Body: 729
    Calls   PolScalarMultipl
    Called by   SystemInitialise
PolOfMinusS   Head: 450 Body: 458
    Called by   PolDelayEmulator
PolPade   Head: 1089 Body: 1100
    Called by   PolDelayEmulator
PolRemove   Head: 359 Body: 369
    Called by   PolTruncate   PolMarkovRecursi IdentifyInitiali
PolScalarMultipl Head: 577 Body: 586
    Called by   PolNormalise   PolUnitGain   PolDerivativeEmu
              DeduceEandF   NormaliseGCD   PolDiophantine
              DesignP   SetDesignKnobs   IdentifyInitiali
PolsDivide   Head: 610 Body: 621

Called by DesignP   SetDesignKnobs   tSystemInitialis
PolsMultiply   Head: 594 Body: 603
Called by PolMarkovRecursi PolDioRecursion SetDesignKnobs
            tSystemInitialis SystemInitialise SetDelayData
PolSqrt   Head: 685 Body: 691
Called by DesignP
PolSquare   Head: 647 Body: 664
Calls   PolZero   Even
Called by DesignP
PolTruncate   Head: 382 Body: 391
Calls   PolRemove
Called by PolEuclid   PolDioRecursion PolInitialCondit
            IdentifySystem
PolUnitGain   Head: 766 Body: 776
Calls   PolGain   PolScalarMultipl
Called by ModelKnobsInitia
PolUnity   Head: 417 Body: 425
Called by PolDivide   DeduceEandF   SetDesignKnobs
            SystemInitialise DesignInitialise STCInitialise
            SelfTuningContro CSTC
PolWeightedAdd   Head: 539 Body: 550
Called by PolMarkovRecursi PolDerivativeEmu PolDioRecursion
            PolDiophantine DesignP   PolInitialCondit
PolWrite   Head: 304 Body: 317
Called by PolLineWrite   WriteData
PolZero   Head: 403 Body: 412
Called by PolMultiply   PolSquare   PolDerivativeEmu
            DeduceEandF   DesignEmulator SystemInitialise
            DesignInitialise STCInitialise   CSTC
PolZeroCancellin Head: 1068 Body: 1083
Calls   PolMultiply   PolDiophantine
Called by PolInitialCondit FindEandF
PreventBump   Head: 3783 Body: 3792
Calls   StateOutput
Called by NoMore
PutComment   Head: 1477 Body: 1483
Called by EnterReal   EnterInteger   EnterBoolean
            EnterPolynomial
PutData   Head: 2876 Body: 2879
Called by SelfTuningContro OneTimeStep
PutDatInitialise Head: 2545 Body: 2548
Calls   EnterReal   EnterBoolean
Called by KnobsInitialise
ReadBoolean   Head: 1598 Body: 1600
Called by EnterBoolean
Run   Head: 3648 Body: 3856
Calls   TimeFor   Splice   OneTimeStep
            WriteLnData   NoMore
Called by CSTC
RunInitialise   Head: 3572 Body: 3577
Calls   WriteTitle   EnterBoolean   EnterReal
            EnterInteger
Called by CSTC
SelfTuningContro Head: 2917 Body: 3494
Calls   PolUnity   Control   PutData
            IdentifySystem SetDesignKnobs DesignEmulator
            TuneLambdaEmulat TunePhiEmulator Emulator
            StateVariableFil

```
    Called by  OneTimeStep
SetData         Head: 3068  Body: 3080
    Called by  IdentifySystem  TunePhiEmulator  TuneLambdaEmulat
SetDelayData    Head: 3299  Body: 3306
    Calls      PolsMultiply   StateOutput
    Called by  IdentifySystem
SetDesignKnobs  Head: 1118  Body: 1149
    Calls      PolUnity       PolEquate      PolsDivide
               PolsMultiply   PolGain        PolScalarMultipl
               PolMultiply    DesignP
    Called by  DesignInitialise  SelfTuningContro
SigGen          Head: 2719  Body: 2725
    Called by  Simulate
SigGenInitialise  Head: 2108  Body: 2111
    Calls      EnterReal
    Called by  SimulationInitia
Simulate        Head: 2827  Body: 2833
    Calls      SigGen         MultiLag       System
               Filter
    Called by  GetData
SimulationInitia  Head: 3611  Body: 3616
    Calls      WriteTitle     SigGenInitialise  tSystemInitialis
               ModelInitialise
    Called by  CSTC
Skip            Head: 1397  Body: 1402
    Called by  GetComment     GetPolynomial
Splice          Head: 3749  Body: 3754
    Calls      FilterInitialise
    Called by  Run
StateInitialise  Head: 2622  Body: 2654
    Calls      InitEmulator   FilterInitialise  TimeDelayInitia
    Called by  STCInitialise
StateOutput     Head: 1992  Body: 2001
    Called by  Filter         DelayFilter    SetDelayData
               PreventBump
StateVariableFil  Head: 1845  Body: 1962
    Calls      cStateVariableFi  dStateVariableFi
    Called by  Filter         DelayFilter    SelfTuningContro
STCInitialise   Head: 2400  Body: 2697
    Calls      PolZero        PolUnity       WriteTitle
               EnterBoolean   KnobsInitialise  StateInitialise
    Called by  CSTC
System          Head: 2744  Body: 2752
    Calls      Delayed        Filter
    Called by  Simulate       OneTimeStep
SystemInitialise  Head: 2255  Body: 2263
    Calls      PolZero        PolUnity       WriteTitle
               EnterPolynomial  PolNormalise    PolLineWrite
               EnterInteger   PolsMultiply    EnterReal
    Called by  KnobsInitialise  CSTC
TimeDelayInitial  Head: 2080  Body: 2087
    Called by  tSystemInitialis  ModelInitialise  StateInitialise
TimeFor         Head: 2096  Body: 2099
    Called by  IdentifySystem  TunePhiEmulator  TuneLambdaEmulat
               Run
tSystemInitialis  Head: 2125  Body: 2137
    Calls      PolEquate      PolsDivide     WriteTitle
               EnterPolynomial  EnterInteger    EnterReal
```

            EnterBoolean   PolsMultiply   FilterInitialise
            TimeDelayInitial
Called by   SimulationInitia
TuneDelay   Head: 3286 Body: 3290
Called by   IdentifySystem
TuneEmInitialise Head: 2459 Body: 2464
Calls   TunerInitialise
Called by   KnobsInitialise
TuneEmulator   Head: 3126 Body: 3137
Called by   IdentifySystem   TunePhiEmulator   TuneLambdaEmulat
TuneLambdaEmulat Head: 3415 Body: 3430
Calls   Filter   DelayFilter   Emulator
            TimeFor   SetData   UpdateLeastSquar
            TuneEmulator
Called by   SelfTuningContro
TunePhiEmulator   Head: 3378 Body: 3386
Calls   Filter   TimeFor   SetData
            UpdateLeastSquar TuneEmulator
Called by   SelfTuningContro
TunerInitialise   Head: 2414 Body: 2422
Calls   EnterReal   EnterBoolean   EnterInteger
Called by   TuneEmInitialise IdentifyInitiali
UpdateLeastSquar Head: 3182 Body: 3227
Calls   UTX
Called by   IdentifySystem   TunePhiEmulator   TuneLambdaEmulat
UTX   Head: 3193 Body: 3200
Called by   UpdateLeastSquar
WriteData   Head: 3655 Body: 3660
Calls   PolWrite
Called by   OneTimeStep
WriteDesign   Head: 1768 Body: 1775
Calls   WriteParameters PolLineWrite
Called by   KnobsInitialise CSTC
WriteLnData   Head: 3706 Body: 3708
Called by   Run
WriteLoopTitle   Head: 1376 Body: 1382
Calls   WriteTitle
Called by   NoMore   CSTC
WriteParameters   Head: 1741 Body: 1748
Calls   PolLineWrite
Called by   WriteDesign   CSTC
WriteTitle   Head: 1368 Body: 1370
Called by   WriteLoopTitle   tSystemInitialis SystemInitialise
            DesignInitialise InitFilterKnobs IdentifyInitiali
            ControlInitialis KnobsInitialise STCInitialise
            RunInitialise   SimulationInitia NoMore

11.3. THE PROGRAMME CODE

```
      1  {$double}  {Oregon Pascal-2 double precision switch}
      2  {[b+]}
      3
      4  PROGRAM CSTC(Input, Output, InLog, OutLog, InData, OutData,
      5  OutSysPar, OutEmPar);
      6
      7  {*****************************************************
c     8   NOTICE OF COPYRIGHT AND OWNERSHIP OF SOFTWARE:
c     9
c    10   Copyright (c) 1990 Research Studies Press Ltd.
c    11   All Rights Reserved.
c    12
c    13   This software is supplied in conjunction with the book:
c    14   "Continuous-Time Self-Tuning Control: Volume II - Implementation"
c    15   written by P.J. Gawthrop and published by:
c    16
c    17       Research Studies Press Ltd.,
c    18       24 Belvedere Road,
c    19       Taunton,
c    20       Somerset,
c    21       England. TA1 1HD
c    22
c    23   The software is provided for use only with this book and
c    24   the software, or any part or extension of it,
c    25   may not be used, marketed or distributed for profit.
c    26
c    27   Copies of the software may be made only for the purposes
c    28   of security or convenience of use and may not be made
c    29   for use dissociated from the copy of the book with
c    30   which is is supplied or for use other than simulation
c    31   of the algorithms described in the book.
c    32
c    33   DISCLAIMER. The software is supplied on the understanding
c    34   that there is NO warranty as to errors, mathematically
c    35   incorrect results or recompilation difficulties.
c    36
c    37   The author and Reseach Studies Press do not accept any
c    38   responsibility for errors, misstatements or omissions
c    39   that may or may not lead to damage or loss of property.
c    40
c    41   Whether this program is copied in whole or in part and
c    42   whether this program is copied in original or in modified
c    43   form, ALL COPIES OF THIS PROGRAM MUST DISPLAY THIS NOTICE
c    44   OF COPYRIGHT AND OWNERSHIP IN FULL.
c    45  *****************************************************}
     46
     47  CONST
     48     Version = 'Version 6.0';
     49
     50     TwoPi = 6.2831853;
     51
     52     MaxParameters = 10;
     53     MaxUFactor = 45;
     54     MaxDegree = 10;
     55     MaxState = 5;
     56     MaxDelay = 100;
```

```
57    MaxLags = 21;
58    MaxNumberInteractions = 2;
59    MaxLoops = 2;
60
61    LengthName = 25;
62    LengthComment = 100;
63    LengthTitle = 15;
64
65    fw = 12; {Output format for real numbers}
66    dp = 6;
67    ChangeSymbol = '#';
68    MultiplySymbol = '*';
69    Pretty = ' ======== ';
70    ProgressReports = 4;
71
72  TYPE
73    TypeName = PACKED ARRAY [1..LengthName] OF CHAR;
74    TypeTitle = PACKED ARRAY [1..LengthTitle] OF CHAR;
75
76    TypeComment =
77    RECORD
78      Str: PACKED ARRAY [1..LengthComment] OF CHAR;
79      Length: INTEGER;
80    END;
81
82    Degree = - 1..MaxDegree;
83
84    Polynomial =
85    RECORD
86      Deg: Degree;
87      Coeff: ARRAY [0..MaxDegree] OF REAL
88    END;
89
90    Vector = ARRAY [1..MaxParameters] OF REAL;
91
92    StateVector = ARRAY [0..MaxState] OF REAL;
93
94    TypeFilterKnobs =
95    RECORD
96      SampleInterval: REAL;
97      ApproximationOrder: INTEGER;
98      ContinuousTime: BOOLEAN;
99      ConstantBetweenSamples: BOOLEAN;
100   END;
101
102   TypeFilterState =
103   RECORD
104     State: StateVector;
105     Old: REAL;
106   END;
107
108   TypeDelayState =
109   RECORD
110     InPointer, OutPointer: 0..MaxDelay;
111     Buffer: ARRAY [0..MaxDelay] OF REAL;
112   END;
113
114   TypeLagState = ARRAY [0..MaxLags] OF REAL;
```

```
115
116    TypeInteraction = ARRAY
117       [1..MaxNumberInteractions] OF REAL;
118
119    InterPolynomial = ARRAY
120       [1..MaxNumberInteractions] OF Polynomial;
121
122    TypeIState = ARRAY
123       [1..MaxNumberInteractions] OF TypeFilterState;
124
125    TypeDesignKnobs =
126       RECORD
127          P, Z, ZPlus, ZMinus, ZMinusPlus, BMinus, BPlus,
128          C: Polynomial;
129          LQWeight: REAL;
130          LQ: BOOLEAN;
131       END;
132
133    TypeSystemKnobs =
134       RECORD
135          A, B, D: Polynomial;
136          NumberInteractions: INTEGER;
137          BInteraction: InterPolynomial;
138          Delay: REAL;
139          Lags: INTEGER;
140          LagTimeConstant: REAL;
141          Interactive: BOOLEAN;
142       END;
143
144    TypeSystemState =
145       RECORD
146          FilterState, ICState: TypeFilterState;
147          DelayState: TypeDelayState;
148          LagState: TypeLagState;
149       END;
150
151    TypeEmKnobs =
152       RECORD
153          F, G, FFilter, GFilter,
154          InitialCondition: Polynomial;
155          GInteraction: InterPolynomial;
156       END;
157
158    TypeEmState =
159       RECORD
160          uState, yState, ICState: TypeFilterState;
161          InterState, InterFState: TypeIState;
162          DelFiltState: TypeDelayState;
163       END;
164
165    TypeErrorPolynomials =
166       RECORD
167          E, ED: Polynomial;
168          EI: InterPolynomial;
169       END;
170
171    TypeControlKnobs =
172       RECORD
```

```
173      qNumerator, qDenominator: Polynomial;
174      rNumerator, rDenominator: Polynomial;
175   END;
176
177   TypeTunerKnobs =
178   RECORD
179      InitialVariance: REAL;
180      ForgetTime, ForgetFactor: REAL;
181      DeadBand: REAL;
182      On: BOOLEAN;
183      TuneInterval: INTEGER;
184   END;
185
186   TypeTunerState =
187   RECORD
188      TuningGain, Variance: ARRAY
189         [1..MaxParameters] OF REAL;
190      UFactor: ARRAY [1..MaxUFactor] OF REAL;
191      EstimationError, Sigma, Sigma1: REAL;
192      TuneCounter: INTEGER;
193   END;
194
195   TypeDataVector =
196   RECORD
197      NumberOfParameters: INTEGER;
198      Data: Vector;
199   END;
200
201   TypeSTCKnobs =
202   RECORD
203      IdentifyingSystem, IdentifyingRational,
204      IdentifyingDelay, SelfTuning, Explicit,
205      UsingLambda, TuningInitialConditions, ZHasFactorB,
206      IntegralAction, Auto: BOOLEAN;
207      DesignKnobs: TypeDesignKnobs;
208      TunerKnobs, IdentifyKnobs: TypeTunerKnobs;
209      ControlKnobs: TypeControlKnobs;
210      PadeOrder: INTEGER;
211      PadeDenominator, PadeNumerator: Polynomial;
212      GCDAZ: Polynomial;
213   END;
214
215   TypeSTCState =
216   RECORD
217      SystemKnobs: TypeSystemKnobs;
218      EmKnobs, SysEmKnobs: TypeEmKnobs;
219      ErrorPolynomials: TypeErrorPolynomials;
220      Phi, PhiHat: REAL;
221      EmState, LambdaEmState, SysEmState: TypeEmState;
222      qState, wState, PhicState, yLambdaState,
223         uLambdaState: TypeFilterState;
224      iLambdaState: TypeIState;
225      uDelayState, yDelayState: TypeDelayState;
226      TunerState, IdentState: TypeTunerState;
227   END;
228
229   TypeSigGenKnobs =
230   RECORD
```

```
231        StepAmplitude, SquareAmplitude, CosAmplitude,
232          Period: REAL;
233        END;
234
235        TypePutDataKnobs =
236        RECORD
237          Max, Min: REAL;
238          Switched: BOOLEAN;
239        END;
240
241        TypeLoopVAR =
242        RECORD
243          ThisLoop: INTEGER;
244          UsingHighGainControl: BOOLEAN;
245
246          SetPointKnobs, InDisturbKnobs,
247          OutDisturbKnobs: TypeSigGenKnobs;
248
249          tSystemKnobs, ModelKnobs: TypeSystemKnobs;
250          PutDataKnobs: TypePutDataKnobs;
251
252          STCKnobs: TypeSTCKnobs;
253          STCState: TypeSTCState;
254
255          tSystemState, ModelState: TypeSystemState;
256          InteractionState: ARRAY
257            [1..MaxLoops] OF TypeFilterState;
258
259          y, y0, u, w, wf, InDist, OutDist: REAL;
260          Interaction: TypeInteraction;
261
262        END {LoopVAR} ;
263
264        TypeRunKnobs =
265        RECORD
266          PrintInterval: INTEGER;
267          LastTime, ExtraTime: REAL;
268          Loops: INTEGER;
269          ExternalData: BOOLEAN;
270          Cascade, OutputCoupled: BOOLEAN;
271          CorrectSystem: BOOLEAN;
272        END;
273
274        LoopVARs = ARRAY [1..MaxLoops] OF TypeLoopVAR;
275
276    VAR
277        All: BOOLEAN;
278        InLog,
279        OutLog {Input and output entry parameters} : TEXT;
280        InData {Input data} : TEXT;
281        OutData {Output data} : TEXT;
282        OutEmPar,
283        OutSysPar {The parameter estimates etc.} : TEXT;
284
285        Small: REAL;
286        Zero, One: Polynomial;
287
288        Time: REAL;
```

```
289     PrintCounter: INTEGER;
290     PrintNow: BOOLEAN;
291
292     RunKnobs: TypeRunKnobs;
293
294     FilterKnobs: TypeFilterKnobs;
295
296     Loop: INTEGER;
297     LoopVAR: LoopVARs;
298     LoopInteraction: TypeInteraction;
299
300     {-------------------------------------------------}
301     {--     Polynomial output procedures        --}
302     {-------------------------------------------------}
303
304     PROCEDURE PolWrite(VAR ListFile: TEXT;
305                        Pol: Polynomial);
306
307 {--     Writes polynomial Pol to ListFile
c   308 --}
309
310     CONST
311       fw = 12;
312       dp = 6;
313
314     VAR
315       i: Degree;
316
317     BEGIN
318       WITH Pol DO
319         FOR i := 0 TO Deg DO
320           Write(ListFile, ' ', Coeff[i]: fw: dp);
321     END;
322
323     PROCEDURE PolLineWrite(VAR ListFile: TEXT;
324                        Pol: Polynomial);
325
326 {--     Writes polynomial Pol to ListFile -
c   327         and appends WriteLn
c   328 --}
329
330     BEGIN
331       PolWrite(ListFile, Pol);
332       WriteLn(ListFile);
333     END;
334
335     {-------------------------------------------------}
336     {--     Polynomial manipulation procedures    --}
337     {-------------------------------------------------}
338
339     FUNCTION PolNorm(Pol: Polynomial): REAL;
340
341 {--     Finds the maximum  absolute value of the
c   342         coefficients ofthe polynomial Pol
c   343 --}
344
345     VAR
346       i: INTEGER;
```

```
347        Max: REAL;
348
349        BEGIN {PolNorm}
350          Max := 0.0;
351
352          WITH Pol DO
353            FOR i := 0 TO Deg DO
354              IF Abs(Coeff[i]) > Max THEN Max := Abs(Coeff[i]);
355
356          PolNorm := Max;
357        END {PolNorm} ;
358
359      PROCEDURE PolRemove(VAR A: Polynomial;
360                          N: INTEGER);
361
362    {-- Removes N leading coefficients from
c  363        polynomial A
c  364    --}
365
366        VAR
367          i: INTEGER;
368
369        BEGIN {PolRemove}
370
371          WITH A DO
372            BEGIN
373
374              A.Deg := A.Deg - N;
375
376              IF N > 0 THEN
377                FOR i := 0 TO Deg DO Coeff[i] := Coeff[i + N];
378
379            END;
380        END {PolRemove} ;
381
382      PROCEDURE PolTruncate(VAR A: Polynomial);
383
384    {-- Removes leading coefficients from
c  385        polynomial A with value <= Small
c  386    --}
387
388        VAR
389          N: INTEGER;
390
391        BEGIN {PolTruncate}
392
393          WITH A DO
394            BEGIN
395              N := 0;
396              WHILE (N <= Deg) AND (Abs(Coeff[N]) <= Small) DO
397                N := N + 1;
398
399              PolRemove(A, N);
400            END;
401        END {PolTruncate} ;
402
403      PROCEDURE PolZero(VAR Result: Polynomial;
404                        Deg: Degree);
```

```
     405
     406    { Sets result to zero polynomial
c    407       of specifed degree }
     408
     409    VAR
     410      i: INTEGER;
     411
     412    BEGIN
     413      Result.Deg := Deg;
     414      WITH Result DO FOR i := 0 TO Deg DO Coeff[i] := 0.0;
     415    END;
     416
     417    PROCEDURE PolUnity(VAR Result: Polynomial;
     418                       Deg: Degree);
     419
     420    { Sets Result to unit polynomial of specified degree }
     421
     422    VAR
     423      i: INTEGER;
     424
     425    BEGIN
     426
     427      Result.Deg := Deg;
     428      WITH Result DO
     429        FOR i := 0 TO Deg - 1 DO Coeff[i] := 0.0;
     430      Result.Coeff[Deg] := 1.0;
     431
     432    END;
     433
     434    PROCEDURE PolEquate(VAR Result: Polynomial;
     435                        Pol: Polynomial);
     436
     437    { Result := Pol }
     438
     439    VAR
     440      i: Degree;
     441
     442    BEGIN
     443
     444      Result.Deg := Pol.Deg;
     445      FOR i := 0 TO Result.Deg DO
     446        Result.Coeff[i] := Pol.Coeff[i];
     447
     448    END;
     449
     450    PROCEDURE PolOfMinusS(VAR Result: Polynomial;
     451                          Pol: Polynomial);
     452
     453    { Result(s) := Pol(-s) }
     454
     455    VAR
     456      Minus, i: INTEGER;
     457
     458    BEGIN
     459      Result.Deg := Pol.Deg;
     460      Minus := - 1;
     461
     462      FOR i := Result.Deg DOWNTO 0 DO
```

```
463       BEGIN
464         Minus := - 1 * Minus;
465         Result.Coeff[i] := Minus * Pol.Coeff[i];
466       END;
467     END;
468
469     PROCEDURE PolAdd(VAR Result: Polynomial;
470                     A, B: Polynomial);
471
472     {Result := A + B}
473
474     VAR
475       i, Shift: Degree;
476
477     BEGIN {PolAdd}
478       IF A.Deg > B.Deg THEN Result.Deg := A.Deg
479       ELSE Result.Deg := B.Deg;
480
481       IF A.Deg > B.Deg THEN
482         BEGIN
483         Shift := A.Deg - B.Deg;
484         FOR i := 0 TO Result.Deg DO
485           IF i - Shift < 0 THEN
486             Result.Coeff[i] := A.Coeff[i]
487           ELSE
488             Result.Coeff[i] := A.Coeff[i] + B.Coeff[i -
489                               Shift];
490         END
491       ELSE
492         BEGIN
493         Shift := B.Deg - A.Deg;
494         FOR i := 0 TO Result.Deg DO
495           IF i - Shift < 0 THEN
496             Result.Coeff[i] := B.Coeff[i]
497           ELSE
498             Result.Coeff[i] := B.Coeff[i] + A.Coeff[i -
499                               Shift];
500         END;
501
502     END {PolAdd} ;
503
504     PROCEDURE PolMinus(VAR Result: Polynomial;
505                       A, B: Polynomial);
506
507     {Result := A - B}
508
509     VAR
510       i, Shift: Degree;
511
512     BEGIN {PolMinus}
513       IF A.Deg > B.Deg THEN Result.Deg := A.Deg
514       ELSE Result.Deg := B.Deg;
515
516       IF A.Deg > B.Deg THEN
517         BEGIN
518         Shift := A.Deg - B.Deg;
519         FOR i := 0 TO Result.Deg DO
520           IF i - Shift < 0 THEN
```

```
521        Result.Coeff[i] := A.Coeff[i]
522      ELSE
523        Result.Coeff[i] := A.Coeff[i] - B.Coeff[i -
524                Shift];
525      END
526    ELSE
527    BEGIN
528      Shift := B.Deg - A.Deg;
529      FOR i := 0 TO Result.Deg DO
530        IF i - Shift < 0 THEN
531          Result.Coeff[i] := - B.Coeff[i]
532        ELSE
533          Result.Coeff[i] := - B.Coeff[i] + A.Coeff[i -
534                Shift];
535      END;
536
537    END {PolMinus} ;
538
539    PROCEDURE PolWeightedAdd(VAR Result: Polynomial;
540                            u: REAL;
541                            A: Polynomial;
542                            v: REAL;
543                            B: Polynomial);
544
545    {Result := uA + vB}
546
547    VAR
548      i, Shift: Degree;
549
550    BEGIN {PolWeightedAdd}
551      IF A.Deg > B.Deg THEN Result.Deg := A.Deg
552      ELSE Result.Deg := B.Deg;
553
554      IF A.Deg > B.Deg THEN
555      BEGIN
556        Shift := A.Deg - B.Deg;
557        FOR i := 0 TO Result.Deg DO
558          IF i - Shift < 0 THEN
559            Result.Coeff[i] := u * A.Coeff[i]
560          ELSE
561            Result.Coeff[i] := u * A.Coeff[i] + v *
562                  B.Coeff[i - Shift];
563      END
564      ELSE
565      BEGIN
566        Shift := B.Deg - A.Deg;
567        FOR i := 0 TO Result.Deg DO
568          IF i - Shift < 0 THEN
569            Result.Coeff[i] := v * B.Coeff[i]
570          ELSE
571            Result.Coeff[i] := v * B.Coeff[i] + u *
572                  A.Coeff[i - Shift];
573      END;
574
575    END {PolWeightedAdd} ;
576
577    PROCEDURE PolScalarMultiply(VAR Result: Polynomial;
578                               A: REAL;
```

```
579                        B: Polynomial);
580
581     { Computes Result = a*B , a real}
582
583     VAR
584        i: INTEGER;
585
586     BEGIN
587
588        FOR i := 0 TO B.Deg DO
589           Result.Coeff[i] := A * B.Coeff[i];
590
591        Result.Deg := B.Deg;
592     END;
593
594  PROCEDURE PolsMultiply(VAR sA: Polynomial;
595                         A: Polynomial);
596
597  {-- Multiplies A by s to give sA
c 598  --}
599
600     VAR
601        i: INTEGER;
602
603     BEGIN {PolsMultiply}
604        FOR i := 0 TO A.Deg DO sA.Coeff[i] := A.Coeff[i];
605
606        sA.Deg := A.Deg + 1;
607        sA.Coeff[sA.Deg] := 0.0;
608     END {PolsMultiply} ;
609
610  PROCEDURE PolsDivide(VAR A: Polynomial;
611                       sA: Polynomial);
612
613  {-- Divides  sA by s to give A.
c 614  sA is assumed to have a zero coefficient
c 615  in the appropriate place.
c 616  --}
617
618     VAR
619        i: INTEGER;
620
621     BEGIN {PolsDivide}
622        A.Deg := sA.Deg - 1;
623
624        FOR i := 0 TO A.Deg DO A.Coeff[i] := sA.Coeff[i];
625
626     END {PolsDivide} ;
627
628  PROCEDURE PolMultiply(VAR Result: Polynomial;
629                        A, B: Polynomial);
630
631     { Computes Result = A*B }
632
633     VAR
634        i, j: INTEGER;
635
636     BEGIN
```

```
637      PolZero(Result, A.Deg + B.Deg);
638
639      WITH Result DO
640        FOR i := 0 TO A.Deg DO
641          FOR j := 0 TO B.Deg DO
642            Coeff[i + j] := Coeff[i + j] + A.Coeff[i] *
643                        B.Coeff[j];
644
645      END;
646
647  PROCEDURE PolSquare(VAR S: Polynomial;
648                    A: Polynomial);
649
650      { Computes S(s^2) = A(s)A(-s)
c   651
c   652      I.e. the coefficients of S are the even index
c   653      coefficients  of A(s)A(-s) }
654
655      VAR
656        i, j, ij, Minus: INTEGER;
657
658      FUNCTION Even(i: INTEGER): BOOLEAN;
659
660      BEGIN {Even}
661        Even := (i MOD 2) = 0;
662      END {Even} ;
663
664      BEGIN {PolSquare}
665      PolZero(S, A.Deg);
666
667      WITH S DO
668        FOR i := A.Deg DOWNTO 0 DO
669          BEGIN
670          Minus := - 1;
671          FOR j := A.Deg DOWNTO 0 DO
672            BEGIN
673            Minus := - Minus;
674            IF Even(i + j) THEN
675              BEGIN
676              ij := (i + j) DIV 2;
677              Coeff[ij] := Coeff[ij] + Minus * A.Coeff[i] *
678                        A.Coeff[j];
679              END;
680            END;
681          END;
682
683      END {PolSquare} ;
684
685  PROCEDURE PolSqrt(VAR A: Polynomial;
686                    S: Polynomial);
687
688  { Computes A(s) where A is stable and A(s)A(-s) = S(s^2)
c   689      Only programmed for degree of A two or less}
690
691      BEGIN {PolSqrt}
692      A.Deg := S.Deg;
693
694      WITH A DO
```

```
695        IF Deg > 2 THEN
696          WriteLn(
697            '*** PolSqrt defined only for degrees up to 2'
698            )
699        ELSE
700          CASE Deg OF
701            0: Coeff[0] := Sqrt(S.Coeff[0]);
702            1:
703              BEGIN
704              Coeff[0] := Sqrt( - S.Coeff[0]);
705              Coeff[1] := Sqrt(S.Coeff[1]);
706              END;
707            2:
708              BEGIN
709              Coeff[0] := Sqrt(S.Coeff[0]);
710              Coeff[2] := Sqrt(S.Coeff[2]);
711              Coeff[1] := Sqrt(Sqr(S.Coeff[1]) + 2 *
712                         Coeff[0] * Coeff[2]);
713              END;
714          END {CASE} ;
715
716      END {PolSqrt} ;
717
718    PROCEDURE PolNormalise(VAR A, B: Polynomial;
719                           i: INTEGER);
720    {-- Normalises both polynomials with respect
c  721      to ith coefficient of A.
c  722      If i> Deg(A) or ith coefficient of A is zero
c  723      then nothing is done.
c  724    --}
725
726      VAR
727        ai: REAL;
728
729      BEGIN {PolNormalise}
730
731        IF (i <= A.Deg) AND (i >= 0) THEN
732          BEGIN
733          ai := A.Coeff[i];
734
735          IF Abs(ai) > Small THEN
736            BEGIN
737            PolScalarMultiply(A, 1.0 / ai, A);
738            PolScalarMultiply(B, 1.0 / ai, B);
739            END;
740          END;
741      END {PolNormalise} ;
742
743    FUNCTION PolGain(VAR A: Polynomial;
744                    ContinuousTime: BOOLEAN): REAL;
745
746    {-- Finds steady state gain of polynomial:
c  747      A(0) in continuous time
c  748      A(1) in discrete-time
c  749    --}
750
751      VAR
752        Gain: REAL;
```

```
753     i: INTEGER;
754
755     BEGIN {PolGain}
756       WITH A DO
757       BEGIN
758         Gain := Coeff[Deg];
759         IF NOT ContinuousTime THEN
760           FOR i := Deg - 1 DOWNTO 0 DO
761             Gain := Gain + Coeff[i];
762         END;
763         PolGain := Gain;
764       END {PolGain} ;
765
766     PROCEDURE PolUnitGain(VAR A: Polynomial;
767                           ContinuousTime: BOOLEAN);
768
769     {-- Normalises polynomial A(s) such that A(0) = 1
770       But nothing is done if A(0)<Small initially.
771     --}
772
773     VAR
774       Gain: REAL;
775
776     BEGIN {PolUnitGain}
777       Gain := PolGain(A, ContinuousTime);
778       IF Abs(Gain) > Small THEN
779         PolScalarMultiply(A, 1.0 / Gain, A);
780     END {PolUnitGain} ;
781
782     PROCEDURE PolMarkovRecursion(VAR MarkovParameter: REAL;
783                           VAR E, F: Polynomial;
784                           A: Polynomial);
785     { Given polynomials A, E and F satisfying:
786       s^i/A = E + F/A
787     computes the new polynomials E and F satisfying
788       s^(i+1)/A = E + F/A
789     together with the (scalar) i+1th Markov
790     parameter of 1/A }
791
792     BEGIN { PolMarkovRecursion }
793
794       IF F.Deg < A.Deg - 1 THEN
795         BEGIN
796         MarkovParameter := 0.0;
797         PolsMultiply(F, F);
798         END
799       ELSE
800         BEGIN
801         MarkovParameter := F.Coeff[0] / A.Coeff[0]; { (2a) }
802
803         PolsMultiply(E, E); { (2b) }
804         WITH E DO Coeff[Deg] := MarkovParameter;
805
806         PolsMultiply(F, F); { (2c) }
807         PolWeightedAdd(F, 1.0, F, - MarkovParameter, A);
808         PolRemove(F, 1); {Highest coeff should be zero}
809         END
810
```

Line markers in left margin:
c 770
c 771
c 786
c 787
c 788
c 789
c 790

```
811    END { PolMarkovRecursion } ;
812
813    PROCEDURE PolDerivativeEmulator
814        (VAR E, F: Polynomial;
815         P, C, A: Polynomial);
816
817    VAR
818        i: INTEGER;
819        hk: REAL;
820        Ek, Fk: Polynomial;
821
822    BEGIN {PolDerivativeEmulator}
823        IF A.Deg = 0 THEN
824          BEGIN
825          PolZero(F, - 1);
826          PolMultiply(E, P, C);
827          END
828        ELSE
829          BEGIN
830          PolZero(Ek, - 1);
831          PolEquate(Fk, C);
832
833          PolEquate(E, Ek);
834          PolEquate(F, Fk);
835          PolScalarMultiply(F, P.Coeff[P.Deg], F);
836
837          WITH P DO
838            FOR i := 1 TO Deg DO
839              BEGIN
840              PolMarkovRecursion(hk, Ek, Fk, A);
841              PolWeightedAdd(E, 1.0, E, Coeff[Deg - i], Ek);
842              PolWeightedAdd(F, 1.0, F, Coeff[Deg - i], Fk);
843              END;
844          END;
845
846    END {PolDerivativeEmulator} ;
847
848    PROCEDURE PolDivide(VAR E, F: Polynomial;
849                        B, A: Polynomial);
850
851    VAR
852        One: Polynomial;
853
854    {--  Computes quotient E and remainder F
855         when B is divided by A:
856
857         B = E*A + F
858    --}
859
860    BEGIN {PolDivide}
861        PolUnity(One, 0);
862        PolDerivativeEmulator(E, F, B, One, A);
863    END {PolDivide} ;
864
865    PROCEDURE PolEuclid(VAR GCD, E, F: Polynomial;
866                        A, B: Polynomial);
867
868    {-- Given a(s) and b(s), finds GCD of a(s) and b(s)
```

```
c   869     and solves for E and F in:
c   870
c   871         Ea + Fb = GCD
c   872
c   873     Small is a small positive number to
c   874     determine termination of Euclids algorithm
c   875
c   876 --}
    877
    878     VAR
    879         Quotient: ARRAY [1..MaxDegree] OF Polynomial;
    880         N: INTEGER;
    881
    882     PROCEDURE FindGCD(AlphaIminus1 {A} ,
    883                       AlphaI {B} : Polynomial);
    884
    885     {Finds the Greates Common Divisor of A and B, together
c   886     with the corresponding quotients E and F,
c   887     using Euclid's algorithm.
c   888     Note that the algorithm terminates when the largest
c   889     absolute value of the coefficients of the remainder
c   890     is < Small;ideally, the remainder should be exactly
c   891     zero}
    892
    893     VAR
    894         i: INTEGER;
    895         Remainder: Polynomial;
    896
    897     BEGIN {FindGCD}
    898         i := 0;
    899
    900         REPEAT
    901             i := i + 1;
    902
    903             PolDivide(Quotient[i], Remainder, AlphaIminus1,
    904                     AlphaI); {I-2.4.5}
    905
    906             IF NOT (PolNorm(Remainder) <= Small) THEN
    907                 BEGIN
    908                 PolEquate(AlphaIminus1, AlphaI);
    909                 PolEquate(AlphaI, Remainder); {I-2.4.6}
    910                 END;
    911
    912         UNTIL PolNorm(Remainder) <= Small;
    913
    914         PolEquate(GCD, AlphaI);
    915         N := i - 1;
    916
    917     END {FindGCD} ;
    918
    919     PROCEDURE DeduceEandF(VAR Beta {F} ,
    920                           Gamma {E} : Polynomial);
    921
    922     VAR
    923         i: INTEGER;
    924         BetaQ, OldBeta: Polynomial;
    925
    926     BEGIN {DeduceEandF}
```

```
927  {--
928          Multiply quotients by -1
929  --}
930          FOR i := 1 TO N DO
931            PolScalarMultiply(Quotient[i], - 1.0,
932                         Quotient[i]);
933
934          IF N < 1 THEN
935            BEGIN
936            PolZero(Beta, - 1);
937            PolUnity(Gamma, 0);
938            Gamma.Coeff[0] := 1.0 / A.Coeff[0];
939            END
940          ELSE
941            BEGIN
942            PolEquate(Beta, Quotient[N]); {beta n = -q n}
943            PolUnity(Gamma, 0); {gamma n = 1}
944            END;
945
946          FOR i := N - 1 DOWNTO 1 DO
947            BEGIN {I-2.4.12}
948            PolEquate(OldBeta, Beta);
949            PolMultiply(BetaQ, Beta, Quotient[i]);
950            PolAdd(Beta, Gamma, BetaQ);
951            PolEquate(Gamma, OldBeta);
952            END;
953
954          END {DeduceEandF} ;
955
956    PROCEDURE NormaliseGCD;
957
958          VAR
959          GCD0: REAL;
960
961          BEGIN {NormaliseGCD}
962          GCD0 := GCD.Coeff[0];
963          PolScalarMultiply(E, 1 / GCD0, E);
964          PolScalarMultiply(F, 1 / GCD0, F);
965          PolScalarMultiply(GCD, 1 / GCD0, GCD);
966          END {NormaliseGCD} ;
967
968    BEGIN {PolEuclid}
969
970          FindGCD(A, B);
971          DeduceEandF(F, E);
972
973  {--    Tidy up
974  --}
975          PolTruncate(E);
976          PolTruncate(F);
977          NormaliseGCD;
978
979    END {PolEuclid} ;
980
981    PROCEDURE PolDioRecursion(VAR E, F: Polynomial;
982                         A, B: Polynomial);
983
984  {-- Diophantine recursion algorithm.
```

```
c  985
c  986    Given E and F solving
c  987       EA + FB = s^k
c  988    this algorithm finds new values of E and F solving
c  989       EA + FB = s^(k+1)
c  990
c  991    The solution is such that F/A is strictly proper
c  992 --}
   993
   994    VAR
   995       MarkovParameter: REAL;
   996
   997    BEGIN { PolDioRecursion }
   998
   999       IF F.Deg < A.Deg - 1 THEN
  1000         BEGIN
  1001         MarkovParameter := 0.0;
  1002         PolsMultiply(E, E);
  1003         PolsMultiply(F, F);
  1004         END
  1005       ELSE
  1006         BEGIN
  1007         MarkovParameter := F.Coeff[0] / A.Coeff[0];
  1008
  1009         PolsMultiply(E, E);
  1010         PolWeightedAdd(E, 1.0, E, MarkovParameter, B);
  1011
  1012         PolsMultiply(F, F);
  1013         PolWeightedAdd(F, 1.0, F, - MarkovParameter, A);
  1014         PolTruncate(F);
  1015         END;
  1016
  1017         PolTruncate(E); {Just in case the order is less than
c 1018                usual}
  1019
  1020    END { PolDioRecursion } ;
  1021
  1022    PROCEDURE PolDiophantine(VAR E, F: Polynomial;
  1023                             VAR GCD: Polynomial;
  1024                             A, B, PC: Polynomial);
  1025
  1026 {-- This procedure gives the controller
c 1027    polynomials E and F
c 1028    for pole placement:
c 1029
c 1030       PC = EA + FB
c 1031
c 1032    A is the open-loop system denominator polynomial
c 1033    B is the open-loop system numerator polynomial
c 1034    PC is the closed-loop system denominator polynomial
c 1035
c 1036       Observer :   phi* = E/C u + F/C y
c 1037
c 1038       Control law: phi* = w
c 1039 --}
  1040
  1041    VAR
  1042       Ek, Fk, E0, F0: Polynomial;
```

```
1043       i: INTEGER;
1044
1045       BEGIN {PolDiophantine}
1046
1047          PolEuclid(GCD, E0, F0, A, B);
1048          PolEquate(E, E0);
1049          PolEquate(F, F0);
1050
1051          WITH PC DO
1052             BEGIN
1053             PolEquate(Ek, E);
1054             PolEquate(Fk, F);
1055             PolScalarMultiply(E, Coeff[Deg], E);
1056             PolScalarMultiply(F, Coeff[Deg], F);
1057
1058             FOR i := 1 TO Deg DO
1059                BEGIN
1060                PolDioRecursion(Ek, Fk, A, B);
1061                PolWeightedAdd(E, 1.0, E, Coeff[Deg - i], Ek);
1062                PolWeightedAdd(F, 1.0, F, Coeff[Deg - i], Fk);
1063                END;
1064             END {WITH PC} ;
1065
1066       END {PolDiophantine} ;
1067
1068    PROCEDURE PolZeroCancellingEmulator
1069          (VAR E, F: Polynomial;
1070          P, C, A: Polynomial;
1071          ZMinus, ZPlus: Polynomial;
1072          VAR GCDAZ: Polynomial {GCD of A and Z-} );
1073
1074    {-- Given open loop system
1075           y = B(s)/A(s) u + C(s)/A(s) v
1076       finds emulator polynomials for
1077           phi = P(s)/(Zplus.Zminus) y
1078    --}
1079
1080       VAR
1081          AZPlus, PC: Polynomial;
1082
1083       BEGIN {PolZeroCancellingEmulator}
1084          PolMultiply(AZPlus, A, ZPlus);
1085          PolMultiply(PC, P, C);
1086          PolDiophantine(E, F, GCDAZ, AZPlus, ZMinus, PC);
1087       END {PolZeroCancellingEmulator} ;
1088
1089    PROCEDURE PolPade(VAR Pade: Polynomial;
1090                   Deg: INTEGER;
1091                   Delay: REAL);
1092
1093    {--      Pade is nth degree Denominator of Pade
1094           approximation to delay
1095    --}
1096
1097       VAR
1098          i: INTEGER;
1099
1100       BEGIN {PolPade}
```

```
1101      Pade.Deg := Deg;
1102
1103      WITH Pade DO
1104        BEGIN
1105        Coeff[Deg] := 1.0;
1106        FOR i := 1 TO Deg DO
1107          Coeff[Deg - i] := Delay / i * (Deg - i + 1) / (2 *
1108                            Deg - i + 1) * Coeff[Deg - i +
1109                            1];
1110        END;
1111
1112      END {PolPade} ;
1113
1114      {-------------------------------------------------}
1115      {--    Emulator design for self-tuning        --}
1116      {-------------------------------------------------}
1117
1118      PROCEDURE SetDesignKnobs(VAR DesignKnobs: TypeDesignKnobs;
1119                    A, B: Polynomial;
1120                    ZeroAtOrigin, ZHasFactorB,
1121                    ContinuousTime: BOOLEAN);
1122
1123      VAR
1124        Gain: REAL;
1125
1126      PROCEDURE DesignP(A, B: Polynomial);
1127
1128        VAR
1129        AA, BB, PP: Polynomial;
1130
1131        BEGIN {DesignP}
1132          WITH DesignKnobs DO
1133            BEGIN
1134            IF ZeroAtOrigin THEN
1135              BEGIN
1136              PolsDivide(A, A);
1137              PolsDivide(B, B);
1138              END;
1139
1140            PolSquare(AA, A);
1141            PolSquare(BB, B);
1142            PolWeightedAdd(PP, 1.0, BB, LQWeight, AA);
1143            PolSqrt(P, PP);
1144
1145            PolScalarMultiply(P, 1 / P.Coeff[P.Deg], P);
1146            END;
1147          END {DesignP} ;
1148
1149        BEGIN {SetDesignKnobs}
1150          WITH DesignKnobs DO
1151            BEGIN
1152
1153            IF NOT ZHasFactorB THEN
1154              BEGIN {Set B+=B; B- = 1}
1155              PolUnity(BMinus, 0);
1156              PolEquate(BPlus, B);
1157              END
1158            ELSE {Set B- = B without s term; B+ = rest}
```

```
1159        BEGIN
1160        PolUnity(BPlus, 0);
1161        IF ZeroAtOrigin THEN
1162          BEGIN
1163          PolsDivide(BMinus, B);
1164          PolsMultiply(BPlus, BPlus);
1165          END
1166        ELSE
1167          BEGIN
1168          PolEquate(BMinus, B);
1169          END;
1170
1171        { Normalise B-, and adjust B+ }
1172        Gain := PolGain(BMinus, ContinuousTime);
1173        PolScalarMultiply(BPlus, Gain, BPlus);
1174        PolScalarMultiply(BMinus, 1.0 / Gain, BMinus);
1175        END;
1176
1177        PolMultiply(ZMinus, BMinus, ZMinusPlus);
1178        PolMultiply(Z, ZMinus, ZPlus);
1179
1180        IF LQ THEN DesignP(A, B);
1181
1182          END {WITH DesignKnobs} ;
1183        END {SetDesignKnobs} ;
1184
1185    PROCEDURE PolInitialConditions
1186        (VAR InitialCondition, ED: Polynomial;
1187        A, D, E: Polynomial;
1188        DesignKnobs: TypeDesignKnobs);
1189
1190 {--    Computes the initial condition for an emulator
c 1191         given the initial condition D of the system B/A.
c 1192
c 1193         ED is the unrealisable part of the
c 1194         initial condition
c 1195 --}
1196
1197    VAR
1198        Rem, AZPlusPlus, ZPlusPlus, FD, EDD, EDC,
1199        GCDAZ: Polynomial;
1200
1201    BEGIN {PolInitialConditions}
1202      WITH DesignKnobs DO
1203        BEGIN
1204        PolMultiply(ZPlusPlus, ZPlus, ZMinusPlus);
1205
1206        IF BMinus.Deg = 0 THEN
1207          BEGIN
1208          PolMultiply(AZPlusPlus, A, ZPlusPlus);
1209          PolDerivativeEmulator(ED, FD, P, D, AZPlusPlus);
1210          END
1211        ELSE
1212          PolZeroCancellingEmulator(ED, FD, P, D, A, BMinus,
1213                              ZPlusPlus, GCDAZ);
1214
1215        PolMultiply(EDD, E, D);
1216        PolMultiply(EDC, ED, C);
```

```
1217        PolWeightedAdd(InitialCondition, 1.0, EDD, - 1.0,
1218            EDC);
1219
1220        PolDivide(InitialCondition, Rem, InitialCondition,
1221            BMinus);
1222        PolTruncate(InitialCondition);
1223      END;
1224    END; {PolInitialConditions}
1225
1226  PROCEDURE PolEmulator(VAR F, G, InitialCondition,
1227    {Emulator numerators}
1228                    FFilter, GFilter {Emulator
1229                         denominators}
1230                    : Polynomial;
1231                    VAR E, ED: {error} Polynomial;
1232                    VAR GCDAZ: Polynomial {GCD of A and
1233                    Z-} ;
1234                    A: Polynomial {System denominator} ;
1235                    D: Polynomial {Initial condition} ;
1236                    DesignKnobs: TypeDesignKnobs);
1237
1238  {-- Given open loop system
1239        y = B(s)/A(s) u + C(s)/A(s) v
1240      finds emulator polynomials for
1241        phi = P(s)/(Zplus.Zminus) y
1242  --}
1243
1244    VAR
1245      Junk, AZPlus: Polynomial;
1246
1247    PROCEDURE FindEandF;
1248
1249      BEGIN {FindEandF}
1250        WITH DesignKnobs DO
1251          IF ZMinus.Deg = 0 THEN
1252            BEGIN
1253            PolMultiply(AZPlus, A, ZPlus);
1254            PolDerivativeEmulator(E, F, P, C, AZPlus);
1255            END
1256          ELSE
1257            BEGIN
1258            PolZeroCancellingEmulator(E, F, P, C, A, ZMinus,
1259                           ZPlus, GCDAZ);
1260            END;
1261      END {FindEandF} ;
1262
1263    BEGIN {PolEmulator}
1264      WITH DesignKnobs DO
1265        BEGIN
1266        FindEandF;
1267
1268        IF GCDAZ.Deg > 0 THEN {Move factor from Z- to Z+,
1269                      and try again}
1270          BEGIN
1271          PolMultiply(ZPlus, GCDAZ, ZPlus);
1272          PolDivide(ZMinus, Junk, GCDAZ, ZMinus);
1273          FindEandF;
1274          END;
```

```
1275
1276  {--
1277          Compute I = (E.D - ED.C)/ Z-
1278  --}
1279          PolInitialConditions(InitialCondition, ED, A, D, E,
1280                           DesignKnobs);
1281
1282  {--
1283          Derive the remaining emulator polynomials
1284  --}
1285          PolMultiply(G, E, BPlus);
1286          PolMultiply(GFilter, C, ZMinusPlus);
1287          PolMultiply(FFilter, C, ZPlus);
1288          END {WITH DesignKnobs} ;
1289      END {PolEmulator} ;
1290
1291    PROCEDURE PolDelayEmulator(VAR F, G, InitialCondition,
1292                           FFilter, GFilter: Polynomial;
1293                           VAR E, ED: Polynomial;
1294                           VAR GCDAZ, PadeDenominator,
1295                           PadeNumerator: Polynomial;
1296                           A, D: Polynomial;
1297                           DesignKnobs: TypeDesignKnobs;
1298                           Delay: REAL;
1299                           PadeOrder: INTEGER);
1300
1301  {--     Computes PadeOrder Pade approximation to e^-sT
c 1302          where T is the time delay.
c 1303
c 1304          Multiplies P polynomial by PadeDenominator.
c 1305          Multiplies B and Z- polynomials by Pade Numerator
c 1306
c 1307          Resultant system (A,B,C) has approximate time delay.
c 1308          Resultant reference model Z/P also has approximate
c 1309          delay.
c 1310
c 1311          Then does pole/Zero placement on modified system
c 1312  --}
  1313
  1314     BEGIN {PolDelayEmulator}
  1315       WITH DesignKnobs DO
  1316         BEGIN
  1317  {--     Compute Pade numerator and denoninator
c 1318  --}
  1319          PolPade(PadeDenominator, PadeOrder, Delay);
  1320          PolOfMinusS(PadeNumerator, PadeDenominator);
  1321
  1322  {--     Adjust design polynomials
c 1323          (N.B. DesignKnobs is passed by value)
c 1324  --}
  1325          PolMultiply(P, P, PadeDenominator);
  1326          PolMultiply(ZMinus, ZMinus, PadeNumerator);
  1327
  1328          PolEmulator(F, G, InitialCondition, FFilter,
  1329                       GFilter, E, ED, GCDAZ, A, D,
  1330                       DesignKnobs);
  1331
  1332          PolMultiply(GFilter, GFilter, PadeDenominator);
```

```
1333        END {WITH DesignKnobs} ;
1334      END {PolDelayEmulator} ;
1335
1336    PROCEDURE DesignEmulator(VAR STCKnobs: TypeSTCKnobs;
1337                             VAR STCState: TypeSTCState);
1338
1339    { Designs the emulator coefficients in terms of
c 1340      the system and design polynomials }
1341
1342    VAR
1343      i: INTEGER;
1344      ZPlusZMinusPlus: Polynomial;
1345
1346    BEGIN {DesignEmulator}
1347      WITH STCKnobs, STCState, SystemKnobs, DesignKnobs,
1348           EmKnobs, ErrorPolynomials DO
1349      BEGIN
1350        PolDelayEmulator(F, G, InitialCondition, FFilter,
1351                         GFilter, E, ED, GCDAZ,
1352                         PadeDenominator, PadeNumerator, A,
1353                         D, DesignKnobs, Delay, PadeOrder);
1354
1355        PolMultiply(ZPlusZMinusPlus, ZPlus, ZMinusPlus);
1356        FOR i := 1 TO NumberInteractions DO
1357        BEGIN
1358          PolMultiply(GInteraction[i], E, BInteraction[i]);
1359          PolZero(EI[i], 0);
1360        END;
1361      END;
1362    END {DesignEmulator} ;
1363
1364    {------------------------------------------------}
1365    {-- Input output  procedures               --}
1366    {------------------------------------------------}
1367
1368    PROCEDURE WriteTitle(Title: TypeTitle);
1369
1370    BEGIN {WriteTitle}
1371      WriteLn(Pretty, Title, Pretty);
1372      WriteLn(OutLog, Pretty, Title, Pretty);
1373      IF NOT Eof(InLog) THEN ReadLn(InLog);
1374    END {WriteTitle} ;
1375
1376    PROCEDURE WriteLoopTitle(Loop, Loops: INTEGER);
1377
1378    VAR
1379      LoopTitle: TypeTitle;
1380      i: INTEGER;
1381
1382    BEGIN {WriteLoopTitle}
1383      IF Loops > 1 THEN
1384      BEGIN
1385        IF Loop = 1 THEN LoopTitle := 'LOOP 1        '
1386        ELSE
1387        BEGIN
1388          LoopTitle := 'LOOP 1        ';
1389          FOR i := 2 TO Loops DO
1390            LoopTitle[6] := Succ(LoopTitle[6]);
```

```
1391          END;
1392          WriteLn;
1393          WriteTitle(LoopTitle);
1394          END;
1395     END {WriteLoopTitle} ;
1396
1397     PROCEDURE Skip(VAR F: TEXT);
1398
1399     VAR
1400       Ch: CHAR;
1401
1402     BEGIN {Skip}
1403       WHILE (F^ = ' ') AND NOT Eoln(F) DO Read(F, Ch);
1404     END {Skip} ;
1405
1406     PROCEDURE GetSymbol(VAR F: TEXT;
1407                     VAR ChangeChar: CHAR);
1408
1409     BEGIN
1410       ChangeChar := ' ';
1411       IF NOT Eof(F) THEN
1412         IF NOT Eoln(F) THEN Read(F, ChangeChar);
1413       IF ChangeChar <> ChangeSymbol THEN ChangeChar := ' ';
1414     END;
1415
1416     FUNCTION NameMatched(i: INTEGER;
1417                     VAR Name: TypeName): BOOLEAN;
1418
1419     VAR
1420       Ch: CHAR;
1421
1422     BEGIN {NameMatched}
1423       IF (i > LengthName) THEN NameMatched := TRUE
1424       ELSE
1425         BEGIN
1426         IF Eoln(InLog) THEN Ch := ' '
1427         ELSE Read(InLog, Ch);
1428
1429         IF (Ch = ' ') AND (InLog^ IN ['-', '0'..'9']) THEN
1430           NameMatched := TRUE
1431         ELSE
1432           BEGIN
1433           IF NOT (Ch = Name[i]) THEN NameMatched := FALSE
1434           ELSE NameMatched := NameMatched(i + 1, Name);
1435           END;
1436
1437         END;
1438
1439     END {NameMatched} ;
1440
1441     FUNCTION NewValue(All: BOOLEAN;
1442                     VAR ChangeChar: CHAR): BOOLEAN;
1443
1444     VAR
1445       NV: BOOLEAN;
1446
1447     BEGIN {NewValue}
1448       NV := NOT Eoln(Input);
```

```
1449
1450        IF NV THEN NewValue := NOT (Input^ = ' ')
1451        ELSE NewValue := FALSE;
1452
1453        IF All THEN
1454          BEGIN
1455          IF NV THEN ChangeChar := ChangeSymbol
1456          ELSE ChangeChar := ' ';
1457          END;
1458
1459      END {NewValue} ;
1460
1461    PROCEDURE GetComment(VAR F: TEXT;
1462                    VAR Comment: TypeComment);
1463
1464      BEGIN {GetComment} ;
1465        Skip(F);
1466        WITH Comment DO
1467          BEGIN
1468          Length := 0;
1469          WHILE NOT Eoln(F) AND (Length < LengthComment) DO
1470            BEGIN
1471            Length := Length + 1;
1472            Read(F, Str[Length]);
1473            END;
1474          END;
1475      END {GetComment} ;
1476
1477    PROCEDURE PutComment(VAR F: TEXT;
1478                    Comment: TypeComment);
1479
1480      VAR
1481        i: INTEGER;
1482
1483      BEGIN {PutComment} ;
1484        Write(F, ' ');
1485        WITH Comment DO
1486          FOR i := 1 TO Length DO
1487            BEGIN
1488            Write(F, Str[i]);
1489            END;
1490      END {PutComment} ;
1491
1492    PROCEDURE EnterReal(VAR x: REAL;
1493                    Default: REAL;
1494                    Name: TypeName;
1495                    All: BOOLEAN);
1496
1497      VAR
1498        ValueFromFile: BOOLEAN;
1499        Comment: TypeComment;
1500        ChangeChar: CHAR;
1501
1502      BEGIN {EnterReal}
1503
1504        x := Default;
1505        GetSymbol(InLog, ChangeChar);
1506        ValueFromFile := FALSE;
```

```
1507      Comment.Length := 0;
1508
1509      IF NOT Eof(InLog) THEN
1510        BEGIN
1511        IF NameMatched(1, Name) THEN
1512          BEGIN
1513          Read(InLog, x);
1514          ValueFromFile := TRUE;
1515          GetComment(InLog, Comment);
1516          END;
1517        ReadLn(InLog);
1518        END;
1519
1520      IF All OR (ChangeChar = ChangeSymbol) OR
1521          NOT ValueFromFile THEN
1522        BEGIN
1523        Write(Name, ' = ', x: fw: dp);
1524        PutComment(Output, Comment);
1525        WriteLn(Output, ' := ');
1526        IF NewValue(All, ChangeChar) THEN
1527          BEGIN
1528          Read(Input, x);
1529          IF NOT Eoln(Input) THEN
1530            GetComment(Input, Comment);
1531          END;
1532        ReadLn(Input);
1533        END;
1534
1535      Write(OutLog, ChangeChar, Name, ' ', x: fw: dp, ' ');
1536      PutComment(OutLog, Comment);
1537      WriteLn(OutLog, ' ');
1538    END {EnterReal} ;
1539
1540  PROCEDURE EnterInteger(VAR x: INTEGER;
1541                    Default: INTEGER;
1542                    Name: TypeName;
1543                    All: BOOLEAN);
1544
1545    VAR
1546      ValueFromFile: BOOLEAN;
1547      Comment: TypeComment;
1548      ChangeChar: CHAR;
1549
1550    BEGIN {EnterInteger}
1551      x := Default;
1552      GetSymbol(InLog, ChangeChar);
1553      ValueFromFile := FALSE;
1554      Comment.Length := 0;
1555
1556      IF NOT Eof(InLog) THEN
1557        BEGIN
1558        IF NameMatched(1, Name) THEN
1559          BEGIN
1560          Read(InLog, x);
1561          ValueFromFile := TRUE;
1562          GetComment(InLog, Comment);
1563          END;
1564        ReadLn(InLog);
```

```
1565     END;
1566
1567     IF All OR (ChangeChar = ChangeSymbol) OR
1568        NOT ValueFromFile THEN
1569     BEGIN
1570        Write(Name, ' = ', x: fw);
1571        PutComment(Output, Comment);
1572        WriteLn(Output, ' := ');
1573        IF NewValue(All, ChangeChar) THEN
1574        BEGIN
1575           Read(Input, x);
1576           IF NOT Eoln(Input) THEN
1577              GetComment(Input, Comment);
1578        END;
1579        ReadLn(Input);
1580     END;
1581
1582     Write(OutLog, ChangeChar, Name, ' ', x: fw, ' ');
1583     PutComment(OutLog, Comment);
1584     WriteLn(OutLog, ' ');
1585     END {EnterInteger} ;
1586
1587  PROCEDURE EnterBoolean(VAR x: BOOLEAN;
1588                        Default: BOOLEAN;
1589                        Name: TypeName;
1590                        All: BOOLEAN);
1591
1592     VAR
1593     Ch: CHAR;
1594     ValueFromFile: BOOLEAN;
1595     Comment: TypeComment;
1596     ChangeChar: CHAR;
1597
1598     PROCEDURE ReadBoolean(VAR F: TEXT);
1599
1600        BEGIN {ReadBoolean}
1601        Ch := ' ';
1602        WHILE (Ch = ' ') AND NOT Eoln(F) DO Read(F, Ch);
1603        x := Ch IN ['T', 't'];
1604        WHILE NOT (F^ = ' ') AND NOT Eoln(F) DO
1605           Read(F, Ch);
1606        END {ReadBoolean} ;
1607
1608     BEGIN {EnterBoolean}
1609     x := Default;
1610     GetSymbol(InLog, ChangeChar);
1611     ValueFromFile := FALSE;
1612     Comment.Length := 0;
1613
1614     IF NOT Eof(InLog) THEN
1615        BEGIN
1616        IF NameMatched(1, Name) THEN
1617           BEGIN
1618           ReadBoolean(InLog);
1619           GetComment(InLog, Comment);
1620           ValueFromFile := TRUE;
1621           END;
1622        ReadLn(InLog);
```

```
1623        END;
1624
1625        IF All OR (ChangeChar = ChangeSymbol) OR
1626          NOT ValueFromFile THEN
1627          BEGIN
1628          Write(Name, ' = ', x);
1629          PutComment(Output, Comment);
1630          WriteLn(Output, ' := ');
1631          IF NewValue(All, ChangeChar) THEN
1632            BEGIN
1633            ReadBoolean(Input);
1634            IF NOT Eoln(Input) THEN
1635              GetComment(Input, Comment);
1636            END;
1637          ReadLn(Input);
1638          END;
1639
1640        IF x THEN Write(OutLog, ChangeChar, Name, ' TRUE ')
1641        ELSE Write(OutLog, ChangeChar, Name, ' FALSE ');
1642        PutComment(OutLog, Comment);
1643        WriteLn(OutLog, ' ');
1644        END {EnterBoolean} ;
1645
1646   PROCEDURE EnterPolynomial(VAR x: Polynomial;
1647                             Default: Polynomial;
1648                             Name: TypeName;
1649                             All: BOOLEAN);
1650
1651        VAR
1652        i: INTEGER;
1653        Factor: Polynomial;
1654        AnotherFactor: BOOLEAN;
1655        ValueFromFile: BOOLEAN;
1656        Comment: TypeComment;
1657        ChangeChar: CHAR;
1658
1659        PROCEDURE GetPolynomial(VAR F: TEXT;
1660                                VAR x: Polynomial;
1661                                VAR AnotherFactor: BOOLEAN);
1662
1663        VAR
1664          Ch: CHAR;
1665
1666        BEGIN {GetPolynomial}
1667          WITH x DO
1668            BEGIN
1669            Deg := - 1;
1670            Skip(F);
1671            WHILE NOT Eoln(F) AND
1672                (F^ IN ['0'..'9', '+', '-']) DO
1673              BEGIN
1674              Deg := Deg + 1;
1675              Read(F, Coeff[Deg]);
1676              Skip(F);
1677              END;
1678            END;
1679
1680          AnotherFactor := F^ = MultiplySymbol;
```

```
1681        IF AnotherFactor THEN Read(F, Ch);
1682
1683        END {GetPolynomial} ;
1684
1685     BEGIN {EnterPolynomial}
1686        WITH x DO
1687        BEGIN
1688        PolEquate(x, Default);
1689        AnotherFactor := FALSE;
1690        ValueFromFile := FALSE;
1691        Comment.Length := 0;
1692        GetSymbol(InLog, ChangeChar);
1693
1694        IF NOT Eof(InLog) THEN
1695           BEGIN
1696           IF NameMatched(1, Name) THEN
1697              BEGIN
1698              GetPolynomial(InLog, x, AnotherFactor);
1699              ValueFromFile := TRUE;
1700              GetComment(InLog, Comment);
1701              END;
1702           ReadLn(InLog);
1703           END;
1704
1705        IF All OR (ChangeChar = ChangeSymbol) OR
1706           NOT ValueFromFile THEN
1707           BEGIN
1708           Write(Name, ' = ');
1709           FOR i := 0 TO Deg DO Write(Coeff[i]: fw: dp);
1710           IF AnotherFactor THEN
1711              Write(Output, ' ', MultiplySymbol);
1712           PutComment(Output, Comment);
1713           WriteLn(' := ');
1714           IF NewValue(All, ChangeChar) THEN
1715              BEGIN
1716              GetPolynomial(Input, x, AnotherFactor);
1717              IF NOT Eoln(Input) THEN
1718                 GetComment(Input, Comment);
1719              END;
1720           ReadLn(Input);
1721           END;
1722
1723        Write(OutLog, ChangeChar, Name);
1724        FOR i := 0 TO Deg DO
1725           Write(OutLog, ' ', Coeff[i]: fw: dp);
1726        IF AnotherFactor THEN
1727           Write(OutLog, ' ', MultiplySymbol);
1728        PutComment(OutLog, Comment);
1729        WriteLn(OutLog);
1730
1731        IF AnotherFactor THEN
1732           BEGIN
1733           WriteLn('Next factor ...');
1734           EnterPolynomial(Factor, Default, Name, All);
1735           PolMultiply(x, x, Factor);
1736           END;
1737        END;
1738
```

```
1739    END {EnterPolynomial} ;
1740
1741    PROCEDURE WriteParameters(VAR LoopVAR: TypeLoopVAR);
1742    {LoopVAR should really be passed by value, but it would
1743    take a lot of stack}
1744
1745    VAR
1746      i: INTEGER;
1747
1748    BEGIN {WriteParameters}
1749      WITH LoopVAR.STCState.SystemKnobs DO
1750      BEGIN
1751        WriteLn('----------------------------------');
1752        WriteLn('      System polynomials');
1753        WriteLn('----------------------------------');
1754        Write(Output, 'A       ');
1755        PolLineWrite(Output, A);
1756        Write(Output, 'B       ');
1757        PolLineWrite(Output, B);
1758        FOR i := 1 TO NumberInteractions DO
1759        BEGIN
1760          Write(Output, 'B[', i: 1, ']    ');
1761          PolLineWrite(Output, BInteraction[i]);
1762        END;
1763        Write(Output, 'D       ');
1764        PolLineWrite(Output, D);
1765      END;
1766    END {WriteParameters} ;
1767
1768    PROCEDURE WriteDesign(VAR LoopVAR: TypeLoopVAR);
1769    {LoopVAR should really be passed by value, but it would
1770    take a lot of stack}
1771
1772    VAR
1773      i: INTEGER;
1774
1775    BEGIN {WriteDesign}
1776      WITH LoopVAR, STCState, EmKnobs, STCKnobs,
1777          DesignKnobs, SystemKnobs, ErrorPolynomials DO
1778      BEGIN
1779        WriteParameters(LoopVAR);
1780        WriteLn('----------------------------------');
1781        WriteLn('      Design polynomials');
1782        WriteLn('----------------------------------');
1783        Write(Output, 'B+      ');
1784        PolLineWrite(Output, BPlus);
1785        Write(Output, 'B-      ');
1786        PolLineWrite(Output, BMinus);
1787        Write(Output, 'C       ');
1788        PolLineWrite(Output, C);
1789        Write(Output, 'P       ');
1790        PolLineWrite(Output, P);
1791        Write(Output, 'Z+      ');
1792        PolLineWrite(Output, ZPlus);
1793        Write(Output, 'Z-      ');
1794        PolLineWrite(Output, ZMinus);
1795        Write(Output, 'Z-+     ');
1796        PolLineWrite(Output, ZMinusPlus);
```

c 1743

c 1770

```
1797        IF SystemKnobs.Delay > 0.0 THEN
1798          BEGIN
1799          Write(Output, 'Pade      ');
1800          PolLineWrite(Output, PadeDenominator);
1801          END;
1802
1803        IF GCDAZ.Deg > 0 THEN
1804          BEGIN
1805          WriteLn('----------------------------------');
1806          Write(Output, 'GCD of A and Z-');
1807          PolLineWrite(Output, GCDAZ);
1808          END;
1809
1810        WriteLn('----------------------------------');
1811        Write(Output, 'F        ');
1812        PolLineWrite(Output, F);
1813        Write(Output, 'F filter ');
1814        PolLineWrite(Output, FFilter);
1815
1816        Write(Output, 'G        ');
1817        PolLineWrite(Output, G);
1818        Write(Output, 'G filter ');
1819        PolLineWrite(Output, GFilter);
1820
1821        FOR i := 1 TO NumberInteractions DO
1822          BEGIN
1823          Write(Output, 'G[', i: 1, ']     ');
1824          PolLineWrite(Output, GInteraction[i]);
1825          END;
1826
1827        Write(Output, 'I        ');
1828        PolLineWrite(Output, InitialCondition);
1829
1830        Write(Output, 'E        ');
1831        PolLineWrite(Output, E);
1832
1833        Write(Output, 'ED       ');
1834        PolLineWrite(Output, ED);
1835
1836        WriteLn('--------------------------------');
1837
1838        END;
1839      END {WriteDesign} ;
1840
1841    {------------------------------------------------}
1842    {-- Data filtering procedures          --}
1843    {------------------------------------------------}
1844
1845    PROCEDURE StateVariableFilter
1846        (u {Signal to be filtered} : REAL;
1847        A: Polynomial;
1848        FilterKnobs: TypeFilterKnobs;
1849        VAR FilterState: TypeFilterState);
1850
1851      PROCEDURE cStateVariableFilter
1852        (u {Signal to be filtered} : REAL;
1853        A: Polynomial;
1854        FilterKnobs: TypeFilterKnobs;
```

```
  1855          VAR FilterState: TypeFilterState);
  1856
  1857 {--     A state variable filter:
c 1858          FilterState[i] := s^-i / a(s^-1) *u
c 1859 --}
  1860
  1861 {--
c 1862    The input u is assumed to be a straight line between
c 1863    uOld and u within the interval.
c 1864    uOld is automatically updated but can be
c 1865    changed if required.
c 1866    For example it can be set equal to the current
c 1867    value of u if the input is constant within one
c 1868    sample
c 1869 --}
  1870
  1871    VAR
  1872      k, Index: INTEGER;
  1873      Sum, hk: REAL;
  1874      Increment: StateVector;
  1875
  1876    BEGIN { cStateVariableFilter }
  1877     WITH FilterKnobs DO
  1878      BEGIN
  1879      IF ConstantBetweenSamples THEN
  1880        FilterState.Old := u;
  1881
  1882      IF A.Deg = 0 THEN
  1883        FilterState.State[0] := u / A.Coeff[0]
  1884      ELSE
  1885        BEGIN
  1886        FilterState.State[0] := 0.0;
  1887        FOR Index := 0 TO A.Deg DO
  1888          Increment[Index] := FilterState.State[Index];
  1889        FOR k := 1 TO ApproximationOrder DO
  1890          BEGIN
  1891          Sum := 0.0;
  1892          hk := SampleInterval / k;
  1893
  1894          BEGIN {Matrix Multiplication}
  1895          FOR Index := 1 TO A.Deg DO
  1896            Sum := Sum - A.Coeff[Index] *
  1897                     Increment[Index];
  1898
  1899          FOR Index := A.Deg DOWNTO 2 DO
  1900            Increment[Index] := hk * Increment[Index -
  1901                       1];
  1902
  1903          Increment[0] := Sum / A.Coeff[0];
  1904          END {Matrix Multiplication} ;
  1905
  1906          IF k = 1 THEN
  1907            Increment[0] := Increment[0] +
  1908                      FilterState.Old /
  1909                      A.Coeff[0];
  1910
  1911          IF k = 2 THEN
  1912            Increment[0] := Increment[0] + (u -
```

```
1913                         FilterState.Old) /
1914                         A.Coeff[0];
1915
1916            Increment[1] := hk * Increment[0];
1917
1918            FOR Index := 0 TO A.Deg DO
1919              FilterState.State[Index] := FilterState.
1920                                State[Index] +
1921                                Increment[Index]
1922                                ;
1923
1924          END;
1925         END;
1926        FilterState.Old := u;
1927
1928        END {WITH FilterKnobs}
1929      END { of cStateVariableFilter } ;
1930
1931    PROCEDURE dStateVariableFilter
1932        (u {Signal to be filtered} : REAL;
1933         A: Polynomial; {Now a discrete-time polynomial}
1934         FilterKnobs: TypeFilterKnobs;
1935         VAR FilterState: TypeFilterState);
1936
1937  {--   A state variable filter:
c 1938  --}
1939
1940      VAR
1941        Index: INTEGER;
1942        Sum: REAL;
1943
1944      BEGIN { dStateVariableFilter }
1945        WITH FilterKnobs DO
1946          BEGIN
1947
1948          FOR Index := A.Deg DOWNTO 1 DO
1949            FilterState.State[Index] := FilterState.State[
1950                              Index - 1];
1951
1952          Sum := u;
1953          FOR Index := 1 TO A.Deg DO
1954            Sum := Sum - A.Coeff[Index] *
1955                FilterState.State[Index];
1956
1957          FilterState.State[0] := Sum / A.Coeff[0];
1958
1959          END {WITH FilterKnobs}
1960      END { of dStateVariableFilter } ;
1961
1962    BEGIN { StateVariableFilter }
1963      WITH FilterKnobs DO
1964        BEGIN
1965        IF ContinuousTime THEN
1966          cStateVariableFilter(u, A, FilterKnobs,
1967                        FilterState)
1968        ELSE
1969          dStateVariableFilter(u, A, FilterKnobs,
1970                        FilterState);
```

```
1971        END {WITH FilterKnobs}
1972        END { of StateVariableFilter } ;
1973
1974    PROCEDURE FilterInitialise(VAR FilterState:
1975                    TypeFilterState;
1976                    ContinuousTime: BOOLEAN;
1977                    InitialValue: REAL);
1978    { Initialises the state of StateVariableFilter }
1979
1980    VAR
1981      j: INTEGER;
1982
1983    BEGIN { FilterInitialise}
1984      FOR j := 0 TO MaxState DO
1985        FilterState.State[j] := 0.0;
1986
1987      IF ContinuousTime THEN
1988        FilterState.State[1] := InitialValue
1989      ELSE FilterState.State[0] := InitialValue;
1990    END { FilterInitialise} ;
1991
1992    FUNCTION StateOutput(FilterState: TypeFilterState;
1993                    Numerator,
1994    Denominator: Polynomial): REAL;
1995
1996    VAR
1997      i, RelativeDegree: INTEGER;
1998      Sum: REAL;
1999    { Computes a scalar system output from the system state }
2000
2001    BEGIN {StateOutput}
2002      Sum := 0.0;
2003
2004      RelativeDegree := Denominator.Deg - Numerator.Deg;
2005
2006      IF RelativeDegree >= 0 THEN
2007        FOR i := 0 TO Numerator.Deg DO
2008          Sum := Sum + FilterState.State[i +
2009              RelativeDegree] * Numerator.Coeff[i];
2010
2011      StateOutput := Sum;
2012    END {StateOutput} ;
2013
2014    FUNCTION Filter(u {Input to filter} : REAL;
2015                    Numerator, Denominator: Polynomial;
2016                    FilterKnobs: TypeFilterKnobs;
2017                    VAR FilterState: TypeFilterState): REAL;
2018    { Implements a continuous-time transfer function }
2019
2020    BEGIN { Filter }
2021      WITH FilterKnobs DO
2022        BEGIN
2023        StateVariableFilter(u, Denominator, FilterKnobs,
2024                    FilterState);
2025        Filter := StateOutput(FilterState, Numerator,
2026                    Denominator);
2027        END {FilterKnobs}
2028    END {of Filter} ;
```

```
      2029
      2030   FUNCTION Delayed(u: REAL;
      2031                 Delay: INTEGER;
      2032                 VAR State: TypeDelayState): REAL;
      2033   { Implements a time delay with input u -
  c   2034     Delay is measured in sample intervals }
      2035
      2036   BEGIN {Delayed}
      2037     WITH State DO
      2038     BEGIN
      2039     InPointer := (InPointer + 1) MOD (MaxDelay + 1);
      2040     OutPointer := (InPointer - Delay + MaxDelay + 1) MOD
      2041            (MaxDelay + 1);
      2042     Buffer[InPointer] := u;
      2043     Delayed := Buffer[OutPointer];
      2044     END;
      2045   END { Delayed } ;
      2046
      2047   FUNCTION DelayFilter(u {Input to filter} : REAL;
      2048                  Numerator, Denominator: Polynomial;
      2049                  Delay: REAL;
      2050                  FilterKnobs: TypeFilterKnobs;
      2051                  VAR FilterState: TypeFilterState;
      2052                  VAR DelFilterState: TypeDelayState):
      2053   REAL;
      2054
      2055   { Implements a time delay in series with a
  c   2056     rational transfer function -
  c   2057     the delay is on the input of the state filter so that
  c   2058     a time varying delay is not correctly handled ; but
  c   2059     the memory requirement is reduced}
      2060
      2061   VAR
      2062     uDelayed: REAL;
      2063
      2064   BEGIN { DelayFilter }
      2065     WITH FilterKnobs DO
      2066     BEGIN
      2067     uDelayed := Delayed(u, Round(Delay / FilterKnobs.
      2068                  SampleInterval),
      2069                  DelFilterState);
      2070
      2071     StateVariableFilter(uDelayed, Denominator,
      2072                  FilterKnobs, FilterState);
      2073
      2074     DelayFilter := StateOutput(FilterState, Numerator,
      2075                  Denominator);
      2076
      2077     END {FilterKnobs}
      2078   END {of DelayFilter} ;
      2079
      2080   PROCEDURE TimeDelayInitialise
      2081     (VAR State: TypeDelayState;
      2082     InitialValue: REAL);
      2083
      2084   VAR
      2085     j: INTEGER;
      2086
```

```
2087    BEGIN {TimeDelayInitialise}
2088      WITH State DO
2089        BEGIN
2090          FOR j := 0 TO MaxDelay DO
2091            Buffer[j] := InitialValue;
2092          InPointer := 0;
2093        END;
2094    END {TimeDelayInitialise} ;
2095
2096    FUNCTION TimeFor(Interval: INTEGER;
2097                    VAR Counter: INTEGER): BOOLEAN;
2098
2099    BEGIN {TimeFor}
2100      TimeFor := Counter = 0;
2101      Counter := (Counter + 1) MOD Interval;
2102    END {TimeFor} ;
2103
2104    {-------------------------------------------------}
2105    {--   CSTC initialisation procedures       --}
2106    {-------------------------------------------------}
2107
2108    PROCEDURE SigGenInitialise(VAR SigGenKnobs:
2109                    TypeSigGenKnobs);
2110
2111    BEGIN {SigGenInitialise}
2112      WITH SigGenKnobs DO
2113        BEGIN
2114        EnterReal(StepAmplitude, 0.0,
2115                'Step amplitude          ', All);
2116        EnterReal(SquareAmplitude, 0.0,
2117                'Square amplitude         ', All);
2118        EnterReal(CosAmplitude, 0.0,
2119                'Cos amplitude            ', All);
2120        EnterReal(Period, 10.0, 'Period                ',
2121                All);
2122        END;
2123    END {SigGenInitialise} ;
2124
2125    PROCEDURE tSystemInitialise(STCKnobs: TypeSTCKnobs;
2126                    STCState: TypeSTCState;
2127                    VAR tSystemKnobs:
2128                    TypeSystemKnobs;
2129                    VAR tSystemState:
2130                    TypeSystemState;
2131                    ContinuousTime: BOOLEAN;
2132                    RunKnobs: TypeRunKnobs);
2133
2134    VAR
2135      i: INTEGER;
2136
2137    BEGIN {tSystemInitialise}
2138      WITH tSystemKnobs DO
2139        BEGIN
2140
2141        PolEquate(A, STCState.SystemKnobs.A);
2142        PolEquate(B, STCState.SystemKnobs.B);
2143        NumberInteractions := STCState.SystemKnobs.
2144                    NumberInteractions;
```

```
2145        FOR i := 1 TO NumberInteractions DO
2146          PolEquate(BInteraction[i],
2147                STCState.SystemKnobs.BInteraction[i]);
2148
2149        PolEquate(D, STCState.SystemKnobs.D);
2150        Delay := STCState.SystemKnobs.Delay;
2151        IF STCKnobs.IntegralAction THEN
2152          BEGIN
2153          PolsDivide(A, A);
2154          PolsDivide(B, B);
2155          FOR i := 1 TO NumberInteractions DO
2156            PolsDivide(BInteraction[i], BInteraction[i]);
2157          PolsDivide(D, D);
2158          END;
2159
2160        IF NOT RunKnobs.CorrectSystem THEN
2161          BEGIN
2162          WriteTitle('Actual system ');
2163          EnterPolynomial(A, A, 'A (system denominator)   ',
2164                All);
2165          EnterPolynomial(B, B, 'B (system numerator)     ',
2166                All);
2167          IF RunKnobs.Loops > 1 THEN
2168            EnterInteger(NumberInteractions,
2169                  RunKnobs.Loops - 1,
2170                  'Number of interactions   ', All)
2171          ELSE NumberInteractions := 0;
2172
2173          FOR i := 1 TO NumberInteractions DO
2174            EnterPolynomial(BInteraction[i],
2175                  STCState.SystemKnobs.
2176                  BInteraction[i],
2177                  'Interaction polynomial   ',
2178                  All);
2179
2180          EnterPolynomial(D, STCState.SystemKnobs.D,
2181                  'D (initial conditions)   ', All);
2182
2183          EnterReal(Delay, 0.0, 'Time delay             ',
2184                All);
2185          EnterInteger(Lags, 0, 'Number of lags         ',
2186                All);
2187          IF Lags > 0 THEN
2188            BEGIN
2189            EnterReal(LagTimeConstant, 0.0,
2190                  'Lag time constant       ', All);
2191            EnterBoolean(Interactive, FALSE,
2192                  'Interactive lags        ', All);
2193
2194            END;
2195          END;
2196
2197        IF NOT ContinuousTime THEN {Multiply by forward
c 2198                shift}
2199          WITH tSystemKnobs DO PolsMultiply(B, B);
2200
2201        FilterInitialise(tSystemState.FilterState,
2202                ContinuousTime, 0.0);
```

```
2203        FilterInitialise(tSystemState.ICState,
2204                    ContinuousTime, 1.0 / A.Coeff[0]);
2205        TimeDelayInitialise(tSystemState.DelayState, 0.0);
2206        FOR i := 0 TO MaxLags DO
2207           tSystemState.LagState[i] := 0.0;
2208        END;
2209     END {tSystemInitialise} ;
2210
2211  PROCEDURE ModelKnobsInitialise
2212        (STCKnobs: TypeSTCKnobs;
2213        tSystemKnobs: TypeSystemKnobs;
2214        VAR ModelKnobs: TypeSystemKnobs;
2215        ContinuousTime: BOOLEAN);
2216
2217     BEGIN {ModelKnobsInitialise}
2218        WITH STCKnobs, ModelKnobs, DesignKnobs DO
2219        BEGIN
2220        IF ZHasFactorB THEN
2221           BEGIN
2222           PolUnitGain(tSystemKnobs.B, ContinuousTime);
2223           PolMultiply(B, tSystemKnobs.B, ZMinusPlus)
2224           END
2225        ELSE PolEquate(B, ZMinusPlus);
2226        PolMultiply(B, B, ZPlus);
2227        PolEquate(A, P);
2228        END;
2229
2230     END {ModelKnobsInitialise} ;
2231
2232  PROCEDURE ModelInitialise(STCKnobs: TypeSTCKnobs;
2233                    STCState: TypeSTCState;
2234                    tSystemKnobs: TypeSystemKnobs;
2235                    VAR ModelKnobs: TypeSystemKnobs;
2236                    VAR ModelState: TypeSystemState;
2237                    ContinuousTime: BOOLEAN);
2238
2239     BEGIN {ModelInitialise}
2240        ModelKnobsInitialise(STCKnobs, tSystemKnobs,
2241                    ModelKnobs, ContinuousTime);
2242        WITH STCKnobs, ModelKnobs, DesignKnobs DO
2243        BEGIN
2244        PolEquate(D, STCState.ErrorPolynomials.ED);
2245        Delay := tSystemKnobs.Delay;
2246        FilterInitialise(ModelState.FilterState,
2247                    ContinuousTime, 0.0);
2248        FilterInitialise(ModelState.ICState, ContinuousTime,
2249                    1.0 / A.Coeff[0]);
2250
2251        TimeDelayInitialise(ModelState.DelayState, 0.0);
2252        END;
2253     END {ModelInitialise} ;
2254
2255  PROCEDURE SystemInitialise(VAR STCKnobs: TypeSTCKnobs;
2256                    VAR STCState: TypeSTCState;
2257                    RunKnobs: TypeRunKnobs);
2258
2259     VAR
2260        i: INTEGER;
```

```
2261     One, Zero: Polynomial;
2262
2263     BEGIN {SystemInitialise}
2264       PolZero(Zero, 0);
2265       PolUnity(One, 0);
2266       WITH STCKnobs, STCState.SystemKnobs DO
2267       BEGIN
2268       WriteTitle('Assumed system ');
2269       PolZero(A, 1);
2270       A.Coeff[0] := 1.0;
2271       EnterPolynomial(A, A, 'A (system denominator)   ',
2272              All);
2273       PolZero(B, 0);
2274       B.Coeff[0] := 1.0;
2275       EnterPolynomial(B, B, 'B (system numerator)    ',
2276              All);
2277
2278       IF A.Coeff[0] <> 1.0 THEN
2279       BEGIN
2280         WriteLn('Normalising A and B so that a0 = 1');
2281         PolNormalise(A, B, 0);
2282         Write('A ');
2283         PolLineWrite(Output, A);
2284         Write('B ');
2285         PolLineWrite(Output, B);
2286       END;
2287
2288       EnterInteger(NumberInteractions, RunKnobs.Loops - 1,
2289              'Number of interactions  ', All);
2290       IF NumberInteractions > MaxNumberInteractions THEN
2291         NumberInteractions := MaxNumberInteractions;
2292       FOR i := 1 TO NumberInteractions DO
2293         EnterPolynomial(BInteraction[i], Zero,
2294              'Interaction polynomial   ', All);
2295       PolZero(D, A.Deg - 1);
2296       EnterPolynomial(D, D, 'D (initial conditions)   ',
2297              All);
2298
2299       IF IntegralAction THEN
2300         WITH STCState.SystemKnobs DO
2301         BEGIN
2302         IF All THEN
2303           WriteLn('Augmenting A, B and D with s');
2304         PolsMultiply(A, A);
2305         PolsMultiply(B, B);
2306         FOR i := 1 TO NumberInteractions DO
2307           PolsMultiply(BInteraction[i],
2308                  BInteraction[i]);
2309         PolsMultiply(D, D);
2310         END;
2311
2312       EnterReal(Delay, 0.0, 'Time delay          ',
2313              All);
2314
2315       END;
2316     END {SystemInitialise} ;
2317
2318     PROCEDURE DesignInitialise(VAR STCKnobs: TypeSTCKnobs;
```

```
2319                         VAR STCState: TypeSTCState;
2320                         ContinuousTime: BOOLEAN);
2321
2322     VAR
2323       One, Zero: Polynomial;
2324
2325     BEGIN {DesignInitialise}
2326       PolZero(Zero, 0);
2327       PolUnity(One, 0);
2328       WITH STCKnobs, STCState.SystemKnobs, DesignKnobs,
2329          STCState.EmKnobs DO
2330       BEGIN
2331         WriteTitle('Emulator design');
2332         EnterBoolean(ZHasFactorB, FALSE,
2333                    'Z has factor B        ', All);
2334         EnterPolynomial(ZMinusPlus, One,
2335                    'Z-+ (Z- not including B) ', All);
2336
2337         EnterPolynomial(ZPlus, One,
2338                    'Z+ (nice model numerator)', All);
2339         WITH ZPlus DO
2340           IF ContinuousTime AND (Coeff[Deg] <> 1.0) THEN
2341             WriteLn('WARNING:  Z+ does not have unit gain ')
2342           ;
2343
2344         EnterBoolean(LQ, FALSE, 'Linear-quadratic poles   ',
2345                    All);
2346
2347         IF LQ THEN
2348           EnterReal(LQWeight, 0,
2349                    'Linear-quadratic weight ', All)
2350         ELSE
2351           BEGIN
2352           PolUnity(P, 1);
2353           P.Coeff[0] := 1.0;
2354           EnterPolynomial(P, P, 'P (model denominator)    ',
2355                    All);
2356           WITH P DO
2357             IF ContinuousTime AND (Coeff[Deg] <> 1.0) THEN
2358               WriteLn('WARNING: P does not have unit gain ')
2359             ;
2360           END;
2361
2362         SetDesignKnobs(DesignKnobs, A, B, IntegralAction,
2363                    ZHasFactorB, ContinuousTime);
2364
2365         EnterPolynomial(C, P, 'C (emulator denominator) ',
2366                    All);
2367         EnterInteger(PadeOrder, 0,
2368                    'Pade approximation order ', All);
2369         IF (PadeOrder > 0) AND
2370            (STCState.SystemKnobs.Delay = 0) THEN
2371         BEGIN
2372           PadeOrder := 0;
2373           WriteLn(
2374 'Setting Pade approximation order to zero as delay is zero'
2375                    );
2376         END;
```

```
2377
2378        EnterReal(Small, 0.0001,
2379                 'Small positive number    ', All);
2380
2381        END;
2382     END {DesignInitialise} ;
2383
2384     PROCEDURE InitFilterKnobs(VAR FilterKnobs: TypeFilterKnobs
2385              );
2386
2387     BEGIN {InitFilterKnobs}
2388        WITH FilterKnobs DO
2389        BEGIN
2390        WriteTitle('Filters     ');
2391        EnterReal(SampleInterval, 0.1,
2392                 'Sample Interval        ', All);
2393        EnterInteger(ApproximationOrder, 5,
2394                 'Approximation Order     ', All);
2395        EnterBoolean(ContinuousTime, TRUE,
2396                 'Continuous-time?        ', All);
2397        END;
2398     END {InitFilterKnobs} ;
2399
2400     PROCEDURE STCInitialise(VAR LoopVAR: TypeLoopVAR;
2401                             FilterKnobs: TypeFilterKnobs;
2402                             RunKnobs: TypeRunKnobs);
2403
2404     VAR
2405        One, Zero: Polynomial;
2406
2407     PROCEDURE KnobsInitialise(FilterKnobs: TypeFilterKnobs;
2408                             RunKnobs: TypeRunKnobs;
2409                             VAR PutDataKnobs:
2410                             TypePutDataKnobs;
2411                             VAR STCKnobs: TypeSTCKnobs;
2412                             VAR STCState: TypeSTCState);
2413
2414        PROCEDURE TunerInitialise
2415           (SampleInterval: REAL;
2416           VAR Knobs: TypeTunerKnobs;
2417           VAR State: TypeTunerState);
2418
2419        VAR
2420           i: INTEGER;
2421
2422        BEGIN {TunerInitialise}
2423           WITH Knobs DO
2424           BEGIN
2425           EnterReal(InitialVariance, 1E5,
2426                    'Initial Variance       ', All);
2427           EnterReal(ForgetTime, 1000.0,
2428                    'Forget time            ', All);
2429           ForgetFactor := 1 - (SampleInterval /
2430                    ForgetTime);
2431
2432           EnterReal(DeadBand, 0.0,
2433                    'Dead band              ', All);
2434
```

```
2435          EnterBoolean(On, TRUE,
2436                   'Estimator on          ', All);
2437
2438          EnterInteger(TuneInterval, 1,
2439                   'Tune interval         ', All);
2440          END;
2441
2442          WITH State, Knobs DO
2443          BEGIN
2444          FOR i := 1 TO MaxParameters DO
2445            BEGIN
2446            TuningGain[i] := 0.0;
2447            Variance[i] := InitialVariance;
2448            END;
2449
2450          FOR i := 1 TO MaxUFactor DO UFactor[i] := 0.0;
2451
2452          EstimationError := 0.0;
2453          Sigma := 0.0;
2454          Sigma1 := 0.0;
2455          TuneCounter := 0;
2456          END;
2457        END {TunerInitialise} ;
2458
2459      PROCEDURE TuneEmInitialise
2460          (SampleInterval: REAL;
2461           VAR TunerKnobs: TypeTunerKnobs;
2462           VAR TunerState: TypeTunerState);
2463
2464      BEGIN {TuneEmInitialise}
2465          TunerInitialise(SampleInterval, TunerKnobs,
2466                   TunerState);
2467      END {TuneEmInitialise} ;
2468
2469      PROCEDURE IdentifyInitialise
2470          (SampleInterval: REAL;
2471           VAR STCKnobs: TypeSTCKnobs;
2472           VAR STCState: TypeSTCState);
2473
2474      VAR
2475          i: INTEGER;
2476          Cs: Polynomial;
2477
2478      BEGIN {IdentifyInitialise}
2479          WITH STCKnobs, STCState DO
2480          BEGIN
2481          WriteTitle('Identification ');
2482          TunerInitialise(SampleInterval, IdentifyKnobs,
2483                   IdentState);
2484
2485          WITH SysEmKnobs, STCState.SystemKnobs DO
2486          BEGIN
2487          EnterPolynomial(Cs, A,
2488                   'Cs (emulator denominator)',
2489                   All);
2490          IF Cs.Coeff[0] <> 1.0 THEN
2491            BEGIN
2492            WriteLn('Normalising Cs so that c0 = 1');
```

```
2493              PolScalarMultiply(Cs, 1.0 / Cs.Coeff[0],
2494                               Cs);
2495              Write('Cs ');
2496              PolLineWrite(Output, Cs);
2497              END;
2498
2499              EnterBoolean(IdentifyingRational, TRUE,
2500                           'Identifying rational part',
2501                           All);
2502              EnterBoolean(IdentifyingDelay, FALSE,
2503                           'Identifying delay       ',
2504                           All);
2505
2506              PolEquate(GFilter, Cs);
2507              PolEquate(FFilter, Cs);
2508              PolEquate(G, B);
2509
2510              FOR i := 1 TO NumberInteractions DO
2511                 PolEquate(GInteraction[i], BInteraction[i]);
2512
2513              PolMinus(F, Cs, A);
2514              PolRemove(F, 1); {Highest coeff should be
c  2515                           zero}
2516
2517              PolEquate(InitialCondition, D);
2518              END;
2519           END;
2520        END {IdentifyInitialise} ;
2521
2522     PROCEDURE ControlInitialise
2523        (VAR ControlKnobs: TypeControlKnobs);
2524
2525        BEGIN {ControlInitialise}
2526        WITH ControlKnobs DO
2527           BEGIN
2528           WriteTitle('Controller     ');
2529
2530           EnterPolynomial(qNumerator, Zero,
2531                           'Q numerator          ',
2532                           All);
2533           EnterPolynomial(qDenominator, One,
2534                           'Q denominator        ',
2535                           All);
2536           EnterPolynomial(rNumerator, One,
2537                           'R numerator          ',
2538                           All);
2539           EnterPolynomial(rDenominator, One,
2540                           'R denominator        ',
2541                           All);
2542           END;
2543        END {ControlInitialise} ;
2544
2545     PROCEDURE PutDatInitialise
2546        (VAR PutDataKnobs: TypePutDataKnobs);
2547
2548        BEGIN {PutDatInitialise}
2549        WITH PutDataKnobs DO
2550           BEGIN
```

```
2551        EnterReal(Max, 1E5, 'Maximum control signal    ',
2552            All);
2553        EnterReal(Min, - 1E5,
2554            'Minimum control signal    ', All);
2555        EnterBoolean(Switched, FALSE,
2556            'Switched control signal ', All);
2557        END;
2558    END {PutDatInitialise} ;
2559
2560    BEGIN {KnobsInitialise}
2561        WITH STCKnobs, STCState DO
2562        BEGIN
2563        SystemInitialise(STCKnobs, STCState, RunKnobs);
2564
2565        IF SelfTuning OR Auto THEN
2566            BEGIN
2567            DesignInitialise(STCKnobs, STCState,
2568                    FilterKnobs.ContinuousTime);
2569            DesignEmulator(STCKnobs, STCState);
2570            WriteDesign(LoopVAR);
2571            END;
2572
2573        IF SelfTuning THEN
2574            WITH DesignKnobs DO
2575            BEGIN
2576            WriteTitle('STC type      ');
2577            EnterBoolean(Explicit, FALSE,
2578                    'Explicit self-tuning     ',
2579                    All);
2580            EnterBoolean(UsingLambda, TRUE,
2581                    'Using lambda filter      ',
2582                    All);
2583            EnterBoolean(IdentifyingSystem, FALSE,
2584                    'Identifying system       ',
2585                    All);
2586            END;
2587
2588        IF SelfTuning OR IdentifyingSystem THEN
2589            EnterBoolean(TuningInitialConditions, FALSE,
2590                    'Tuning initial conditions', All);
2591
2592        IF IdentifyingSystem THEN
2593            BEGIN
2594            IdentifyInitialise(FilterKnobs.SampleInterval,
2595                    STCKnobs, STCState);
2596            END;
2597
2598        IF SelfTuning AND NOT Explicit THEN
2599            BEGIN
2600            WriteTitle('Tuner          ');
2601            TuneEmInitialise(FilterKnobs.SampleInterval,
2602                    TunerKnobs, TunerState);
2603            END;
2604
2605        IF Auto THEN ControlInitialise(ControlKnobs);
2606
2607        PutDatInitialise(PutDataKnobs);
2608
```

```
2609            IF NOT Auto THEN
2610              BEGIN
2611              WITH ControlKnobs DO
2612                BEGIN
2613                PolEquate(qNumerator, One);
2614                PolEquate(qDenominator, One);
2615                PolEquate(rNumerator, One);
2616                PolEquate(rDenominator, One);
2617                END;
2618              END;
2619            END;
2620          END {KnobsInitialise} ;
2621
2622          PROCEDURE StateInitialise(STCKnobs: TypeSTCKnobs;
2623                          VAR STCState: TypeSTCState;
2624                          ContinuousTime: BOOLEAN);
2625
2626          VAR
2627            i: INTEGER;
2628
2629            PROCEDURE InitEmulator(EmKnobs: TypeEmKnobs;
2630                          VAR EmState: TypeEmState;
2631                          ContinuousTime: BOOLEAN);
2632
2633            VAR
2634              i: INTEGER;
2635
2636            BEGIN {InitEmulator}
2637              WITH EmState, EmKnobs DO
2638                BEGIN
2639                FilterInitialise(uState, ContinuousTime, 0.0);
2640                FilterInitialise(yState, ContinuousTime, 0.0);
2641                FilterInitialise(ICState, ContinuousTime,
2642                          1.0 / FFilter.Coeff[0]);
2643
2644                FOR i := 1 TO MaxNumberInteractions DO
2645                  BEGIN
2646                  FilterInitialise(InterState[i],
2647                          ContinuousTime, 0.0);
2648                  FilterInitialise(InterFState[i],
2649                          ContinuousTime, 0.0);
2650                  END;
2651                END;
2652            END {InitEmulator} ;
2653
2654          BEGIN {StateInitialise}
2655            WITH STCKnobs, STCState DO
2656              BEGIN
2657              Phi := 0.0;
2658              PhiHat := 0.0;
2659
2660              IF IdentifyingSystem THEN
2661                InitEmulator(SysEmKnobs, SysEmState,
2662                          ContinuousTime);
2663
2664              IF Auto THEN
2665                InitEmulator(EmKnobs, EmState, ContinuousTime);
2666
```

```
2667        IF SelfTuning AND UsingLambda THEN
2668            InitEmulator(EmKnobs, LambdaEmState,
2669                    ContinuousTime);
2670
2671        WITH STCKnobs, STCState, DesignKnobs,
2672            ControlKnobs DO
2673        BEGIN
2674        FilterInitialise(qState, ContinuousTime, 0.0);
2675        FilterInitialise(wState, ContinuousTime, 0.0);
2676        FilterInitialise(PhicState, ContinuousTime,
2677                    0.0);
2678        FilterInitialise(uLambdaState, ContinuousTime,
2679                    0.0);
2680        FilterInitialise(yLambdaState, ContinuousTime,
2681                    0.0);
2682        FOR i := 1 TO MaxNumberInteractions DO
2683            FilterInitialise(iLambdaState[i],
2684                    ContinuousTime, 0.0);
2685        TimeDelayInitialise(uDelayState, 0.0);
2686        TimeDelayInitialise(yDelayState, 0.0);
2687        TimeDelayInitialise(EmState.DelFiltState, 0.0);
2688        TimeDelayInitialise(LambdaEmState.DelFiltState,
2689                    0.0);
2690        TimeDelayInitialise(SysEmState.DelFiltState,
2691                    0.0);
2692        END;
2693
2694        END;
2695    END {StateInitialise} ;
2696
2697    BEGIN {STCInitialise}
2698    PolZero(Zero, 0);
2699    PolUnity(One, 0);
2700
2701    WITH LoopVAR, STCKnobs DO
2702    BEGIN
2703    WriteTitle('Control action ');
2704    EnterBoolean(Auto, TRUE,
2705            'Automatic controller mode', All);
2706    EnterBoolean(IntegralAction, TRUE,
2707            'Integral action        ', All);
2708    KnobsInitialise(FilterKnobs, RunKnobs, PutDataKnobs,
2709            STCKnobs, STCState);
2710    StateInitialise(STCKnobs, STCState,
2711            FilterKnobs.ContinuousTime);
2712    END;
2713    END {STCInitialise} ;
2714
2715    {------------------------------------------------}
2716    {--    System simulation procedures        --}
2717    {------------------------------------------------}
2718
2719    FUNCTION SigGen(SigGenKnobs: TypeSigGenKnobs;
2720            Time: REAL): REAL;
2721
2722    VAR
2723    Sig, NormalisedTime: REAL;
2724
```

```
2725    BEGIN {SigGen}
2726      WITH SigGenKnobs DO
2727      BEGIN
2728      Sig := StepAmplitude;
2729      NormalisedTime := Time / Period;
2730
2731      IF ((NormalisedTime - Trunc(NormalisedTime)) <
2732        0.5) THEN
2733        Sig := Sig + SquareAmplitude
2734      ELSE Sig := Sig - SquareAmplitude;
2735
2736      IF NOT (CosAmplitude = 0.0) THEN
2737        Sig := Sig + CosAmplitude * Sin(TwoPi * Time /
2738                            Period);
2739
2740      SigGen := Sig;
2741      END;
2742    END {SigGen} ;
2743
2744    FUNCTION System(u: REAL;
2745                    Knobs: TypeSystemKnobs;
2746                    FilterKnobs: TypeFilterKnobs;
2747                    VAR State: TypeSystemState): REAL;
2748
2749    VAR
2750      y, uD: REAL;
2751
2752    BEGIN {System}
2753      WITH Knobs, FilterKnobs, State DO
2754      BEGIN
2755      uD := Delayed(u, Round(Delay / SampleInterval),
2756                    DelayState);
2757      y := Filter(uD, B, A, FilterKnobs, FilterState);
2758
2759      IF D.Deg >= 0 THEN
2760        y := y + Filter(0.0, D, A, FilterKnobs, ICState);
2761
2762      System := y;
2763      END;
2764    END {System} ;
2765
2766    FUNCTION MultiLag(u: REAL;
2767                      Lags: INTEGER;
2768                      TimeConstant: REAL;
2769                      Interactive: BOOLEAN;
2770                      FilterKnobs: TypeFilterKnobs;
2771                      VAR State: TypeLagState): REAL;
2772
2773    VAR
2774      i: INTEGER;
2775
2776    BEGIN {MultiLag}
2777      State[0] := u;
2778      WITH FilterKnobs DO
2779      FOR i := 1 TO Lags DO
2780        IF Interactive THEN
2781          State[i] := State[i] + (State[i - 1] + State[i +
2782            1] - 2 * State[i]) *
```

```
2783                         SampleInterval * Sqr(Lags) /
2784                         TimeConstant
2785              ELSE
2786              State[i] := State[i] + (State[i - 1] -
2787                         State[i]) * SampleInterval * Lags /
2788                         TimeConstant;
2789
2790          MultiLag := State[Lags];
2791
2792          IF Interactive THEN State[Lags + 1] := State[Lags];
2793          END {MultiLag} ;
2794
2795     {-------------------------------------------------}
2796     {--    Self-tuner input/output procedures      --}
2797     {-------------------------------------------------}
2798
2799     PROCEDURE GetData(VAR ThisLoopVAR: TypeLoopVAR;
2800                       VAR LoopVAR: LoopVARs;
2801                       VAR InData: TEXT;
2802                       VAR Time: REAL;
2803                       RunKnobs: TypeRunKnobs;
2804                       FilterKnobs: TypeFilterKnobs);
2805
2806          PROCEDURE GetDataFromFile(VAR InData: TEXT);
2807
2808          VAR
2809            i: INTEGER;
2810
2811          BEGIN {GetDataFromFile}
2812          WITH ThisLoopVAR DO
2813            BEGIN
2814            Read(InData, Time, u, y);
2815            FOR i := 1 TO tSystemKnobs.NumberInteractions DO
2816              IF NOT Eoln(InData) THEN
2817                Read(InData, Interaction[i])
2818              ELSE Interaction[i] := 0.0;
2819
2820            IF NOT Eoln(InData) THEN Read(InData, w)
2821            ELSE w := 0.0;
2822
2823            ReadLn(InData);
2824            END;
2825          END {GetDataFromFile} ;
2826
2827          PROCEDURE Simulate;
2828
2829          VAR
2830            uD: REAL;
2831            j, Loop: INTEGER;
2832
2833          BEGIN {Simulate}
2834          WITH ThisLoopVAR, RunKnobs DO
2835            BEGIN
2836            InDist := SigGen(InDisturbKnobs, Time);
2837            OutDist := SigGen(OutDisturbKnobs, Time);
2838
2839            IF NOT Cascade OR (ThisLoop = 1) THEN uD := u
2840            ELSE uD := LoopVAR[ThisLoop - 1].y;
```

```
2841
2842        uD := uD + InDist;
2843
2844        WITH tSystemKnobs, tSystemState DO
2845          uD := MultiLag(uD, Lags, LagTimeConstant,
2846                         Interactive, FilterKnobs,
2847                         LagState);
2848
2849        y := System(uD, tSystemKnobs, FilterKnobs,
2850                    tSystemState) + OutDist;
2851
2852        j := 0;
2853        FOR Loop := 1 TO Loops DO
2854          IF NOT (Loop = ThisLoop) THEN
2855            WITH tSystemKnobs DO
2856            BEGIN
2857              j := j + 1;
2858              y := y + Filter(Interaction[j],
2859                              BInteraction[j], A,
2860                              FilterKnobs,
2861                              InteractionState[j + 1]);
2862            END;
2863
2864          IF NOT Cascade OR (ThisLoop = Loops) THEN
2865            w := SigGen(SetPointKnobs, Time)
2866          ELSE w := LoopVAR[ThisLoop + 1].u;
2867
2868        END;
2869      END {Simulate} ;
2870
2871    BEGIN {GetData}
2872      IF RunKnobs.ExternalData THEN GetDataFromFile(InData)
2873      ELSE Simulate;
2874    END {GetData} ;
2875
2876  PROCEDURE PutData(VAR u: REAL;
2877                    PutDataKnobs: TypePutDataKnobs);
2878
2879    BEGIN {PutData}
2880      WITH PutDataKnobs DO
2881      BEGIN
2882        IF u > Max THEN u := Max
2883        ELSE IF u < Min THEN u := Min;
2884
2885        IF Switched THEN
2886          IF Abs(u - Min) < Abs(u - Max) THEN u := Min
2887          ELSE u := Max;
2888      END;
2889    END {PutData} ;
2890
2891    {--------------------------------------------------}
2892    {--   High-gain (emulator-free) control      --}
2893    {--------------------------------------------------}
2894
2895  PROCEDURE HighGainControl(VAR u: REAL;
2896                    w, y: REAL;
2897                    FilterKnobs: TypeFilterKnobs;
2898                    VAR STCKnobs: TypeSTCKnobs;
```

```
2899                    VAR STCState: TypeSTCState);
2900
2901    BEGIN {HighGainControl}
2902      WITH STCKnobs, STCState, DesignKnobs, FilterKnobs,
2903          ControlKnobs DO
2904        BEGIN
2905        Phi := Filter(y, P, Z, FilterKnobs, PhicState);
2906
2907        u := Filter(w - Phi, qDenominator, qNumerator,
2908                    FilterKnobs, qState);
2909
2910        END;
2911    END {HighGainControl} ;
2912
2913    {-------------------------------------------------}
2914    {--    Self-tuning  control              --}
2915    {-------------------------------------------------}
2916
2917    PROCEDURE SelfTuningControl(VAR u: REAL
2918      { The control signal } ;
2919                        w, y: REAL
2920                        { The setpoint and system output }
2921                        ;
2922                        Interaction: TypeInteraction
2923                        {Interaction terms} ;
2924                        FilterKnobs: TypeFilterKnobs
2925                        { The digital filter parameters }
2926                        ;
2927                        ExternalData: BOOLEAN;
2928                        VAR PutDataKnobs:
2929                        TypePutDataKnobs
2930                        { The control signal limits etc.  }
2931                        ;
2932                        VAR STCKnobs: TypeSTCKnobs
2933                        { The user defined STC variables }
2934                        ;
2935                        VAR STCState: TypeSTCState
2936                        { The internal state of the STC }
2937                        );
2938
2939    VAR
2940      One: Polynomial; { A unit polynomial of zero order }
2941
2942  { The continuous-time self-tuning controller implementing
c 2943    many possible algorithms }
2944
2945        {-------------------------------------------------}
2946        {--    Emulator-based control procedures    --}
2947        {-------------------------------------------------}
2948
2949    FUNCTION Emulator(y, u: REAL;
2950                        Interaction: TypeInteraction;
2951                        NumberInteractions: INTEGER;
2952                        F, FFilter, G, GFilter,
2953                        InitialCondition: Polynomial;
2954                        GInteraction: InterPolynomial;
2955                        InputDelay: REAL;
2956                        FilterKnobs: TypeFilterKnobs;
```

```
2957                        VAR EmState: TypeEmState): REAL;
2958
2959   { Implements a tuneable emulator including
c  2960  initial condition and interaction terms }
2961
2962        VAR
2963          i: INTEGER;
2964          Em: REAL;
2965
2966        BEGIN {Emulator}
2967          WITH FilterKnobs, EmState DO
2968            BEGIN
2969              Em := 0.0;
2970
2971          {--    System input component of emulator output --}
2972            IF InputDelay > 0.0 THEN
2973              Em := Em + DelayFilter(u, G, GFilter,
2974                              InputDelay, FilterKnobs,
2975                              uState, DelFiltState)
2976            ELSE
2977              Em := Em + Filter(u, G, GFilter, FilterKnobs,
2978                              uState);
2979
2980          {--    System output component of emulator output --}
2981            Em := Em + Filter(y, F, FFilter, FilterKnobs,
2982                              yState);
2983
2984  {--    Initial condition  component of emulator output --}
2985            Em := Em + Filter(0.0, InitialCondition, FFilter,
2986                              FilterKnobs, ICState);
2987
2988          {--    Interaction  component of emulator output --}
2989            FOR i := 1 TO NumberInteractions DO
2990              Em := Em + Filter(Interaction[i],
2991                              GInteraction[i], FFilter,
2992                              FilterKnobs, InterState[i]);
2993            END;
2994
2995          Emulator := Em;
2996          END { Emulator} ;
2997
2998        FUNCTION Control(y, w: REAL;
2999                        Interaction: TypeInteraction;
3000                        STCKnobs: TypeSTCKnobs;
3001                        VAR STCState: TypeSTCState;
3002                        FilterKnobs: TypeFilterKnobs): REAL;
3003
3004        FUNCTION ImplicitSolution
3005            (y, w: REAL;
3006            Interaction: TypeInteraction;
3007            Em0State, Em1State: TypeEmState;
3008            Q0State, Q1State: TypeFilterState;
3009            STCKnobs: TypeSTCKnobs;
3010            VAR STCState: TypeSTCState;
3011            FilterKnobs: TypeFilterKnobs): REAL;
3012
3013        VAR
3014          PhiQ0Hat, PhiQ1Hat, u: REAL;
```

```
3015
3016        BEGIN {ImplicitSolution}
3017          WITH STCKnobs, STCState, EmKnobs, DesignKnobs,
3018              SystemKnobs, FilterKnobs, ControlKnobs DO
3019          BEGIN
3020          PhiQ0Hat := Emulator(y, 0.0, Interaction,
3021                               NumberInteractions, F,
3022                               FFilter, G, GFilter,
3023                               InitialCondition,
3024                               GInteraction, 0.0,
3025                               FilterKnobs,
3026                    Em0State) + Filter(0.0, qNumerator,
3027                               qDenominator,
3028                               FilterKnobs,
3029                               Q0State);
3030
3031          PhiQ1Hat := Emulator(y, 1.0, Interaction,
3032                               NumberInteractions, F,
3033                               FFilter, G, GFilter,
3034                               InitialCondition,
3035                               GInteraction, 0.0,
3036                               FilterKnobs,
3037                    Em1State) + Filter(1.0, qNumerator,
3038                               qDenominator,
3039                               FilterKnobs,
3040                               Q1State);
3041
3042          u := (w - PhiQ0Hat) / (PhiQ1Hat - PhiQ0Hat);
3043
3044          ImplicitSolution := u;
3045
3046          END;
3047        END {ImplicitSolution} ;
3048
3049        BEGIN {Control}
3050          WITH STCKnobs, ControlKnobs, STCState DO
3051          IF qNumerator.Deg = qDenominator.Deg THEN
3052          Control := ImplicitSolution(y, w, Interaction,
3053                               EmState, EmState,
3054                               qState, qState,
3055                               STCKnobs, STCState,
3056                               FilterKnobs)
3057          ELSE
3058            WITH FilterKnobs DO
3059            Control := Filter(w - PhiHat, qDenominator,
3060                               qNumerator, FilterKnobs,
3061                               qState);
3062        END {Control} ;
3063
3064    {----------------------------------------------}
3065    {--     Emulator tuning procedures         --}
3066    {----------------------------------------------}
3067
3068    PROCEDURE SetData(VAR DataVector: TypeDataVector;
3069                          State: TypeEmState;
3070                          Knobs: TypeEmKnobs;
3071                          TuningInitialConditions,
3072                          IntegralAction: BOOLEAN;
```

```
3073                     NumberInteractions: INTEGER);
3074
3075      VAR
3076       i, k, j: INTEGER;
3077       Integrating: INTEGER; { Set to one if Integral
c 3078                             action, else zéro }
3079
3080      BEGIN {SetData}
3081       IF IntegralAction THEN Integrating := 1
3082       ELSE Integrating := 0;
3083
3084       j := 0;
3085       WITH State, Knobs, DataVector DO
3086        BEGIN
3087        IF TuningInitialConditions THEN
3088         WITH ICState DO
3089          FOR k := FFilter.Deg -
3090           InitialCondition.Deg TO FFilter.Deg DO
3091           BEGIN
3092           j := j + 1;
3093           Data[j] := State[k];
3094           END;
3095
3096        WITH uState DO
3097         FOR k := GFilter.Deg - G.Deg TO GFilter.Deg -
3098          Integrating DO
3099          BEGIN
3100          j := j + 1;
3101          Data[j] := State[k];
3102          END;
3103
3104        WITH yState DO
3105         FOR k := FFilter.Deg - F.Deg TO FFilter.Deg -
3106          Integrating DO
3107          BEGIN
3108          j := j + 1;
3109          Data[j] := State[k];
3110          END;
3111
3112        FOR i := 1 TO NumberInteractions DO
3113         WITH InterState[i] DO
3114          FOR k := GFilter.Deg -
3115           GInteraction[i].Deg TO GFilter.Deg -
3116           Integrating DO
3117           BEGIN
3118           j := j + 1;
3119           Data[j] := State[k];
3120           END;
3121
3122        NumberOfParameters := j;
3123        END;
3124      END {SetData} ;
3125
3126      PROCEDURE TuneEmulator(VAR Knobs: TypeEmKnobs;
3127                     State: TypeTunerState;
3128                     TuningInitialConditions,
3129                      IntegralAction: BOOLEAN;
3130                      NumberInteractions: INTEGER);
```

```
3131
3132      VAR
3133        i, k, j: INTEGER;
3134        Integrating: INTEGER; { Set to one if Integral
c 3135                           action, else zero }
3136
3137      BEGIN {TuneEmulator}
3138        IF IntegralAction THEN Integrating := 1
3139        ELSE Integrating := 0;
3140        j := 0;
3141
3142        WITH Knobs, State DO
3143          BEGIN
3144          IF TuningInitialConditions THEN
3145            WITH InitialCondition DO
3146            FOR k := 0 TO Deg DO
3147              BEGIN
3148              j := j + 1;
3149              Coeff[k] := Coeff[k] - (TuningGain[j] /
3150                         Sigma1) * EstimationError;
3151
3152            END;
3153
3154          WITH G DO
3155            FOR k := 0 TO Deg - Integrating DO
3156              BEGIN
3157              j := j + 1;
3158              Coeff[k] := Coeff[k] - (TuningGain[j] /
3159                         Sigma1) * EstimationError;
3160            END;
3161
3162          WITH F DO
3163            FOR k := 0 TO Deg - Integrating DO
3164              BEGIN
3165              j := j + 1;
3166              Coeff[k] := Coeff[k] - (TuningGain[j] /
3167                         Sigma1) * EstimationError;
3168            END;
3169
3170          FOR i := 1 TO NumberInteractions DO
3171            WITH GInteraction[i] DO
3172            FOR k := 0 TO Deg - Integrating DO
3173              BEGIN
3174              j := j + 1;
3175              Coeff[k] := Coeff[k] - (TuningGain[j] /
3176                         Sigma1) * EstimationError;
3177            END;
3178
3179          END;
3180      END {TuneEmulator} ;
3181
3182      PROCEDURE UpdateLeastSquaresGain
3183          (VAR TunerState: TypeTunerState;
3184          TunerKnobs: TypeTunerKnobs;
3185          DataVector: TypeDataVector);
3186
3187      VAR
3188        j, UIndex1, UIndex2: INTEGER;
```

```
3189        fj, bj, OldSigma1, Lambda: REAL;
3190        i: INTEGER;
3191        UFac: REAL;
3192
3193        FUNCTION UTX(j: INTEGER): REAL; { computes jth element
c 3194                          of UT * X }
3195
3196        VAR
3197          i: INTEGER;
3198          Sum, UFac: REAL;
3199
3200        BEGIN { UTX }
3201
3202          Sum := 0.0;
3203
3204          WITH TunerState, TunerKnobs, DataVector DO
3205            BEGIN
3206            FOR i := 1 TO j DO
3207              BEGIN
3208
3209              IF i = j THEN { use unit Diagonal term }
3210                UFac := 1.0
3211              ELSE
3212                BEGIN
3213                UIndex1 := UIndex1 + 1;
3214                UFac := UFactor[UIndex1]
3215                END;
3216
3217              Sum := Sum + Data[i] * UFac;
3218
3219              END;
3220
3221            UTX := Sum
3222            END
3223
3224          END;
3225        { of UTX }
3226
3227        BEGIN { UpdateLeastSquaresGain }
3228
3229          WITH TunerState, TunerKnobs, DataVector DO
3230            BEGIN
3231
3232            UIndex1 := 0;
3233            UIndex2 := 0;
3234            Sigma1 := 1.0;
3235
3236            FOR j := 1 TO NumberOfParameters DO
3237              BEGIN
3238              OldSigma1 := Sigma1;
3239              fj := UTX(j);
3240
3241              bj := Variance[j] * fj;
3242              fj := fj / ForgetFactor;
3243              Sigma1 := OldSigma1 + fj * bj;
3244              Variance[j] := OldSigma1 / Sigma1 *
3245                          Variance[j] / ForgetFactor;
3246              TuningGain[j] := bj; { jth element of normalised
```

```
c  3247                          Kalman TuningGain }
   3248
   3249          Lambda := - fj / OldSigma1;
   3250
   3251 {--    Update jth column of UFactor
c  3252        and 1-jth element of TuningGain
c  3253 --}
   3254          FOR i := 1 TO j - 1 DO
   3255          BEGIN
   3256            UIndex2 := UIndex2 + 1;
   3257            UFac := UFactor[UIndex2];
   3258            UFactor[UIndex2] := UFac + Lambda *
   3259                               TuningGain[i];
   3260            TuningGain[i] := TuningGain[i] + UFac * bj;
   3261          END;
   3262          END;
   3263
   3264          { Set Sigma1 to value required in 'Tune' }
   3265          Sigma1 := (Sigma1 - 1.0) * ForgetFactor +
   3266                     ForgetFactor;
   3267
   3268          { Set Sigma to XT P X }
   3269          Sigma := (Sigma1 - ForgetFactor) / Sigma1;
   3270
   3271          END;
   3272
   3273      END { of UpdateLeastSquaresGain } ;
   3274
   3275    PROCEDURE IdentifySystem(y, u: REAL;
   3276                   Interaction: TypeInteraction;
   3277                   FilterKnobs: TypeFilterKnobs;
   3278                   VAR STCKnobs: TypeSTCKnobs;
   3279                   VAR STCState: TypeSTCState);
   3280
   3281    VAR
   3282      yHat: REAL;
   3283      i: INTEGER;
   3284      DataVector: TypeDataVector;
   3285
   3286    PROCEDURE TuneDelay(VAR Delay: REAL;
   3287                   State: TypeTunerState;
   3288                   NumberOfParameters: INTEGER);
   3289
   3290      BEGIN {TuneDelay}
   3291      WITH State DO
   3292        Delay := Delay -
   3293                (TuningGain[NumberOfParameters] /
   3294                 Sigma1) * EstimationError;
   3295        IF Delay < 0.0 THEN Delay := 0.0; {Negative
c  3296        delays are not allowed}
   3297      END {TuneDelay} ;
   3298
   3299    PROCEDURE SetDelayData(VAR DataVector: TypeDataVector;
   3300                   State: TypeEmState;
   3301                   Knobs: TypeEmKnobs);
   3302
   3303    VAR
   3304      sG: Polynomial;
```

```
3305
3306    BEGIN {SetDelayData}
3307
3308      WITH DataVector, Knobs, State DO
3309      BEGIN
3310      NumberOfParameters := NumberOfParameters + 1;
3311      PolsMultiply(sG, G);
3312      Data[NumberOfParameters] := - StateOutput(uState
3313                          , sG, GFilter);
3314      END
3315    END {SetDelayData} ;
3316
3317    BEGIN {IdentifySystem}
3318
3319      WITH STCKnobs, STCState, SysEmState, SysEmKnobs,
3320          SystemKnobs, IdentState DO
3321      BEGIN
3322
3323      yHat := Emulator(y, u, Interaction,
3324              NumberInteractions, F, FFilter,
3325              G, GFilter, InitialCondition,
3326              GInteraction, SystemKnobs.Delay,
3327              FilterKnobs, SysEmState);
3328
3329      EstimationError := yHat - y;
3330
3331      WITH IdentifyKnobs DO
3332        IF (Abs(EstimationError) >= DeadBand) AND On AND
3333        TimeFor(TuneInterval, TuneCounter) THEN
3334        BEGIN
3335
3336          IF IdentifyingRational THEN
3337            SetData(DataVector, SysEmState, SysEmKnobs,
3338                TuningInitialConditions,
3339                IntegralAction,
3340                SystemKnobs.NumberInteractions)
3341          ELSE DataVector.NumberOfParameters := 0;
3342
3343          IF IdentifyingDelay THEN
3344            SetDelayData(DataVector, SysEmState,
3345                SysEmKnobs);
3346
3347          UpdateLeastSquaresGain(IdentState,
3348                IdentifyKnobs,
3349                DataVector);
3350
3351          IF IdentifyingRational THEN
3352            TuneEmulator(SysEmKnobs, IdentState,
3353                TuningInitialConditions,
3354                IntegralAction,
3355                SystemKnobs.NumberInteractions
3356                );
3357          IF IdentifyingDelay THEN
3358            TuneDelay(SystemKnobs.Delay, IdentState,
3359                DataVector.NumberOfParameters);
3360
3361        END;
3362    END;
```

```
3363
3364        WITH STCKnobs, STCState, SysEmKnobs, IdentState,
3365            STCState.SystemKnobs DO
3366        BEGIN
3367        PolMinus(A, FFilter, F);
3368        PolEquate(B, G);
3369        PolTruncate(B);
3370        PolEquate(D, InitialCondition);
3371
3372        FOR i := 1 TO NumberInteractions DO
3373          PolEquate(BInteraction[i], GInteraction[i]);
3374        END;
3375
3376        END {IdentifySystem} ;
3377
3378    PROCEDURE TunePhiEmulator(y: REAL;
3379                    FilterKnobs: TypeFilterKnobs;
3380                    VAR STCKnobs: TypeSTCKnobs;
3381                    VAR STCState: TypeSTCState);
3382
3383    VAR
3384      DataVector: TypeDataVector;
3385
3386    BEGIN {TunePhiEmulator}
3387
3388      WITH STCKnobs, STCState, EmKnobs, EmState,
3389          TunerState, SystemKnobs DO
3390      BEGIN
3391
3392      WITH DesignKnobs, FilterKnobs DO
3393        Phi := Filter(y, P, Z, FilterKnobs, PhicState);
3394
3395      EstimationError := PhiHat - Phi;
3396
3397      WITH TunerKnobs DO
3398        IF (Abs(EstimationError) >= DeadBand) AND On AND
3399          TimeFor(TuneInterval, TuneCounter) THEN
3400        BEGIN
3401        SetData(DataVector, EmState, EmKnobs,
3402                TuningInitialConditions,
3403                IntegralAction, NumberInteractions);
3404
3405        UpdateLeastSquaresGain(TunerState, TunerKnobs,
3406                            DataVector);
3407        TuneEmulator(EmKnobs, TunerState,
3408                    TuningInitialConditions,
3409                    IntegralAction,
3410                    NumberInteractions);
3411        END;
3412      END;
3413      END {TunePhiEmulator} ;
3414
3415    PROCEDURE TuneLambdaEmulator
3416        (y, u: REAL;
3417        Interaction: TypeInteraction;
3418        FilterKnobs: TypeFilterKnobs;
3419        LambdaNumerator, LambdaDenominator: Polynomial;
3420        ZLambda, PLambda: Polynomial;
```

```
3421          VAR STCKnobs: TypeSTCKnobs;
3422          VAR STCState: TypeSTCState);
3423
3424      VAR
3425          uLambda, yLambda, PhiLambda, PhiLamHat: REAL;
3426          InterLambda: TypeInteraction;
3427          DataVector: TypeDataVector;
3428          i: INTEGER;
3429
3430      BEGIN {TuneLambdaEmulator}
3431
3432          WITH STCKnobs, STCState, EmKnobs, LambdaEmState,
3433              TunerState, SystemKnobs DO
3434          BEGIN
3435
3436          WITH FilterKnobs DO
3437          BEGIN
3438          PhiLambda := Filter(y, PLambda, ZLambda,
3439                              FilterKnobs, PhicState);
3440
3441          uLambda := DelayFilter(u, LambdaNumerator,
3442                              LambdaDenominator, Delay,
3443                              FilterKnobs,
3444                              uLambdaState,
3445                              uDelayState);
3446          yLambda := DelayFilter(y, LambdaNumerator,
3447                              LambdaDenominator, Delay,
3448                              FilterKnobs,
3449                              yLambdaState,
3450                              yDelayState);
3451
3452          FOR i := 1 TO SystemKnobs.NumberInteractions DO
3453              InterLambda[i] := Filter(Interaction[i],
3454                              LambdaNumerator,
3455                              LambdaDenominator,
3456                              FilterKnobs,
3457                              iLambdaState[i]);
3458
3459          WITH DesignKnobs DO
3460          PhiLamHat := Emulator(yLambda, uLambda,
3461                              InterLambda,
3462                              NumberInteractions, F,
3463                              FFilter, G, GFilter,
3464                              InitialCondition,
3465                              GInteraction, 0.0,
3466                              FilterKnobs,
3467                              LambdaEmState);
3468          END;
3469
3470          EstimationError := PhiLamHat - PhiLambda;
3471
3472          WITH TunerKnobs DO
3473          IF (Abs(EstimationError) >= DeadBand) AND On AND
3474              TimeFor(TuneInterval, TuneCounter) THEN
3475          BEGIN
3476          SetData(DataVector, LambdaEmState, EmKnobs,
3477                              TuningInitialConditions,
3478                              IntegralAction, NumberInteractions);
```

```
3479              UpdateLeastSquaresGain(TunerState, TunerKnobs,
3480                         DataVector);
3481              TuneEmulator(EmKnobs, TunerState,
3482                         TuningInitialConditions,
3483                         IntegralAction,
3484                         NumberInteractions);
3485
3486          END;
3487        END;
3488      END {TuneLambdaEmulator} ;
3489
3490   {--------------------------------------------------}
3491   {--     Self-tuning control: procedure body    --}
3492   {--------------------------------------------------}
3493
3494   BEGIN {SelfTuningControl}
3495     WITH STCKnobs, STCState, ControlKnobs DO
3496       BEGIN
3497
3498       PolUnity(One, 0);
3499
3500       IF NOT FilterKnobs.ContinuousTime THEN
3501         IF NOT ExternalData THEN
3502           BEGIN
3503           IF NOT Auto THEN u := w
3504           ELSE
3505             u := Control(y, w, Interaction, STCKnobs,
3506                         STCState, FilterKnobs);
3507           PutData(u, PutDataKnobs);
3508           END;
3509
3510       IF IdentifyingSystem THEN
3511         BEGIN
3512         IdentifySystem(y, u, Interaction, FilterKnobs,
3513                     STCKnobs, STCState);
3514         IF SelfTuning THEN
3515           WITH STCState.SystemKnobs DO
3516             SetDesignKnobs(DesignKnobs, A, B,
3517                         IntegralAction, ZHasFactorB,
3518                         FilterKnobs.ContinuousTime);
3519         END;
3520
3521       IF SelfTuning THEN
3522         BEGIN
3523         IF Explicit THEN
3524           DesignEmulator(STCKnobs, STCState)
3525         ELSE IF UsingLambda THEN
3526           WITH DesignKnobs DO
3527             TuneLambdaEmulator(y, u, Interaction,
3528                         FilterKnobs, Z, P, One,
3529                         One, STCKnobs, STCState)
3530         ELSE
3531           TunePhiEmulator(y, FilterKnobs, STCKnobs,
3532                         STCState);
3533         END;
3534
3535       IF FilterKnobs.ContinuousTime THEN
3536         IF NOT ExternalData THEN
```

```
3537          BEGIN
3538          IF NOT Auto THEN u := w
3539          ELSE
3540            u := Control(y, w, Interaction, STCKnobs,
3541                        STCState, FilterKnobs);
3542          PutData(u, PutDataKnobs);
3543          END;
3544
3545          IF SelfTuning OR Auto THEN
3546            WITH DesignKnobs, EmKnobs, SystemKnobs DO
3547            BEGIN
3548            PhiHat := Emulator(y, u, Interaction,
3549                              NumberInteractions, F,
3550                              FFilter, G, GFilter,
3551                              InitialCondition,
3552                              GInteraction, 0.0,
3553                              FilterKnobs, EmState);
3554
3555            END;
3556
3557          WITH ControlKnobs DO
3558            IF Auto AND
3559              (qNumerator.Deg = qDenominator.Deg) THEN {Update
c  3560              Q filter}
3561              WITH STCState DO
3562              StateVariableFilter(u, qDenominator,
3563                                  FilterKnobs, qState);
3564
3565          END;
3566        END {SelfTuningControl} ;
3567
3568   {-------------------------------------------------}
3569   {--      Simulation initialisation              --}
3570   {-------------------------------------------------}
3571
3572   PROCEDURE RunInitialise;
3573
3574   VAR
3575     Loop, i: INTEGER;
3576
3577   BEGIN {RunInitialise}
3578     WITH RunKnobs DO
3579     BEGIN
3580     WriteTitle('Data Source   ');
3581     EnterBoolean(ExternalData, FALSE,
3582                  'External data          ', All);
3583
3584     EnterReal(LastTime, 10.0,
3585               'Last time             ', All);
3586
3587     EnterInteger(PrintInterval, 1,
3588                  'Print interval        ', All);
3589
3590     IF ExternalData THEN
3591       BEGIN
3592       WriteTitle('Real data     ');
3593       Reset(InData, 'indata.dat');
3594       END;
```

```
3595
3596        FOR Loop := 1 TO Loops DO
3597          WITH LoopVAR[Loop] DO
3598          BEGIN
3599            ThisLoop := Loop;
3600            u := 0.0;
3601            y0 := 0.0;
3602            w := 0.0;
3603            InDist := 0.0;
3604            LoopInteraction[Loop] := 0.0;
3605            FOR i := 1 TO Loops DO Interaction[i] := 0.0;
3606          END;
3607
3608        END;
3609      END {RunInitialise} ;
3610
3611    PROCEDURE SimulationInitialise
3612        (VAR ThisLoopVAR: TypeLoopVAR;
3613        FilterKnobs: TypeFilterKnobs;
3614        RunKnobs: TypeRunKnobs);
3615
3616    BEGIN {SimulationInitialise}
3617      WITH ThisLoopVAR, STCKnobs, ControlKnobs, RunKnobs DO
3618        IF NOT ExternalData THEN
3619        BEGIN
3620          WriteTitle('Simulation       ');
3621          IF NOT Cascade OR (Loop = Loops) THEN
3622          BEGIN
3623            WriteTitle('Setpoint        ');
3624            SigGenInitialise(SetPointKnobs);
3625          END;
3626          WriteTitle('In Disturbance ');
3627          SigGenInitialise(InDisturbKnobs);
3628          WriteTitle('Out Disturbance');
3629          SigGenInitialise(OutDisturbKnobs);
3630
3631          tSystemInitialise(STCKnobs, STCState,
3632                            tSystemKnobs, tSystemState,
3633                            FilterKnobs.ContinuousTime,
3634                            RunKnobs);
3635          IF Auto THEN
3636            ModelInitialise(STCKnobs, STCState,
3637                            tSystemKnobs, ModelKnobs,
3638                            ModelState,
3639                            FilterKnobs.ContinuousTime);
3640
3641        END;
3642      END {SimulationInitialise} ;
3643
3644    {-------------------------------------------------}
3645    {-- Execution of the simulation and control --}
3646    {-------------------------------------------------}
3647
3648    PROCEDURE Run;
3649
3650      VAR
3651      Loop, OtherLoop, j: INTEGER;
3652      ReportCount: INTEGER;
```

```
3653    FirstTime, ReportInterval: REAL;
3654
3655    PROCEDURE WriteData(VAR ThisLoopVAR: TypeLoopVAR);
3656
3657    VAR
3658      i: INTEGER;
3659
3660    BEGIN {WriteData}
3661      WITH ThisLoopVAR, STCState, STCKnobs, SystemKnobs DO
3662      BEGIN
3663        Write(OutData, Time: fw: dp, ' ', u: fw: dp, ' ',
3664          y: fw: dp, ' ');
3665        FOR i := 1 TO tSystemKnobs.NumberInteractions DO
3666          Write(OutData, Interaction[i]: fw: dp, ' ');
3667        Write(OutData, w: fw: dp, ' ', y0: fw: dp, ' ',
3668          PhiHat: fw: dp, ' ', Phi: fw: dp);
3669
3670        IF IdentifyingSystem AND
3671          NOT UsingHighGainControl THEN
3672          WITH STCState.SystemKnobs, IdentState DO
3673          BEGIN
3674            Write(OutSysPar, Time: fw: dp, ' ',
3675              EstimationError: fw: dp, ' ', Sigma: fw:
3676              dp, ' ');
3677            Write(OutSysPar, Delay: fw: dp, ' ');
3678
3679            PolWrite(OutSysPar, B);
3680            PolWrite(OutSysPar, A);
3681            FOR i := 1 TO NumberInteractions DO
3682              PolWrite(OutSysPar, BInteraction[i]);
3683            IF TuningInitialConditions THEN
3684              PolWrite(OutSysPar, D);
3685          END;
3686
3687        IF SelfTuning AND NOT UsingHighGainControl THEN
3688          WITH EmKnobs, TunerState DO
3689          BEGIN
3690            Write(OutEmPar, Time: fw: dp, ' ',
3691              EstimationError: fw: dp, ' ', Sigma: fw:
3692              dp, ' ');
3693            PolWrite(OutEmPar, F);
3694            PolWrite(OutEmPar, G);
3695            FOR i := 1 TO NumberInteractions DO
3696              PolWrite(OutEmPar, GInteraction[i]);
3697
3698            IF TuningInitialConditions THEN
3699              PolWrite(OutEmPar, InitialCondition);
3700          END;
3701
3702      END;
3703
3704    END {WriteData} ;
3705
3706    PROCEDURE WriteLnData;
3707
3708    BEGIN {WriteLnData}
3709      WriteLn(OutData);
3710      WriteLn(OutSysPar);
```

```
3711        WriteLn(OutEmPar);
3712        END {WriteLnData} ;
3713
3714        PROCEDURE OneTimeStep(VAR ThisLoopVAR: TypeLoopVAR);
3715
3716        BEGIN {OneTimeStep}
3717
3718          WITH ThisLoopVAR, RunKnobs, FilterKnobs DO
3719          BEGIN
3720            GetData(ThisLoopVAR, LoopVAR, InData, Time,
3721                 RunKnobs, FilterKnobs);
3722
3723            WITH STCKnobs.ControlKnobs, STCState DO
3724              wf := Filter(w, rNumerator, rDenominator,
3725                   FilterKnobs, wState);
3726
3727            WITH STCKnobs DO
3728              IF Auto THEN
3729                y0 := System(wf, ModelKnobs, FilterKnobs,
3730                     ModelState);
3731
3732            IF UsingHighGainControl THEN
3733              BEGIN
3734              HighGainControl(u, wf, y, FilterKnobs, STCKnobs,
3735                   STCState);
3736              PutData(u, PutDataKnobs);
3737              END
3738            ELSE
3739              SelfTuningControl(u, wf, y, Interaction,
3740                   FilterKnobs, ExternalData,
3741                   PutDataKnobs, STCKnobs,
3742                   STCState);
3743
3744            IF PrintNow THEN WriteData(ThisLoopVAR);
3745
3746          END;
3747        END {OneTimeStep} ;
3748
3749        PROCEDURE Splice(VAR ThisLoopVAR: TypeLoopVAR);
3750
3751        VAR
3752          k, j: INTEGER;
3753
3754        BEGIN {Splice}
3755          WITH ThisLoopVAR, STCKnobs DO
3756            IF TuningInitialConditions THEN
3757              WITH STCState, SysEmState, SysEmKnobs,
3758                   IdentState DO
3759              BEGIN
3760              WriteLn('Splicing data');
3761              j := 0;
3762              FOR k := FFilter.Deg -
3763                   InitialCondition.Deg TO FFilter.Deg DO
3764                BEGIN
3765                j := j + 1;
3766                Variance[j] := Variance[j] + IdentifyKnobs.
3767                         InitialVariance;
3768                END;
```

```
3769
3770            FilterInitialise(ICState,
3771                            FilterKnobs.ContinuousTime,
3772                            1.0 / FFilter.Coeff[0]);
3773            END
3774          ELSE WriteLn('Not splicing data');
3775          END {Splice} ;
3776
3777    FUNCTION NoMore: BOOLEAN;
3778
3779      VAR
3780        More: BOOLEAN;
3781        Loop: INTEGER;
3782
3783      PROCEDURE PreventBump;
3784      {Preserves continuity in system output
c 3785        when B changes -
c 3786        Initial conditions are ignored}
3787
3788        VAR
3789          yNew: REAL;
3790          i: INTEGER;
3791
3792        BEGIN {PreventBump}
3793          WITH LoopVAR[Loop], tSystemKnobs, tSystemState DO
3794          BEGIN
3795            yNew := StateOutput(FilterState, B, A);
3796            IF yNew <> 0.0 THEN
3797            WITH FilterState DO
3798              FOR i := 0 TO A.Deg DO
3799                State[i] := State[i] * y / yNew;
3800            END;
3801          END {PreventBump} ;
3802
3803      BEGIN {NoMore}
3804        WITH RunKnobs DO
3805        BEGIN
3806          IF ExternalData THEN More := NOT Eof(InData)
3807          ELSE More := TRUE;
3808
3809          IF More THEN
3810          BEGIN
3811            WriteLn('Time now is ', Time: fw: dp);
3812            EnterBoolean(More, FALSE,
3813                        'More time              ', All);
3814            IF More THEN
3815            BEGIN
3816              EnterReal(ExtraTime, 10.0,
3817                        'Extra time            ', All);
3818              LastTime := LastTime + ExtraTime;
3819
3820              FOR Loop := 1 TO Loops DO
3821                WITH LoopVAR[Loop], tSystemKnobs,
3822                  STCKnobs DO
3823                BEGIN
3824                  WriteLoopTitle(Loop, Loops);
3825                  IF NOT ExternalData THEN
3826                  BEGIN
```

```
3827                    WriteTitle('Actual system  ');
3828                    EnterPolynomial(A, A,
3829                           'A (system denominator)  '
3830                           , All);
3831                    EnterPolynomial(B, B,
3832                           'B (system numerator)   '
3833                           , All);
3834                    EnterReal(Delay, 0.0,
3835                           'Time delay             ',
3836                           All);
3837                    PreventBump;
3838                    END;
3839                 IF NOT Explicit THEN
3840                 WITH TunerKnobs DO
3841                    EnterBoolean(On, TRUE,
3842                           'Estimator on           '
3843                           , All);
3844                 IF IdentifyingSystem THEN
3845                 WITH IdentifyKnobs DO
3846                    EnterBoolean(On, TRUE,
3847                           'System estimator on    '
3848                           , All);
3849              END;
3850           END;
3851        END;
3852        END;
3853     NoMore := NOT More;
3854     END { NoMore } ;
3855
3856  BEGIN {Run}
3857
3858     Time := FilterKnobs.SampleInterval;
3859     PrintCounter := 0;
3860
3861     WITH RunKnobs DO
3862      IF ExternalData THEN
3863
3864        REPEAT
3865        WriteLn('Processing data in file ...');
3866        WHILE NOT Eof(InData) AND (Time < LastTime) DO
3867           BEGIN
3868           PrintNow := TimeFor(PrintInterval,
3869                               PrintCounter);
3870           IF Eoln(InData) THEN
3871              BEGIN
3872              Splice(LoopVAR[1]);
3873              ReadLn(InData);
3874              END
3875           ELSE OneTimeStep(LoopVAR[1]);
3876
3877           IF PrintNow THEN WriteLnData;
3878           Time := Time + FilterKnobs.SampleInterval;
3879           END;
3880        UNTIL NoMore
3881      ELSE
3882        REPEAT
3883        ReportCount := 1;
3884        FirstTime := Time;
```

```
3885            ReportInterval := (LastTime - FirstTime) /
3886                        ProgressReports;
3887            FirstTime := FirstTime -
3888                        FilterKnobs.SampleInterval;
3889            WriteLn('Simulation running:');
3890            WHILE (Time < LastTime) DO
3891              BEGIN
3892              IF (Time - FirstTime) >=
3893                ReportCount * ReportInterval THEN
3894                BEGIN
3895                Write('     ');
3896                Write((100 * ReportCount) DIV
3897                    ProgressReports: 3);
3898                WriteLn('% complete');
3899                ReportCount := ReportCount + 1;
3900                END;
3901
3902              PrintNow := TimeFor(PrintInterval,
3903                        PrintCounter);
3904              FOR Loop := 1 TO Loops DO
3905                OneTimeStep(LoopVAR[Loop]);
3906
3907              FOR Loop := 1 TO Loops DO
3908                IF OutputCoupled THEN
3909                  LoopInteraction[Loop] := LoopVAR[Loop].y
3910                ELSE
3911                  LoopInteraction[Loop] := LoopVAR[Loop].u;
3912
3913              FOR Loop := 1 TO Loops DO
3914                BEGIN
3915                j := 0;
3916                FOR OtherLoop := 1 TO Loops DO
3917                  IF NOT (OtherLoop = Loop) THEN
3918                    BEGIN
3919                    j := j + 1;
3920                    LoopVAR[Loop].Interaction[j] :=
3921                    LoopInteraction[OtherLoop];
3922                    END;
3923                END;
3924              IF PrintNow THEN WriteLnData;
3925              Time := Time + FilterKnobs.SampleInterval;
3926              END;
3927            UNTIL NoMore;
3928
3929          WriteLnData; {Once more for luck}
3930
3931          END {Run} ;
3932
3933        {-----------------------------------------------}
3934        {--    Selection of appropriate chapter      --}
3935        {-----------------------------------------------}
3936
3937        FUNCTION Chapter(VAR All: BOOLEAN): INTEGER;
3938
3939          VAR
3940            What: INTEGER;
3941            Ch: CHAR;
3942
```

```
3943    BEGIN {Chapter}
3944      WriteLn;
3945      WriteLn(Pretty, 'C S T C ', Version, Pretty);
3946      WriteLn;
3947
3948      WriteLn('Enter all variables (y/n, default n)?');
3949      IF Eoln(Input) THEN All := FALSE
3950      ELSE
3951        BEGIN
3952          Read(Input, Ch);
3953          All := Ch IN ['y', 'Y'];
3954        END;
3955      ReadLn(Input);
3956
3957      EnterInteger(What, 1, 'Chapter              ',
3958               All);
3959      WriteLn;
3960      Chapter := What;
3961    END {Chapter} ;
3962
3963  {----------------------------------------------}
3964  {--     Body of CSTC                        --}
3965  {----------------------------------------------}
3966
3967  BEGIN {CSTC}
3968    Reset(InLog, 'inlog.dat');
3969    Rewrite(OutLog, 'outlog.dat');
3970
3971    Rewrite(OutData, 'outdata.dat');
3972    Rewrite(OutEmPar, 'outempar.dat');
3973    Rewrite(OutSysPar, 'outsyspar.dat');
3974
3975    PolZero(Zero, 0);
3976    PolUnity(One, 0);
3977
3978    WITH RunKnobs DO
3979      BEGIN
3980        Loops := 1;
3981        Cascade := FALSE;
3982        FilterKnobs.ConstantBetweenSamples := FALSE;
3983
3984        CASE Chapter(All) OF
3985          1:
3986            WITH LoopVAR[1], STCKnobs, STCState DO
3987              BEGIN
3988                UsingHighGainControl := FALSE;
3989                tSystemKnobs.NumberInteractions := 0;
3990                SystemKnobs.NumberInteractions := 0;
3991                IdentifyingSystem := FALSE;
3992                CorrectSystem := TRUE;
3993                SelfTuning := FALSE;
3994                RunInitialise;
3995                InitFilterKnobs(FilterKnobs);
3996                STCInitialise(LoopVAR[1], FilterKnobs,
3997                         RunKnobs);
3998                SimulationInitialise(LoopVAR[1], FilterKnobs,
3999                         RunKnobs);
4000                EnterBoolean(FilterKnobs.ConstantBetweenSamples,
```

```
4001                        FALSE, 'Constant between samples ',
4002                        All);
4003            Run;
4004            END;
4005      2:
4006        WITH LoopVAR[1], STCKnobs, STCState DO
4007        BEGIN
4008          EnterBoolean(FilterKnobs.ContinuousTime, TRUE,
4009                       'Continuous-time?        ', All);
4010          EnterBoolean(STCKnobs.IntegralAction, TRUE,
4011                       'Integral action        ', All);
4012          tSystemKnobs.NumberInteractions := 0;
4013          SystemKnobs.NumberInteractions := 0;
4014          SystemInitialise(STCKnobs, STCState, RunKnobs);
4015          DesignInitialise(STCKnobs, STCState,
4016                          FilterKnobs.ContinuousTime);
4017          DesignEmulator(STCKnobs, STCState);
4018          WriteDesign(LoopVAR[1]);
4019          END;
4020      3:
4021        WITH LoopVAR[1], STCKnobs, STCState DO
4022        BEGIN
4023          UsingHighGainControl := FALSE;
4024          tSystemKnobs.NumberInteractions := 0;
4025          SystemKnobs.NumberInteractions := 0;
4026          IdentifyingSystem := FALSE;
4027          CorrectSystem := TRUE;
4028          SelfTuning := FALSE;
4029          RunInitialise;
4030          InitFilterKnobs(FilterKnobs);
4031          STCInitialise(LoopVAR[1], FilterKnobs,
4032                   RunKnobs);
4033          SimulationInitialise(LoopVAR[1], FilterKnobs,
4034                   RunKnobs);
4035          Run;
4036          END;
4037      4:
4038        WITH LoopVAR[1], STCKnobs, STCState DO
4039        BEGIN
4040          UsingHighGainControl := FALSE;
4041          tSystemKnobs.NumberInteractions := 0;
4042          SystemKnobs.NumberInteractions := 0;
4043          IdentifyingSystem := FALSE;
4044          CorrectSystem := FALSE;
4045          SelfTuning := FALSE;
4046          RunInitialise;
4047          InitFilterKnobs(FilterKnobs);
4048          STCInitialise(LoopVAR[1], FilterKnobs,
4049                   RunKnobs);
4050          SimulationInitialise(LoopVAR[1], FilterKnobs,
4051                   RunKnobs);
4052          Run;
4053          END;
4054      5:
4055        WITH LoopVAR[1], STCKnobs, STCState DO
4056        BEGIN
4057          UsingHighGainControl := FALSE;
4058          tSystemKnobs.NumberInteractions := 0;
```

```
4059        SystemKnobs.NumberInteractions := 0;
4060        Small := 0.000001;
4061        IdentifyingSystem := TRUE;
4062        CorrectSystem := FALSE;
4063        SelfTuning := FALSE;
4064        RunInitialise;
4065        InitFilterKnobs(FilterKnobs);
4066        STCInitialise(LoopVAR[1], FilterKnobs,
4067                  RunKnobs);
4068        SimulationInitialise(LoopVAR[1], FilterKnobs,
4069                  RunKnobs);
4070        Run;
4071        WriteParameters(LoopVAR[1]);
4072        END;
4073
4074    6, 7:
4075        WITH LoopVAR[1], STCKnobs, STCState DO
4076        BEGIN
4077        UsingHighGainControl := FALSE;
4078        tSystemKnobs.NumberInteractions := 0;
4079        SystemKnobs.NumberInteractions := 0;
4080        CorrectSystem := FALSE;
4081        SelfTuning := TRUE;
4082        RunInitialise;
4083        InitFilterKnobs(FilterKnobs);
4084        STCInitialise(LoopVAR[1], FilterKnobs,
4085                  RunKnobs);
4086        SimulationInitialise(LoopVAR[1], FilterKnobs,
4087                  RunKnobs);
4088        Run;
4089        WriteDesign(LoopVAR[1]);
4090        END;
4091
4092    8:
4093        WITH LoopVAR[1], STCKnobs, STCState DO
4094        BEGIN
4095        tSystemKnobs.NumberInteractions := 0;
4096        SystemKnobs.NumberInteractions := 0;
4097        CorrectSystem := FALSE;
4098        SelfTuning := TRUE;
4099        UsingHighGainControl := TRUE;
4100        RunInitialise;
4101        InitFilterKnobs(FilterKnobs);
4102        STCInitialise(LoopVAR[1], FilterKnobs,
4103                  RunKnobs);
4104        SimulationInitialise(LoopVAR[1], FilterKnobs,
4105                  RunKnobs);
4106        Run;
4107        END;
4108
4109    9:
4110        BEGIN
4111        Cascade := TRUE;
4112        OutputCoupled := FALSE;
4113        EnterInteger(Loops, 2,
4114                  'Number of loops       ', All);
4115        RunInitialise;
4116        InitFilterKnobs(FilterKnobs);
```

```
4117        FOR Loop := 1 TO Loops DO
4118          WITH LoopVAR[Loop], STCKnobs DO
4119          BEGIN
4120          WriteLoopTitle(Loop, Loops);
4121          CorrectSystem := FALSE;
4122          EnterBoolean(SelfTuning, TRUE,
4123                     'Self-tuning control     ',
4124                     All);
4125          EnterBoolean(UsingHighGainControl, FALSE,
4126                     'Using high-gain control  ',
4127                     All);
4128          STCInitialise(LoopVAR[Loop], FilterKnobs,
4129                     RunKnobs);
4130          SimulationInitialise(LoopVAR[Loop],
4131                     FilterKnobs, RunKnobs);
4132          END;
4133
4134        Run;
4135        FOR Loop := 1 TO Loops DO
4136          BEGIN
4137          WriteLoopTitle(Loop, Loops);
4138          WriteDesign(LoopVAR[Loop]);
4139          END;
4140        END;
4141
4142    10:
4143        BEGIN
4144        EnterInteger(Loops, 2,
4145                   'Number of loops         ', All);
4146        EnterBoolean(OutputCoupled, FALSE,
4147                   'Output coupled          ', All);
4148
4149        RunInitialise;
4150        InitFilterKnobs(FilterKnobs);
4151        FOR Loop := 1 TO Loops DO
4152          WITH LoopVAR[Loop], STCKnobs DO
4153          BEGIN
4154          WriteLoopTitle(Loop, Loops);
4155          CorrectSystem := FALSE;
4156          EnterBoolean(SelfTuning, TRUE,
4157                     'Self-tuning control     ',
4158                     All);
4159          EnterBoolean(UsingHighGainControl, FALSE,
4160                     'Using high-gain control  ',
4161                     All);
4162          STCInitialise(LoopVAR[Loop], FilterKnobs,
4163                     RunKnobs);
4164          SimulationInitialise(LoopVAR[Loop],
4165                     FilterKnobs, RunKnobs);
4166          END;
4167
4168        Run;
4169
4170        FOR Loop := 1 TO Loops DO
4171          BEGIN
4172          WriteLoopTitle(Loop, Loops);
4173          WriteDesign(LoopVAR[Loop]);
4174          END;
```

```
4175          END;
4176
4177          END {CASE} ;
4178          END {WITH RunKnobs} ;
4179    END.
```

Variable Index

Procedure Index